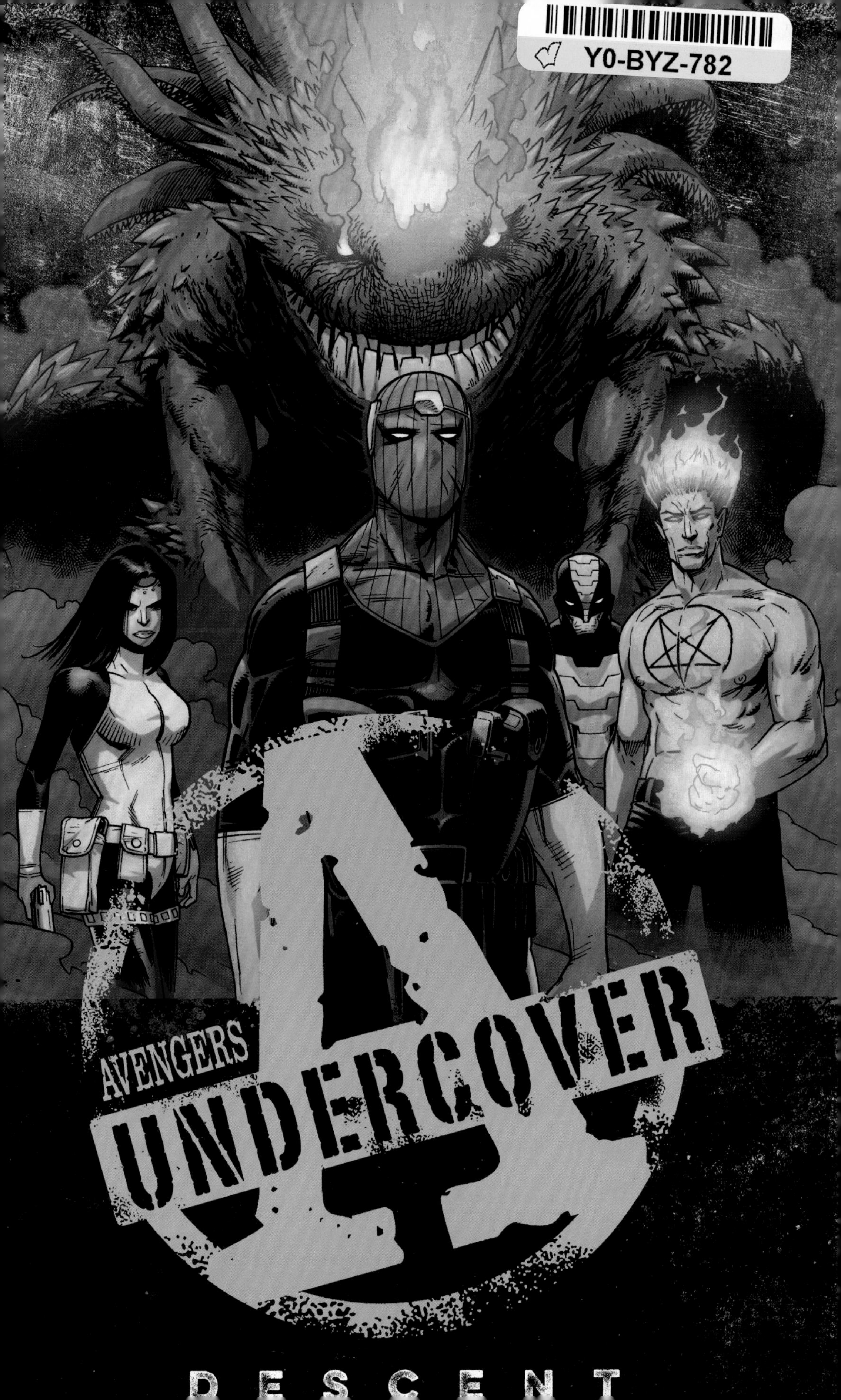
AVENGERS
UNDERCOVER
DESCENT

HAZMAT

CHASE

NICO

DEATH LOCKET

CAMMI

ANACHRONISM

BLOODSTONE

COLLECTION EDITOR: **JENNIFER GRÜNWALD**
ASSISTANT EDITOR: **SARAH BRUNSTAD**   ASSOCIATE MANAGING EDITOR: **ALEX STARBUCK**
EDITOR, SPECIAL PROJECTS: **MARK D. BEAZLEY**   SENIOR EDITOR, SPECIAL PROJECTS: **JEFF YOUNGQUIST**
BOOK DESIGN: **RODOLFO MURAGUCHI**   SVP PRINT, SALES & MARKETING: **DAVID GABRIEL**

EDITOR IN CHIEF: **AXEL ALONSO**   CHIEF CREATIVE OFFICER: **JOE QUESADA**
PUBLISHER: **DAN BUCKLEY**   EXECUTIVE PRODUCER: **ALAN FINE**

AVENGERS UNDERCOVER VOL. 1: DESCENT. Contains material originally published in magazine form as AVENGERS UNDERCOVER #1-5. First printing 2014. ISBN# 978-0-7851-8940-4. Publi
by MARVEL WORLDWIDE, INC., a subsidiary of MARVEL ENTERTAINMENT, LLC. OFFICE OF PUBLICATION: 135 West 50th Street, New York, NY 10020. Copyright © 2014 Marvel Characters, In
rights reserved. All characters featured in this issue and the distinctive names and likenesses thereof, and all related indicia are trademarks of Marvel Characters, Inc. No similarity between a
the names, characters, persons, and/or institutions in this magazine with those of any living or dead person or institution is intended, and any such similarity which may exist is purely coincide
Printed in Canada. ALAN FINE, EVP - Office of the President, Marvel Worldwide, Inc. and EVP & CMO Marvel Characters B.V.; DAN BUCKLEY, Publisher & President - Print, Animation & Digital Divis
JOE QUESADA, Chief Creative Officer; TOM BREVOORT, SVP of Publishing; DAVID BOGART, SVP of Operations & Procurement, Publishing; C.B. CEBULSKI, SVP of Creator & Content Developm
DAVID GABRIEL, SVP Print, Sales & Marketing; JIM O'KEEFE, VP of Operations & Logistics; DAN CARR, Executive Director of Publishing Technology; SUSAN CRESPI, Editorial Operations Manager;
MORALES, Publishing Operations Manager; STAN LEE, Chairman Emeritus. For information regarding advertising in Marvel Comics or on Marvel.com, please contact Niza Disla, Director of M
Partnerships, at ndisla@marvel.com. For Marvel subscription inquiries, please call 800-217-9158. **Manufactured between 7/4/2014 and 8/11/2014 by SOLISCO PRINTERS, SCOTT, QC, CAN**

10 9 8 7 6 5 4 3 2 1

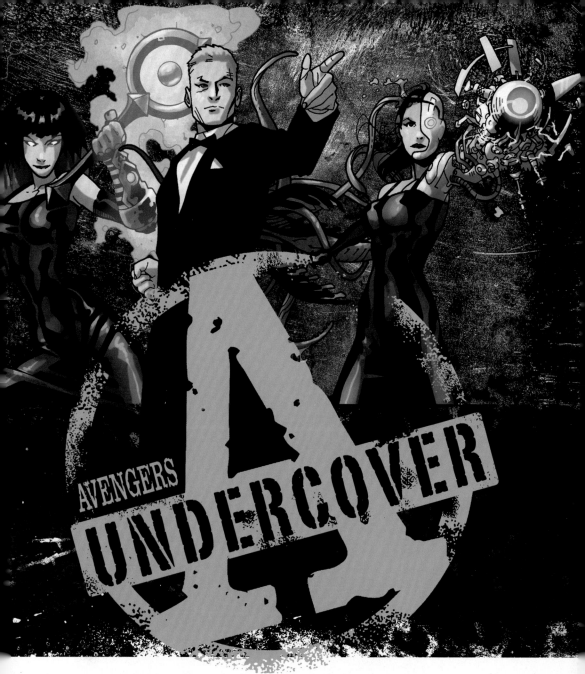

DESCENT

WRITER:
DENNIS HOPELESS

ARTISTS:
KEVIN WALKER (#1-2 & #4-5)
& TIMOTHY GREEN II (#3)

INKER, #4-5: JASON GORDER
COLOR ARTIST: JEAN-FRANCOIS BEAULIEU
LETTERER: VC'S JOE CARAMAGNA
COVER ART: FRANCESCO MATTINA
ASSISTANT EDITOR: JON MOISAN
EDITOR: BILL ROSEMANN

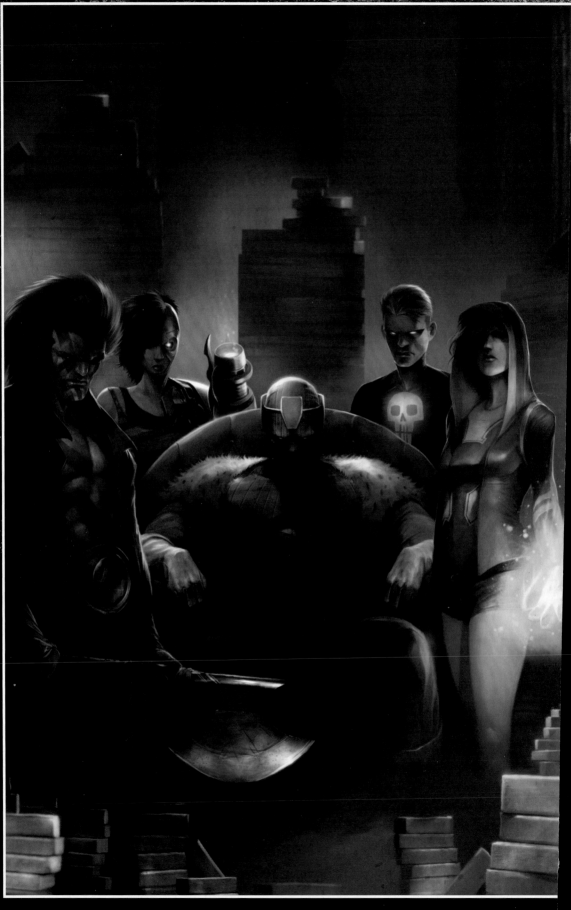

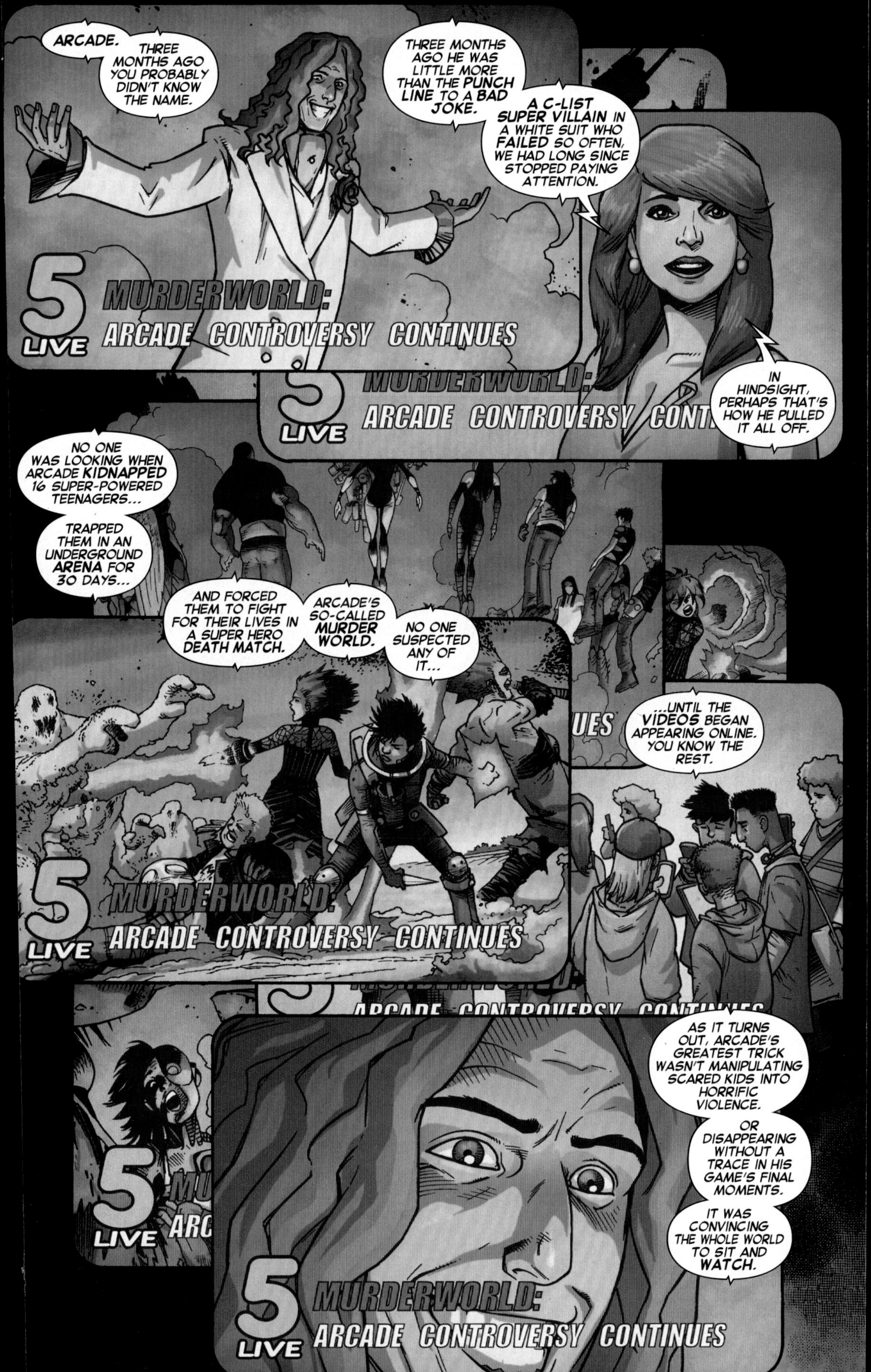
ARCADE.
THREE MONTHS AGO YOU PROBABLY DIDN'T KNOW THE NAME.
THREE MONTHS AGO HE WAS LITTLE MORE THAN THE PUNCH LINE TO A BAD JOKE.
A C-LIST SUPER VILLAIN IN A WHITE SUIT WHO FAILED SO OFTEN, WE HAD LONG SINCE STOPPED PAYING ATTENTION.
5 LIVE
MURDERWORLD:
ARCADE CONTROVERSY CONTINUES
IN HINDSIGHT, PERHAPS THAT'S HOW HE PULLED IT ALL OFF.
NO ONE WAS LOOKING WHEN ARCADE KIDNAPPED 16 SUPER-POWERED TEENAGERS...
TRAPPED THEM IN AN UNDERGROUND ARENA FOR 30 DAYS...
AND FORCED THEM TO FIGHT FOR THEIR LIVES IN A SUPER HERO DEATH MATCH.
ARCADE'S SO-CALLED MURDER WORLD.
NO ONE SUSPECTED ANY OF IT...
...UNTIL THE VIDEOS BEGAN APPEARING ONLINE. YOU KNOW THE REST.
AS IT TURNS OUT, ARCADE'S GREATEST TRICK WASN'T MANIPULATING SCARED KIDS INTO HORRIFIC VIOLENCE.
OR DISAPPEARING WITHOUT A TRACE IN HIS GAME'S FINAL MOMENTS.
IT WAS CONVINCING THE WHOLE WORLD TO SIT AND WATCH.

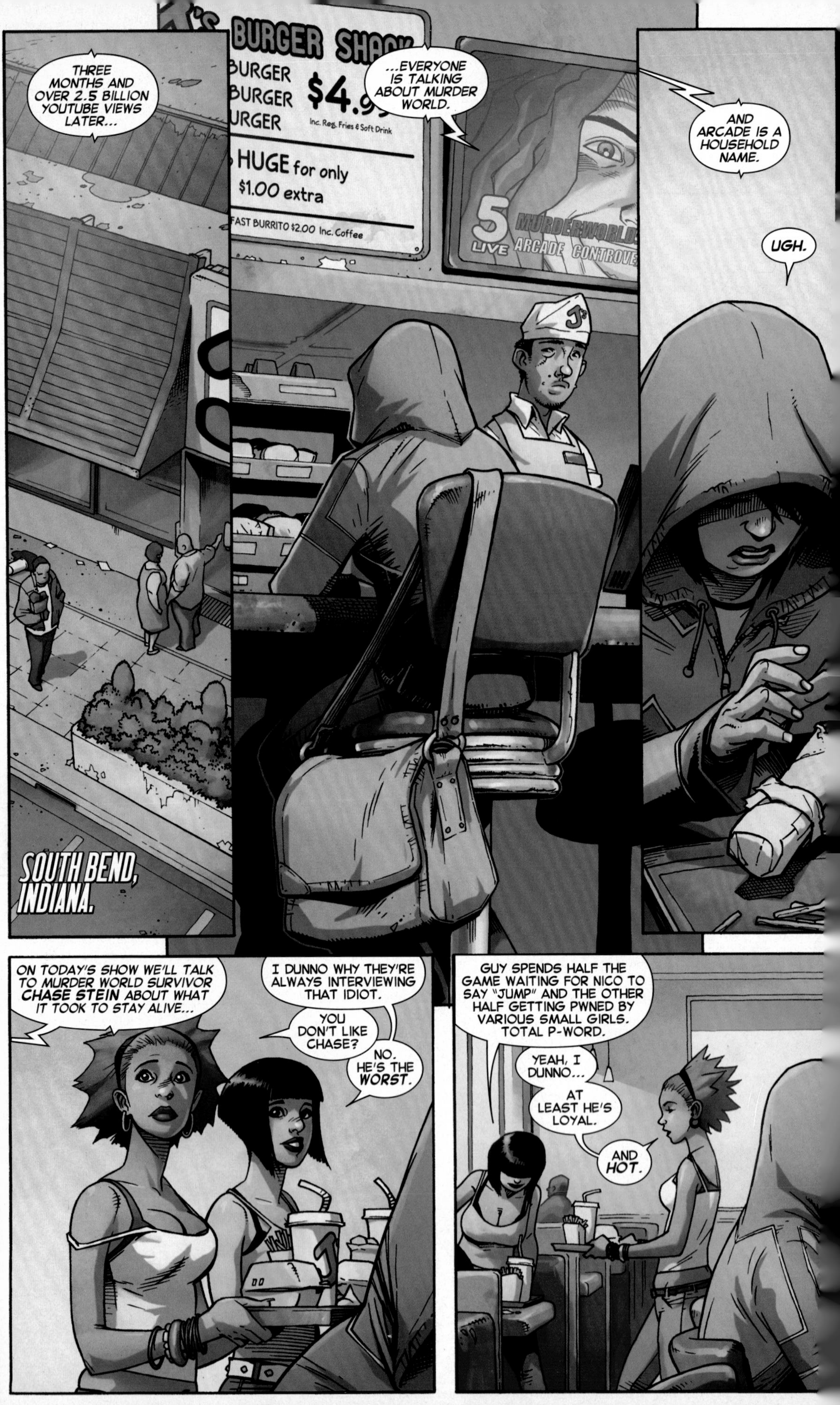
THREE MONTHS AND OVER 2.5 BILLION YOUTUBE VIEWS LATER...
SOUTH BEND, INDIANA.
BURGER SHACK
BURGER
BURGER
URGER
$4.9
Inc. Reg. Fries & Soft Drink
HUGE for only $1.00 extra
FAST BURRITO $2.00 Inc. Coffee
...EVERYONE IS TALKING ABOUT MURDER WORLD.
5 LIVE
MURDERWORLD
ARCADE CONTROVE
AND ARCADE IS A HOUSEHOLD NAME.
UGH.
ON TODAY'S SHOW WE'LL TALK TO MURDER WORLD SURVIVOR CHASE STEIN ABOUT WHAT IT TOOK TO STAY ALIVE...
I DUNNO WHY THEY'RE ALWAYS INTERVIEWING THAT IDIOT.
YOU DON'T LIKE CHASE?
NO. HE'S THE WORST.
GUY SPENDS HALF THE GAME WAITING FOR NICO TO SAY "JUMP" AND THE OTHER HALF GETTING PWNED BY VARIOUS SMALL GIRLS. TOTAL P-WORD.
YEAH, I DUNNO...
AT LEAST HE'S LOYAL.
AND HOT.

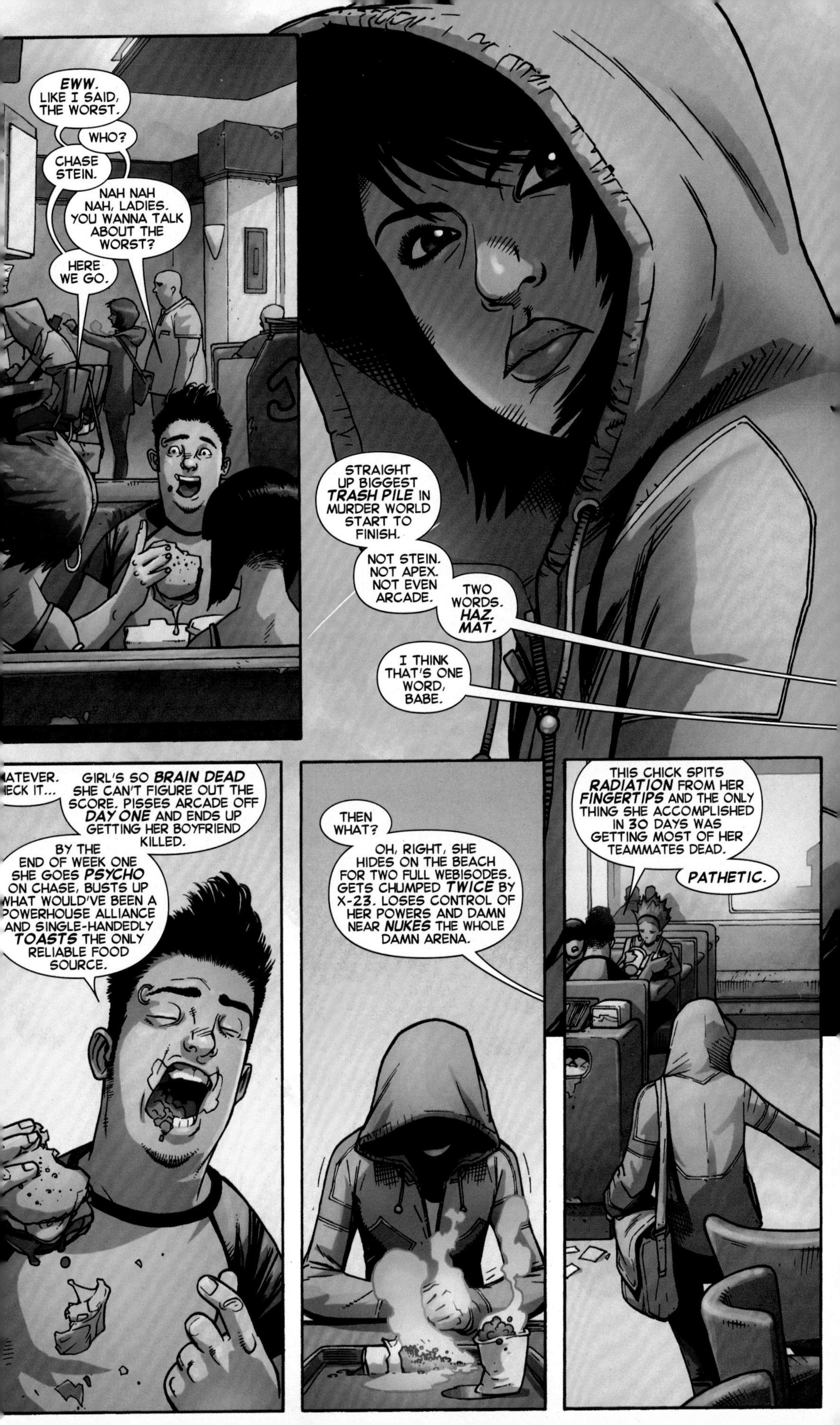
EWW. LIKE I SAID, THE WORST.
WHO?
CHASE STEIN.
NAH NAH NAH, LADIES. YOU WANNA TALK ABOUT THE WORST?
HERE WE GO.
STRAIGHT UP BIGGEST TRASH PILE IN MURDER WORLD START TO FINISH.
NOT STEIN. NOT APEX. NOT EVEN ARCADE.
TWO WORDS. HAZ. MAT.
I THINK THAT'S ONE WORD, BABE.
ATEVER. ECK IT...
GIRL'S SO BRAIN DEAD SHE CAN'T FIGURE OUT THE SCORE. PISSES ARCADE OFF DAY ONE AND ENDS UP GETTING HER BOYFRIEND KILLED.
BY THE END OF WEEK ONE SHE GOES PSYCHO ON CHASE, BUSTS UP WHAT WOULD'VE BEEN A POWERHOUSE ALLIANCE AND SINGLE-HANDEDLY TOASTS THE ONLY RELIABLE FOOD SOURCE.
THEN WHAT?
OH, RIGHT, SHE HIDES ON THE BEACH FOR TWO FULL WEBISODES. GETS CHUMPED TWICE BY X-23. LOSES CONTROL OF HER POWERS AND DAMN NEAR NUKES THE WHOLE DAMN ARENA.
THIS CHICK SPITS RADIATION FROM HER FINGERTIPS AND THE ONLY THING SHE ACCOMPLISHED IN 30 DAYS WAS GETTING MOST OF HER TEAMMATES DEAD.
PATHETIC.

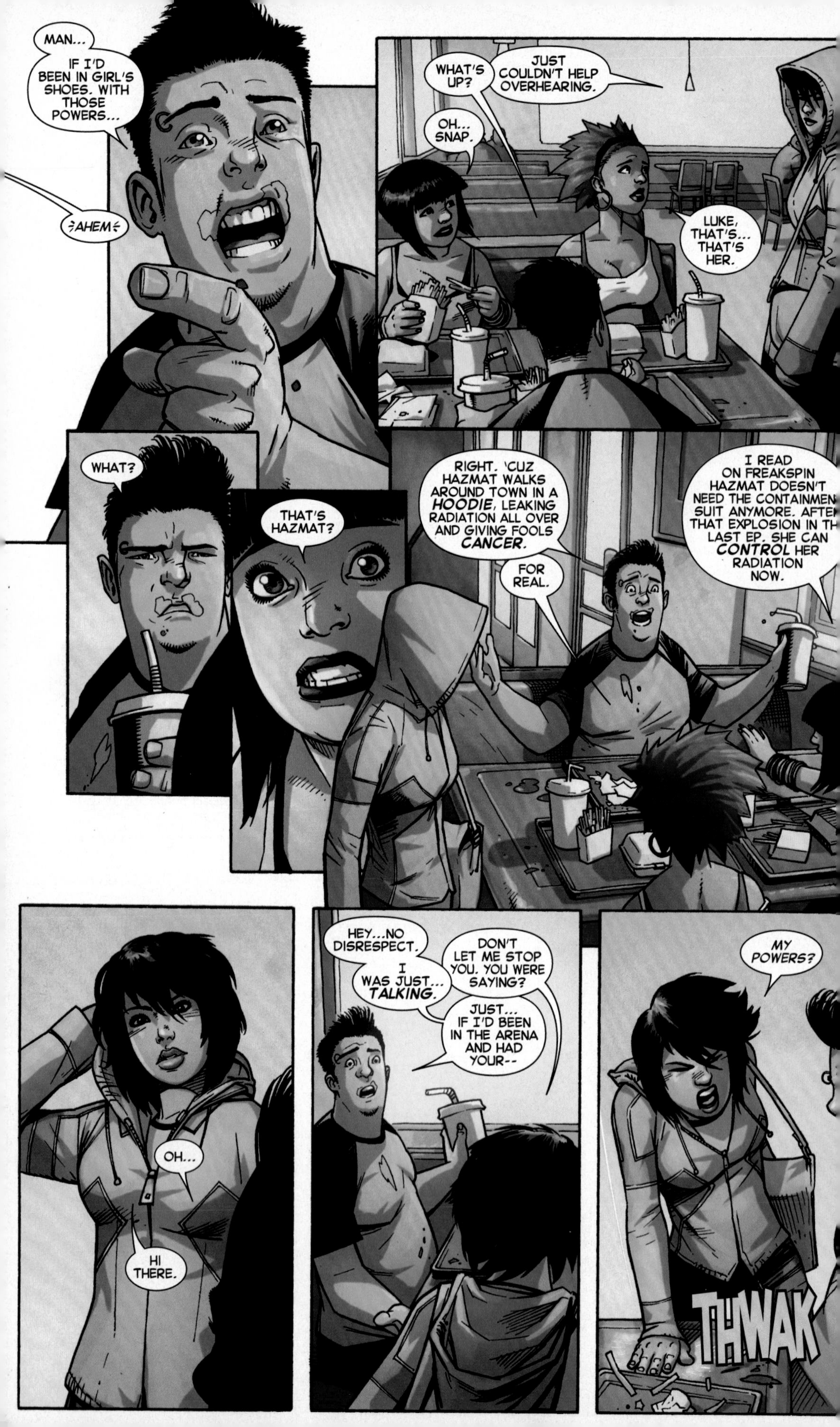
MAN...
IF I'D BEEN IN GIRL'S SHOES. WITH THOSE POWERS...
AHEM
WHAT'S UP?
JUST COULDN'T HELP OVERHEARING.
OH... SNAP.
LUKE, THAT'S... THAT'S HER.
WHAT?
THAT'S HAZMAT?
RIGHT. 'CUZ HAZMAT WALKS AROUND TOWN IN A HOODIE, LEAKING RADIATION ALL OVER AND GIVING FOOLS CANCER.
FOR REAL.
I READ ON FREAKSPIN HAZMAT DOESN'T NEED THE CONTAINMEN SUIT ANYMORE. AFTE THAT EXPLOSION IN TH LAST EP. SHE CAN CONTROL HER RADIATION NOW.
OH...
HI THERE.
HEY...NO DISRESPECT.
I WAS JUST... TALKING.
DON'T LET ME STOP YOU. YOU WERE SAYING?
JUST... IF I'D BEEN IN THE ARENA AND HAD YOUR--
MY POWERS?
THWAK

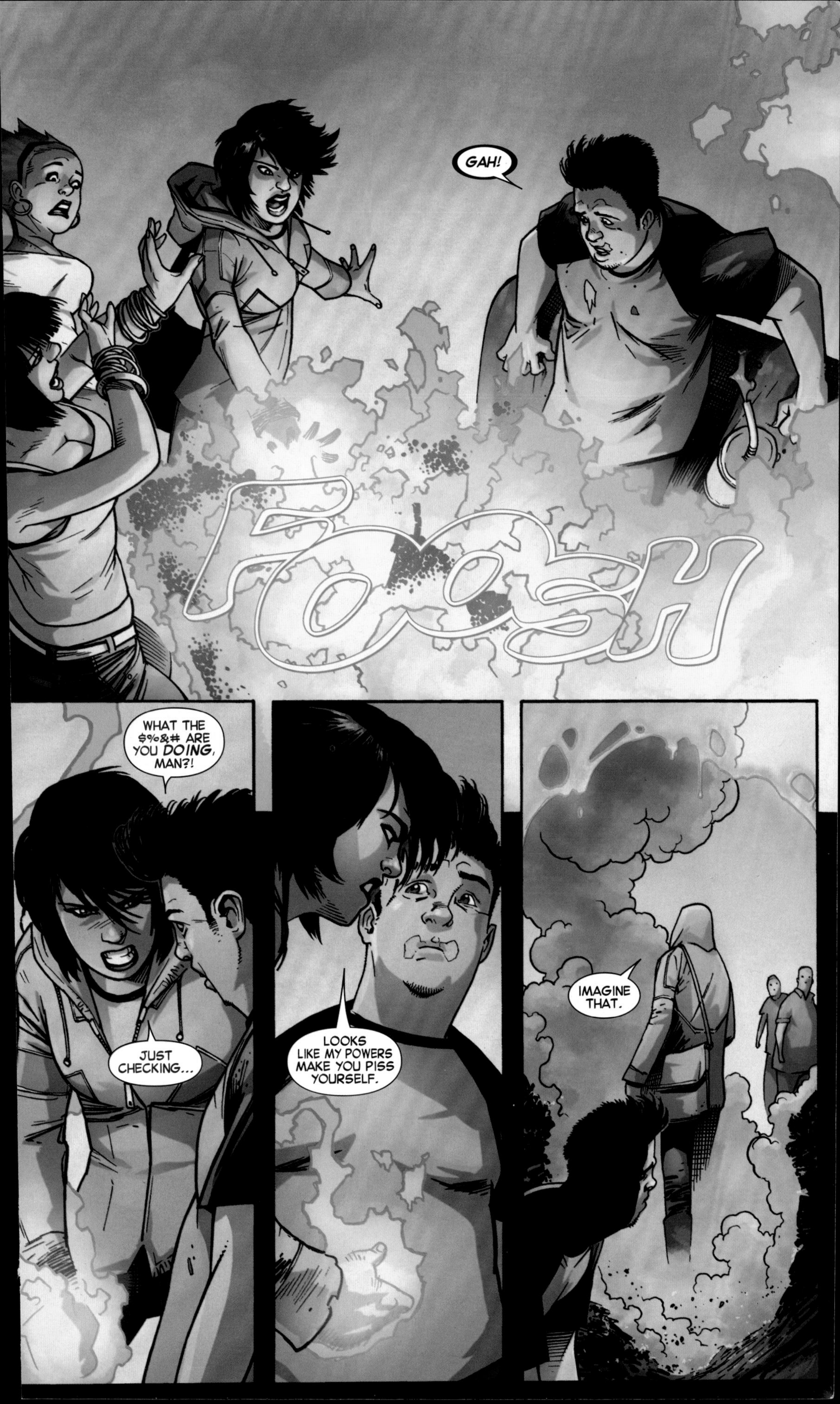
GAH!
FOOSH
WHAT THE $%&# ARE YOU DOING, MAN?!
JUST CHECKING...
LOOKS LIKE MY POWERS MAKE YOU PISS YOURSELF.
IMAGINE THAT.

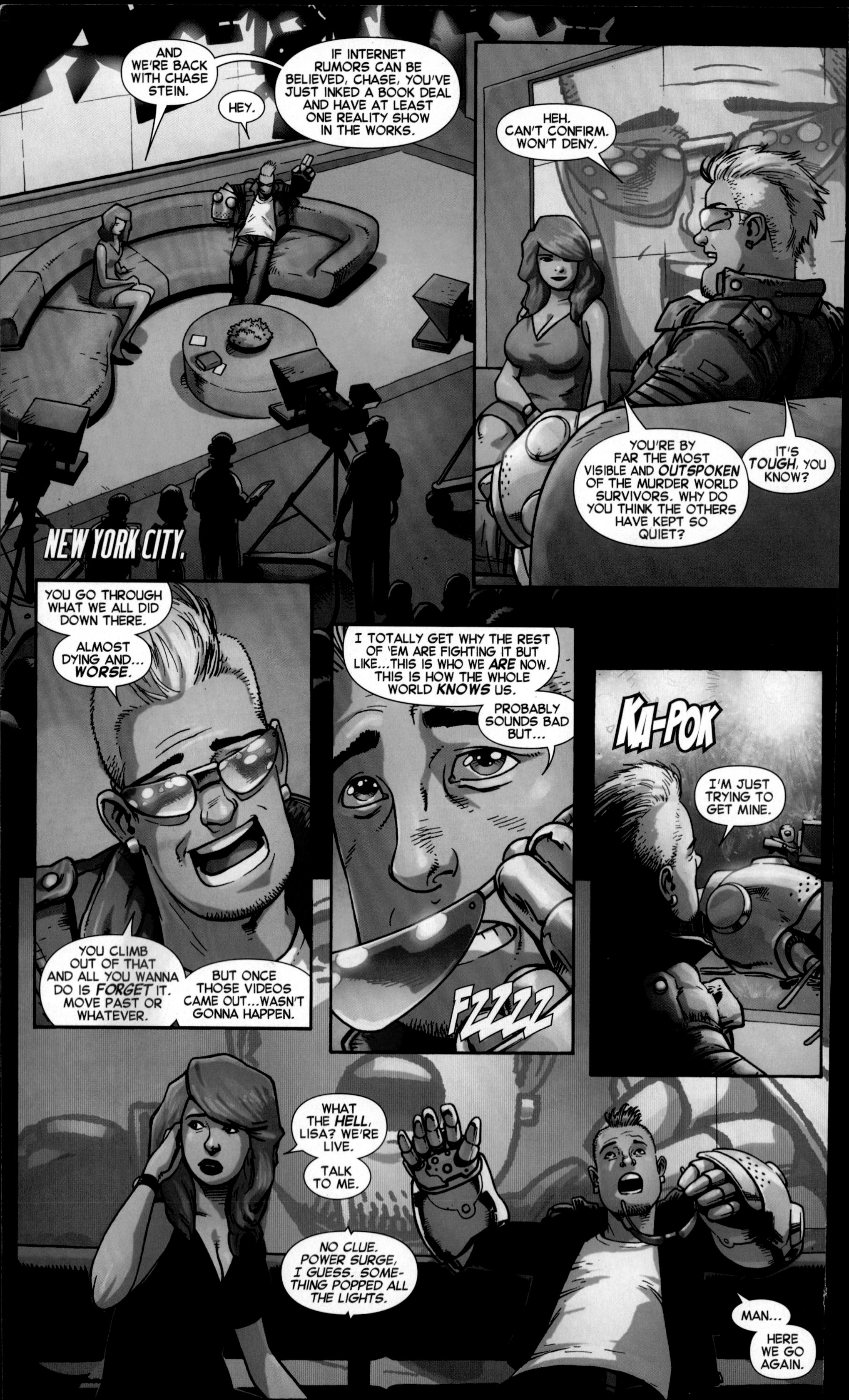
AND WE'RE BACK WITH CHASE STEIN.
HEY.
IF INTERNET RUMORS CAN BE BELIEVED, CHASE, YOU'VE JUST INKED A BOOK DEAL AND HAVE AT LEAST ONE REALITY SHOW IN THE WORKS.
NEW YORK CITY.
HEH. CAN'T CONFIRM. WON'T DENY.
YOU'RE BY FAR THE MOST VISIBLE AND OUTSPOKEN OF THE MURDER WORLD SURVIVORS. WHY DO YOU THINK THE OTHERS HAVE KEPT SO QUIET?
IT'S TOUGH, YOU KNOW?
YOU GO THROUGH WHAT WE ALL DID DOWN THERE.
ALMOST DYING AND... WORSE.
YOU CLIMB OUT OF THAT AND ALL YOU WANNA DO IS FORGET IT. MOVE PAST OR WHATEVER.
BUT ONCE THOSE VIDEOS CAME OUT...WASN'T GONNA HAPPEN.
I TOTALLY GET WHY THE REST OF 'EM ARE FIGHTING IT BUT LIKE...THIS IS WHO WE ARE NOW. THIS IS HOW THE WHOLE WORLD KNOWS US.
PROBABLY SOUNDS BAD BUT...
FZZZZ
KA-POK
I'M JUST TRYING TO GET MINE.
WHAT THE HELL, LISA? WE'RE LIVE.
TALK TO ME.
NO CLUE. POWER SURGE, I GUESS. SOMETHING POPPED ALL THE LIGHTS.
MAN...
HERE WE GO AGAIN.

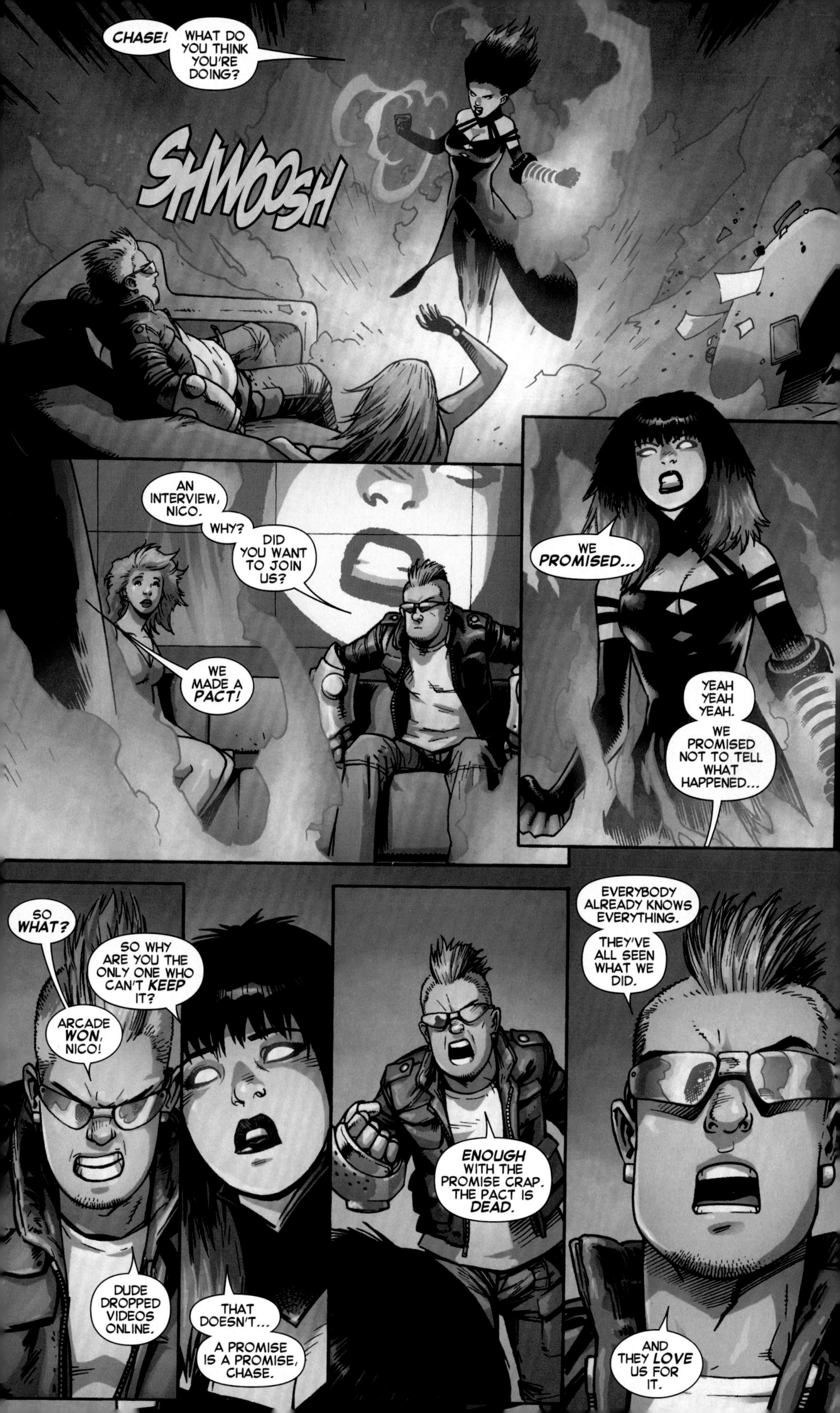
CHASE!
WHAT DO YOU THINK YOU'RE DOING?
SHWOOSH
AN INTERVIEW, NICO.
WHY?
DID YOU WANT TO JOIN US?
WE MADE A PACT!
WE PROMISED...
YEAH YEAH YEAH.
WE PROMISED NOT TO TELL WHAT HAPPENED...
SO WHAT?
SO WHY ARE YOU THE ONLY ONE WHO CAN'T KEEP IT?
ARCADE WON, NICO!
DUDE DROPPED VIDEOS ONLINE.
THAT DOESN'T...
A PROMISE IS A PROMISE, CHASE.
ENOUGH WITH THE PROMISE CRAP. THE PACT IS DEAD.
EVERYBODY ALREADY KNOWS EVERYTHING.
THEY'VE ALL SEEN WHAT WE DID.
AND THEY LOVE US FOR IT.

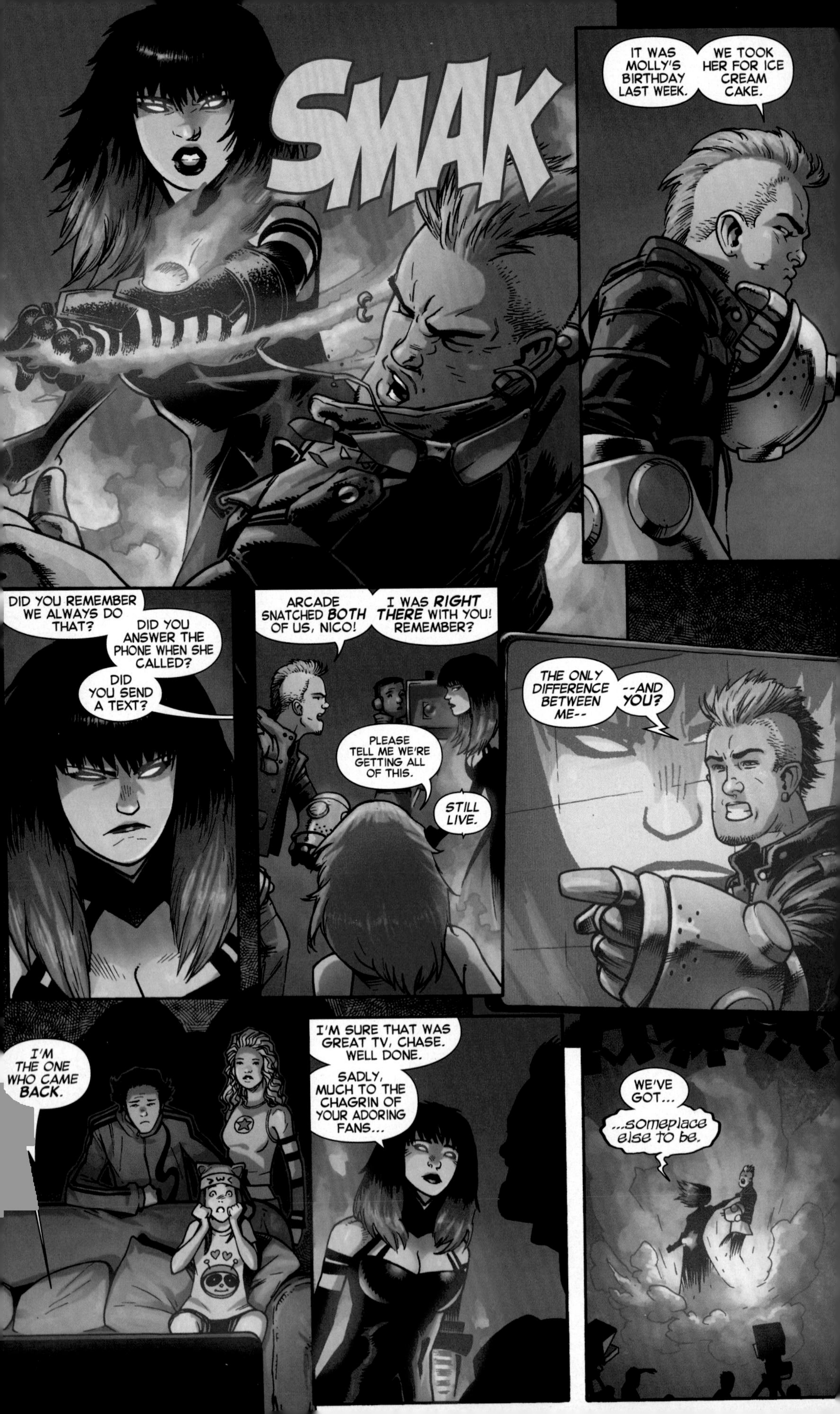
SMAK
IT WAS MOLLY'S BIRTHDAY LAST WEEK.
WE TOOK HER FOR ICE CREAM CAKE.
DID YOU REMEMBER WE ALWAYS DO THAT?
DID YOU ANSWER THE PHONE WHEN SHE CALLED?
DID YOU SEND A TEXT?
ARCADE SNATCHED **BOTH** OF US, NICO!
I WAS **RIGHT THERE** WITH YOU! REMEMBER?
PLEASE TELL ME WE'RE GETTING ALL OF THIS.
STILL LIVE.
THE ONLY DIFFERENCE BETWEEN ME--
--AND **YOU?**
I'M THE ONE WHO CAME **BACK**.
I'M SURE THAT WAS GREAT TV, CHASE. WELL DONE.
SADLY, MUCH TO THE CHAGRIN OF YOUR ADORING FANS...
WE'VE GOT...
...someplace else to be.

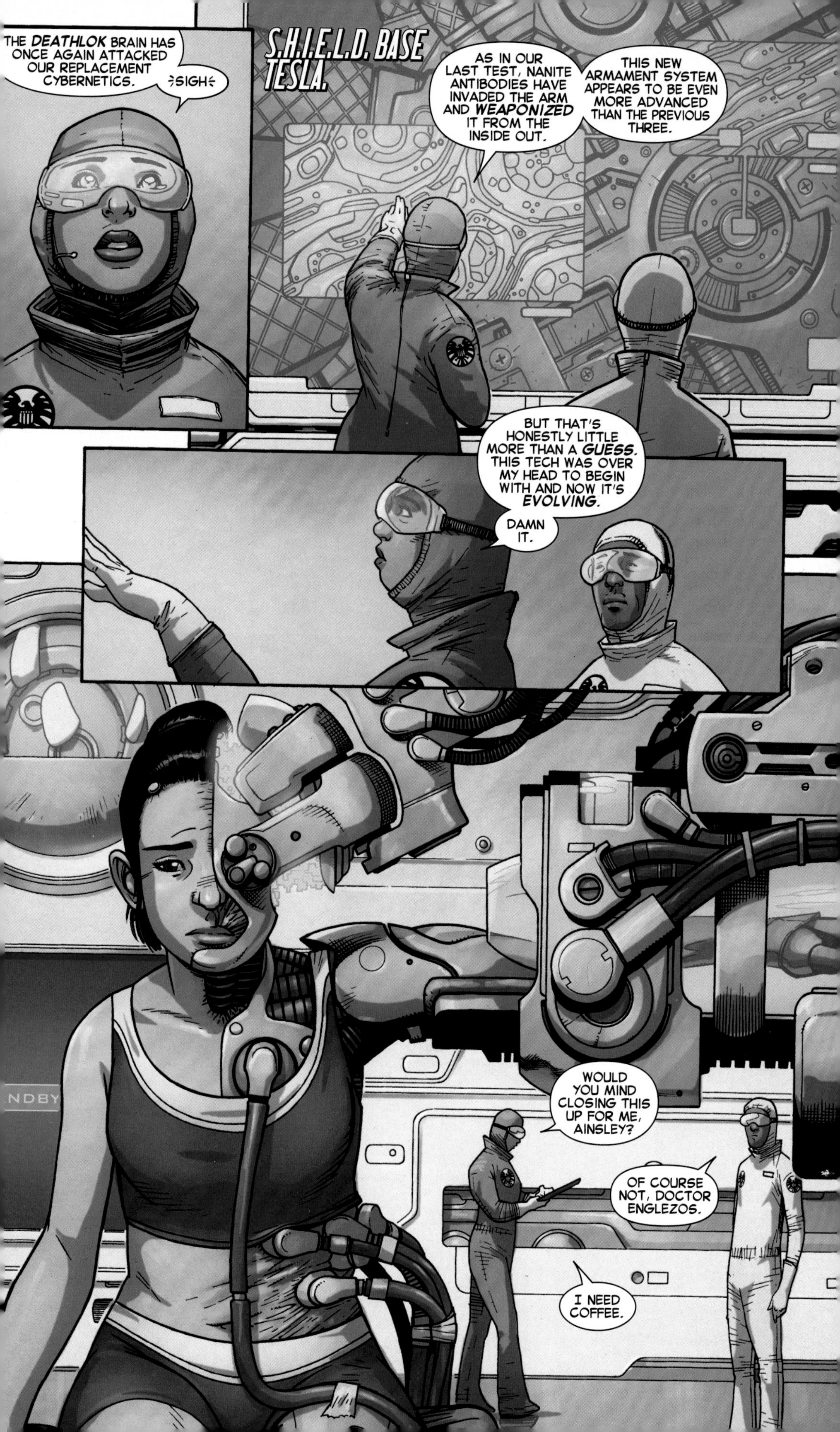
THE DEATHLOK BRAIN HAS ONCE AGAIN ATTACKED OUR REPLACEMENT CYBERNETICS.
SIGH
S.H.I.E.L.D. BASE TESLA.
AS IN OUR LAST TEST, NANITE ANTIBODIES HAVE INVADED THE ARM AND WEAPONIZED IT FROM THE INSIDE OUT.
THIS NEW ARMAMENT SYSTEM APPEARS TO BE EVEN MORE ADVANCED THAN THE PREVIOUS THREE.
BUT THAT'S HONESTLY LITTLE MORE THAN A GUESS. THIS TECH WAS OVER MY HEAD TO BEGIN WITH AND NOW IT'S EVOLVING.
DAMN IT.
WOULD YOU MIND CLOSING THIS UP FOR ME, AINSLEY?
OF COURSE NOT, DOCTOR ENGLEZOS.
I NEED COFFEE.

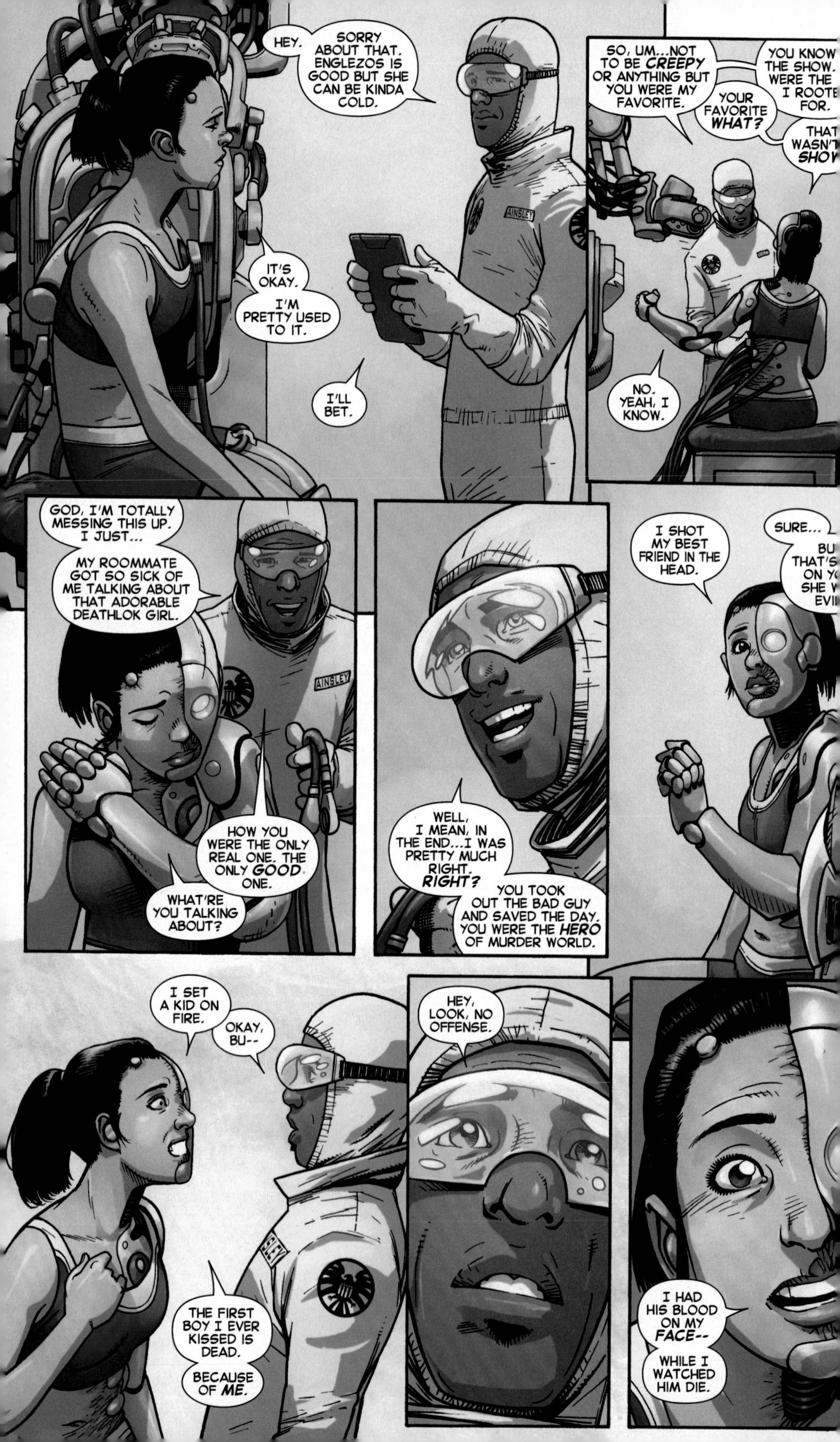
HEY.
SORRY ABOUT THAT. ENGLEZOS IS GOOD BUT SHE CAN BE KINDA COLD.
IT'S OKAY.
I'M PRETTY USED TO IT.
I'LL BET.
SO, UM...NOT TO BE CREEPY OR ANYTHING BUT YOU WERE MY FAVORITE.
YOUR FAVORITE WHAT?
NO. YEAH, I KNOW.
GOD, I'M TOTALLY MESSING THIS UP. I JUST...
MY ROOMMATE GOT SO SICK OF ME TALKING ABOUT THAT ADORABLE DEATHLOK GIRL.
HOW YOU WERE THE ONLY REAL ONE. THE ONLY GOOD ONE.
WHAT'RE YOU TALKING ABOUT?
WELL, I MEAN, IN THE END...I WAS PRETTY MUCH RIGHT. RIGHT?
YOU TOOK OUT THE BAD GUY AND SAVED THE DAY. YOU WERE THE HERO OF MURDER WORLD.
I SHOT MY BEST FRIEND IN THE HEAD.
SURE...
I SET A KID ON FIRE.
OKAY, BU--
THE FIRST BOY I EVER KISSED IS DEAD.
BECAUSE OF ME.
HEY, LOOK, NO OFFENSE.
I HAD HIS BLOOD ON MY FACE--
WHILE I WATCHED HIM DIE.

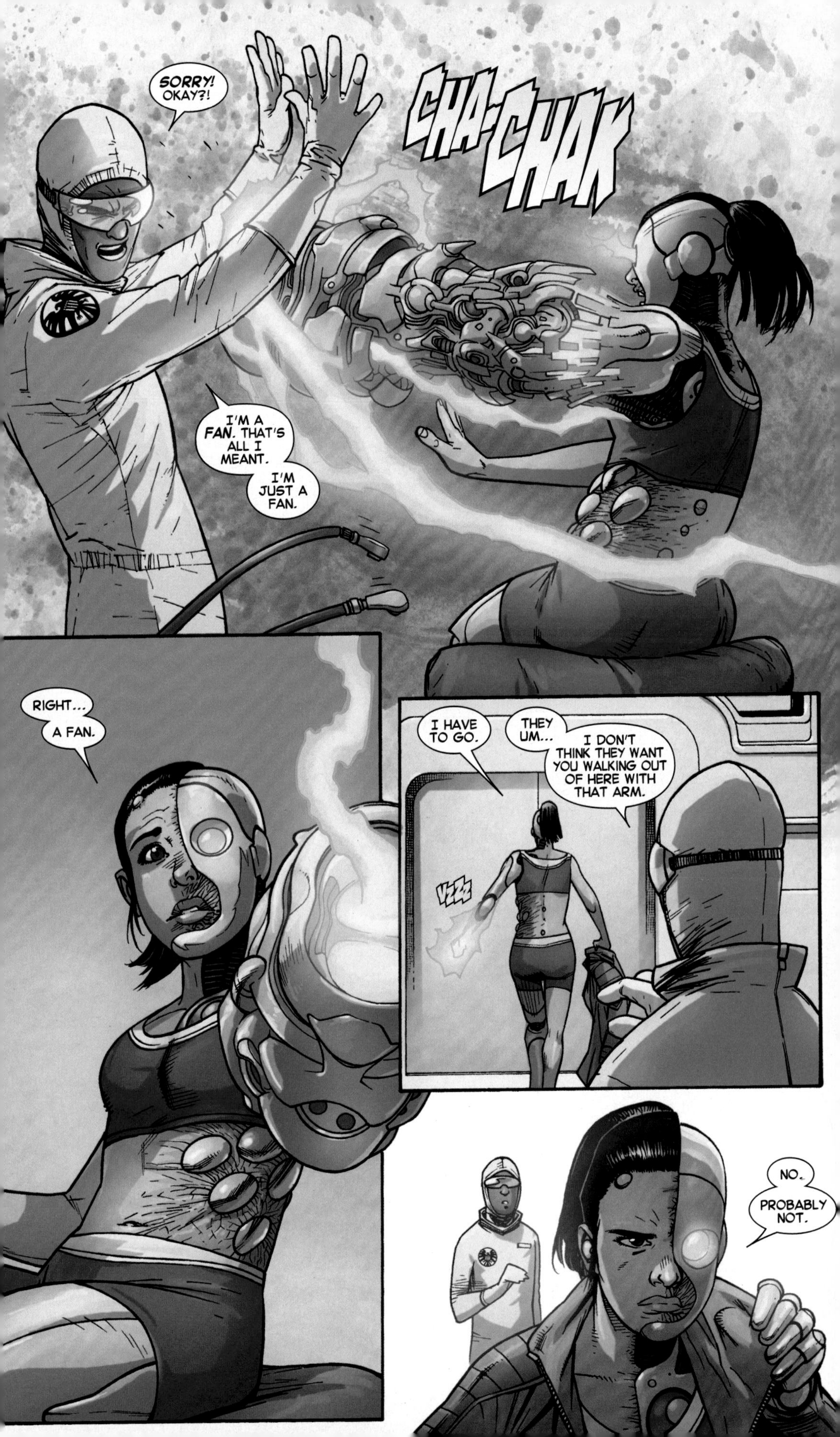
SORRY! OKAY?!
CHA-CHAK
I'M A FAN. THAT'S ALL I MEANT.
I'M JUST A FAN.
RIGHT...
A FAN.
I HAVE TO GO.
THEY UM...
I DON'T THINK THEY WANT YOU WALKING OUT OF HERE WITH THAT ARM.
VZZZ
NO.
PROBABLY NOT.

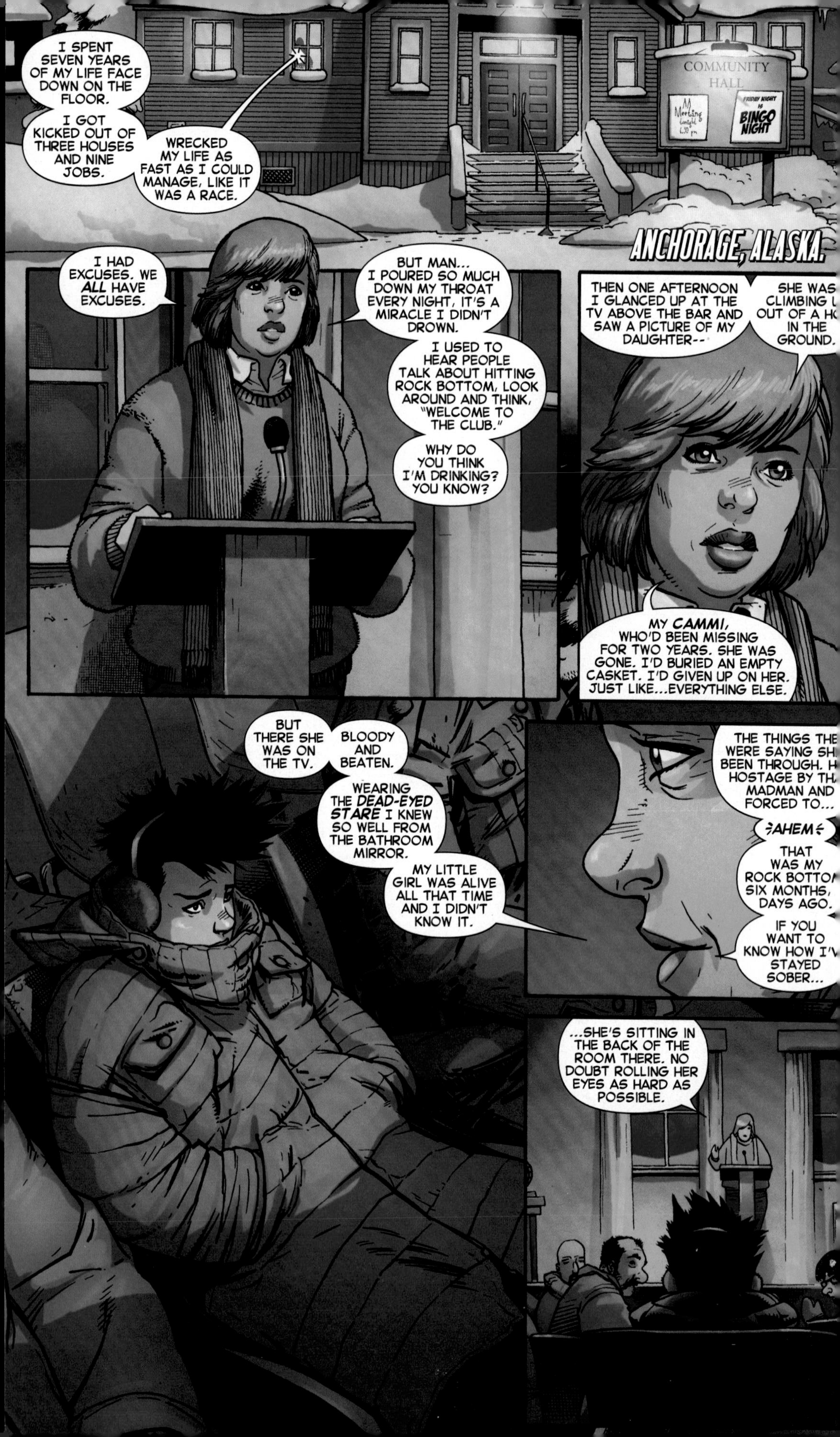
I SPENT SEVEN YEARS OF MY LIFE FACE DOWN ON THE FLOOR.
I GOT KICKED OUT OF THREE HOUSES AND NINE JOBS.
WRECKED MY LIFE AS FAST AS I COULD MANAGE, LIKE IT WAS A RACE.
COMMUNITY HALL
FRIDAY NIGHT IS BINGO NIGHT
ANCHORAGE, ALASKA.
I HAD EXCUSES. WE ALL HAVE EXCUSES.
BUT MAN... I POURED SO MUCH DOWN MY THROAT EVERY NIGHT, IT'S A MIRACLE I DIDN'T DROWN.
I USED TO HEAR PEOPLE TALK ABOUT HITTING ROCK BOTTOM, LOOK AROUND AND THINK, "WELCOME TO THE CLUB."
WHY DO YOU THINK I'M DRINKING? YOU KNOW?
THEN ONE AFTERNOON I GLANCED UP AT THE TV ABOVE THE BAR AND SAW A PICTURE OF MY DAUGHTER--
SHE WAS CLIMBING OUT OF A HO IN THE GROUND.
MY CAMMI, WHO'D BEEN MISSING FOR TWO YEARS. SHE WAS GONE. I'D BURIED AN EMPTY CASKET. I'D GIVEN UP ON HER. JUST LIKE...EVERYTHING ELSE.
BUT THERE SHE WAS ON THE TV.
BLOODY AND BEATEN.
WEARING THE DEAD-EYED STARE I KNEW SO WELL FROM THE BATHROOM MIRROR.
MY LITTLE GIRL WAS ALIVE ALL THAT TIME AND I DIDN'T KNOW IT.
THE THINGS THE WERE SAYING SH BEEN THROUGH. H HOSTAGE BY TH MADMAN AND FORCED TO...
AHEM
THAT WAS MY ROCK BOTTO SIX MONTHS, DAYS AGO.
IF YOU WANT TO KNOW HOW I'V STAYED SOBER...
...SHE'S SITTING IN THE BACK OF THE ROOM THERE. NO DOUBT ROLLING HER EYES AS HARD AS POSSIBLE.

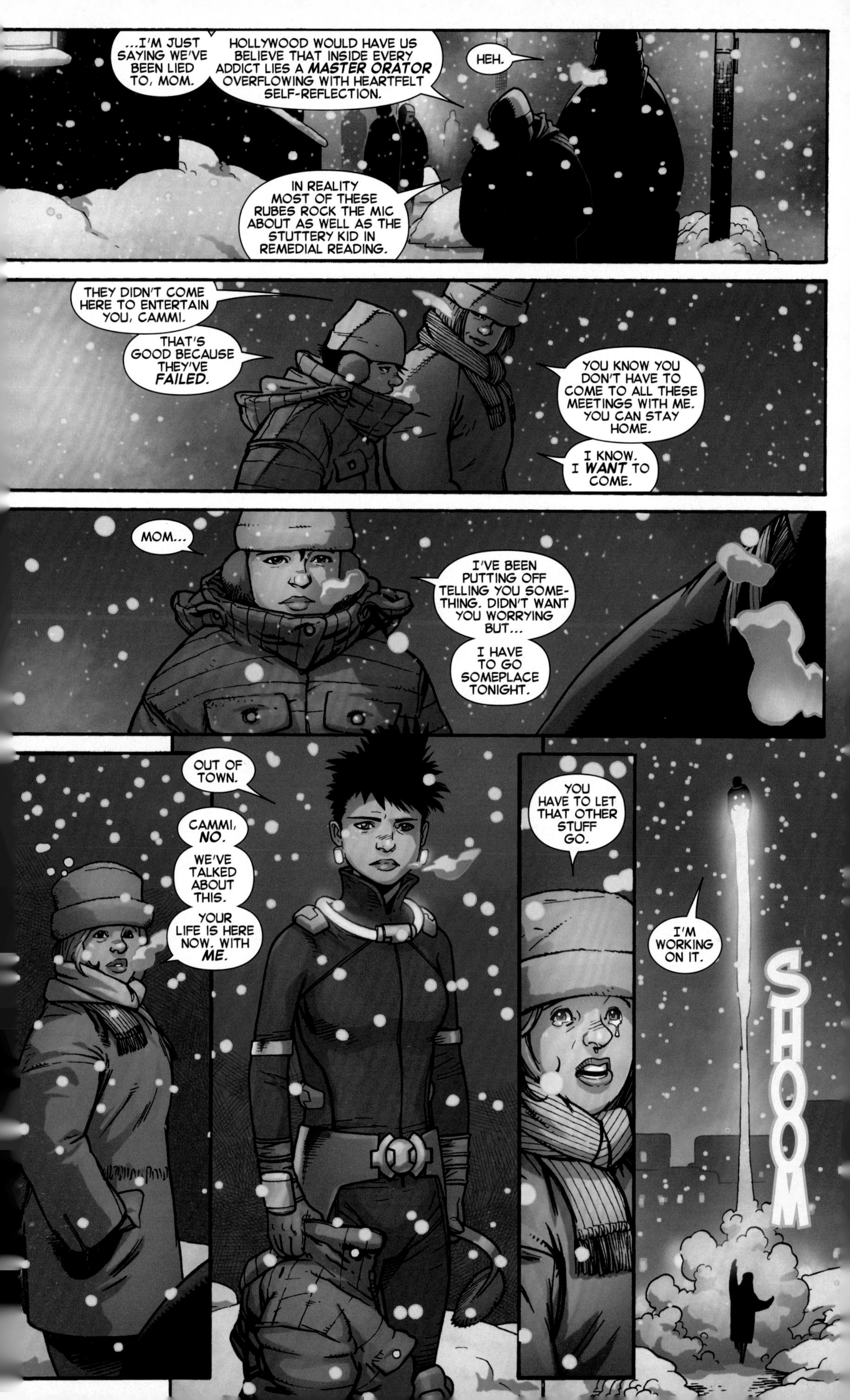
...I'M JUST SAYING WE'VE BEEN LIED TO, MOM.
HOLLYWOOD WOULD HAVE US BELIEVE THAT INSIDE EVERY ADDICT LIES A MASTER ORATOR OVERFLOWING WITH HEARTFELT SELF-REFLECTION.
HEH.
IN REALITY MOST OF THESE RUBES ROCK THE MIC ABOUT AS WELL AS THE STUTTERY KID IN REMEDIAL READING.
THEY DIDN'T COME HERE TO ENTERTAIN YOU, CAMMI.
THAT'S GOOD BECAUSE THEY'VE FAILED.
YOU KNOW YOU DON'T HAVE TO COME TO ALL THESE MEETINGS WITH ME. YOU CAN STAY HOME.
I KNOW. I WANT TO COME.
MOM...
I'VE BEEN PUTTING OFF TELLING YOU SOME-THING. DIDN'T WANT YOU WORRYING BUT...
I HAVE TO GO SOMEPLACE TONIGHT.
OUT OF TOWN.
CAMMI, NO.
WE'VE TALKED ABOUT THIS.
YOUR LIFE IS HERE NOW. WITH ME.
YOU HAVE TO LET THAT OTHER STUFF GO.
I'M WORKING ON IT.
SHOOM

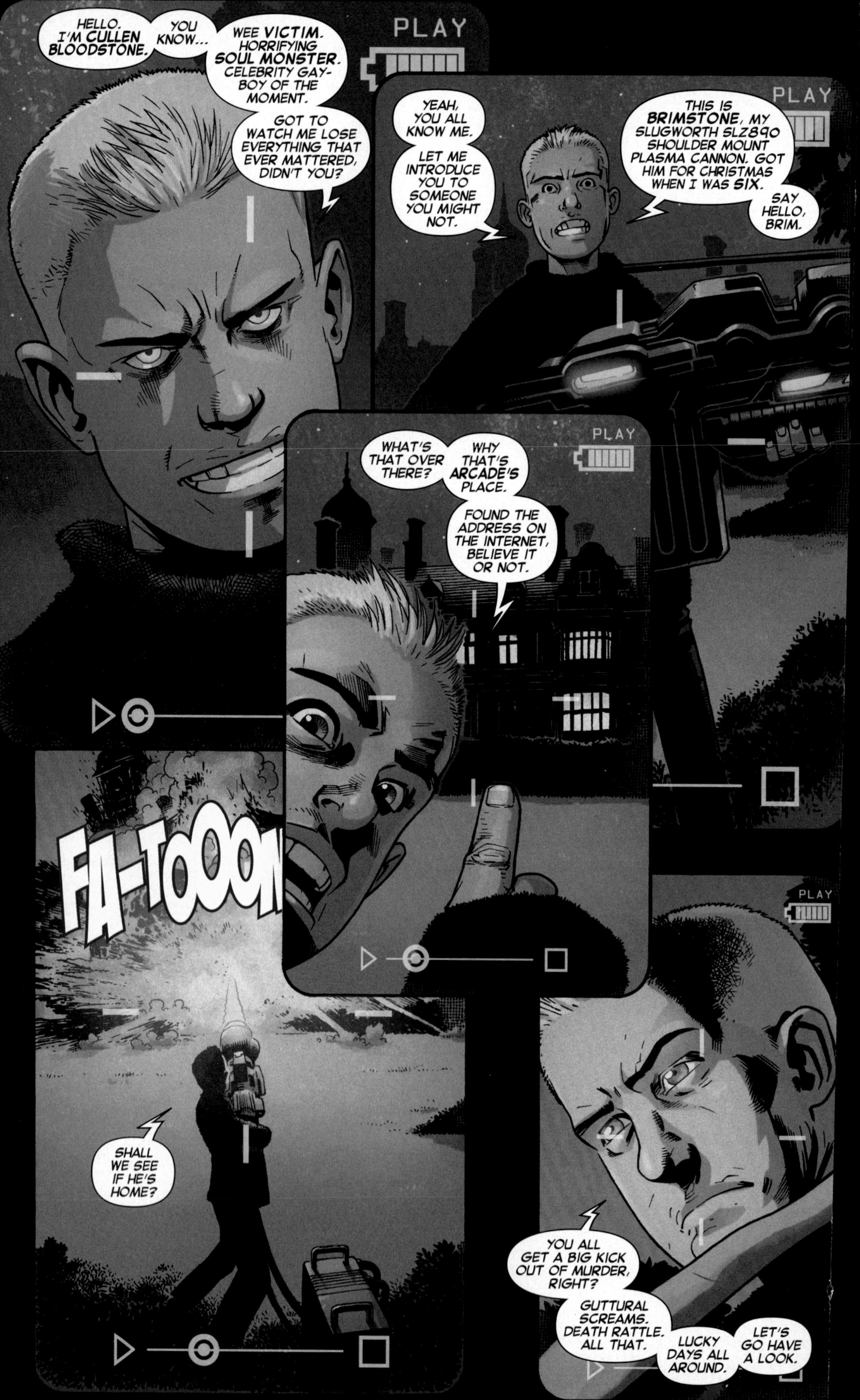
PLAY
HELLO. I'M CULLEN BLOODSTONE.
YOU KNOW...
WEE VICTIM. HORRIFYING SOUL MONSTER. CELEBRITY GAY-BOY OF THE MOMENT.
GOT TO WATCH ME LOSE EVERYTHING THAT EVER MATTERED, DIDN'T YOU?
PLAY
YEAH, YOU ALL KNOW ME.
LET ME INTRODUCE YOU TO SOMEONE YOU MIGHT NOT.
THIS IS BRIMSTONE, MY SLUGWORTH SLZ890 SHOULDER MOUNT PLASMA CANNON. GOT HIM FOR CHRISTMAS WHEN I WAS SIX.
SAY HELLO, BRIM.
PLAY
WHAT'S THAT OVER THERE?
WHY THAT'S ARCADE'S PLACE.
FOUND THE ADDRESS ON THE INTERNET, BELIEVE IT OR NOT.
FA-TOOOM
SHALL WE SEE IF HE'S HOME?
PLAY
YOU ALL GET A BIG KICK OUT OF MURDER, RIGHT?
GUTTURAL SCREAMS. DEATH RATTLE. ALL THAT.
LUCKY DAYS ALL AROUND.
LET'S GO HAVE A LOOK.

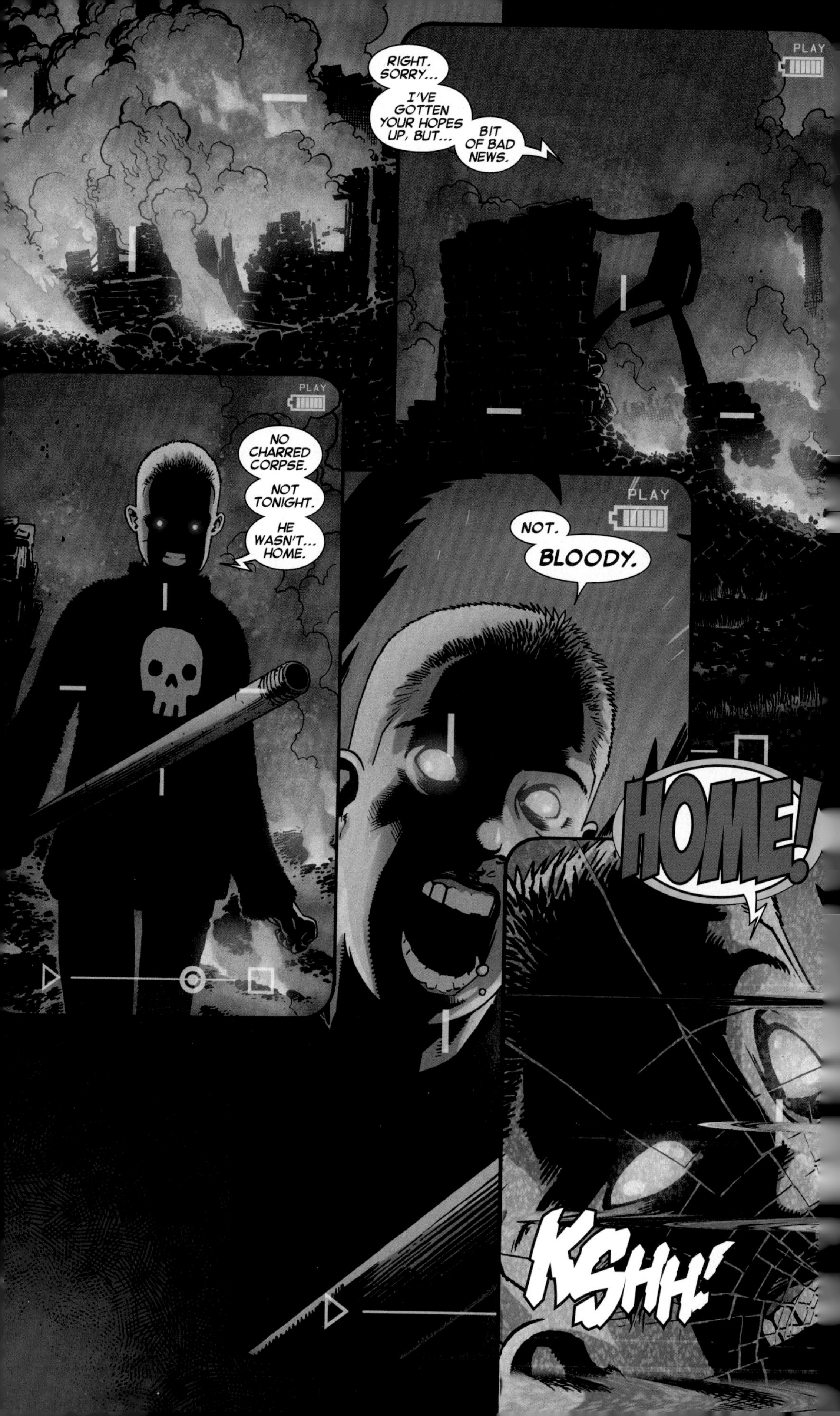
RIGHT. SORRY...
I'VE GOTTEN YOUR HOPES UP, BUT...
BIT OF BAD NEWS.
PLAY
NO CHARRED CORPSE.
NOT TONIGHT.
HE WASN'T... HOME.
PLAY
NOT.
BLOODY.
HOME!
KSHH!

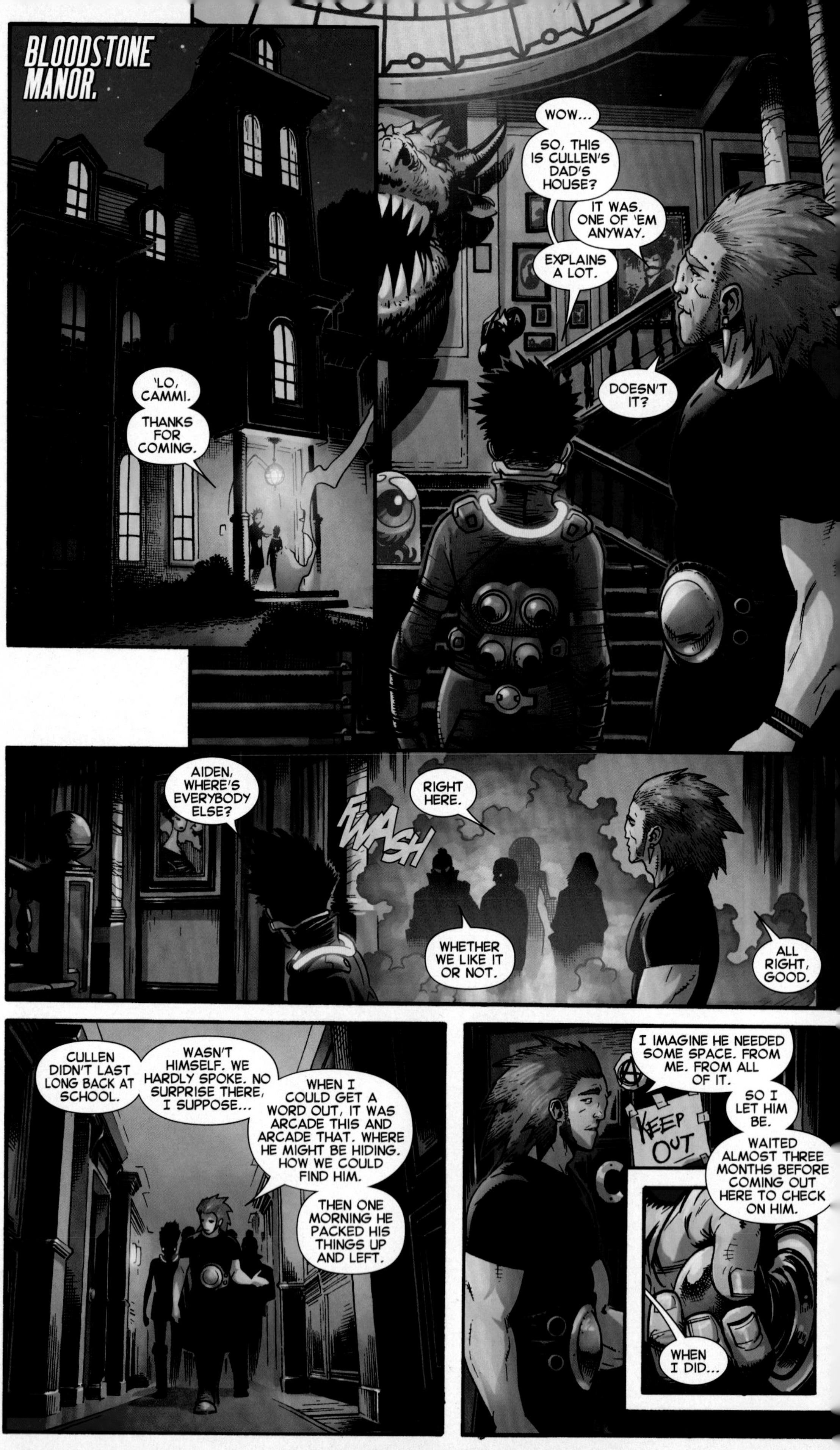
BLOODSTONE MANOR.
'LO, CAMMI.
THANKS FOR COMING.
WOW...
SO, THIS IS CULLEN'S DAD'S HOUSE?
IT WAS. ONE OF 'EM ANYWAY.
EXPLAINS A LOT.
DOESN'T IT?
AIDEN, WHERE'S EVERYBODY ELSE?
FWASH
RIGHT HERE.
WHETHER WE LIKE IT OR NOT.
ALL RIGHT, GOOD.
CULLEN DIDN'T LAST LONG BACK AT SCHOOL.
WASN'T HIMSELF. WE HARDLY SPOKE. NO SURPRISE THERE, I SUPPOSE...
WHEN I COULD GET A WORD OUT, IT WAS ARCADE THIS AND ARCADE THAT. WHERE HE MIGHT BE HIDING. HOW WE COULD FIND HIM.
THEN ONE MORNING HE PACKED HIS THINGS UP AND LEFT.
I IMAGINE HE NEEDED SOME SPACE. FROM ME. FROM ALL OF IT.
KEEP OUT
SO I LET HIM BE.
WAITED ALMOST THREE MONTHS BEFORE COMING OUT HERE TO CHECK ON HIM.
WHEN I DID...

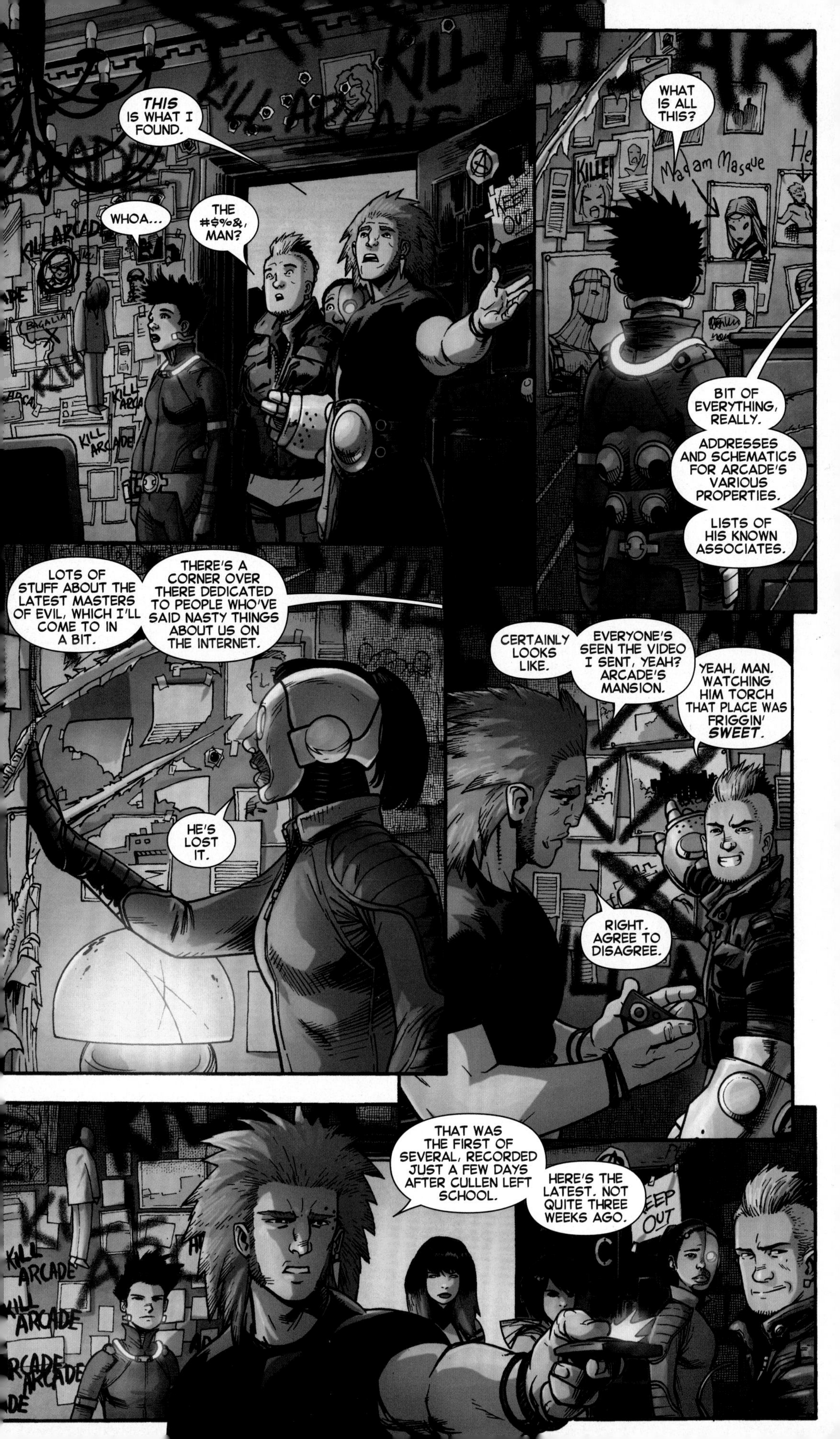
THIS IS WHAT I FOUND.
WHOA...
THE #$%&, MAN?
WHAT IS ALL THIS?
KILLET
Madam Masque
BIT OF EVERYTHING, REALLY.
ADDRESSES AND SCHEMATICS FOR ARCADE'S VARIOUS PROPERTIES.
LISTS OF HIS KNOWN ASSOCIATES.
LOTS OF STUFF ABOUT THE LATEST MASTERS OF EVIL, WHICH I'LL COME TO IN A BIT.
THERE'S A CORNER OVER THERE DEDICATED TO PEOPLE WHO'VE SAID NASTY THINGS ABOUT US ON THE INTERNET.
HE'S LOST IT.
CERTAINLY LOOKS LIKE.
EVERYONE'S SEEN THE VIDEO I SENT, YEAH? ARCADE'S MANSION.
YEAH, MAN. WATCHING HIM TORCH THAT PLACE WAS FRIGGIN' SWEET.
RIGHT. AGREE TO DISAGREE.
THAT WAS THE FIRST OF SEVERAL, RECORDED JUST A FEW DAYS AFTER CULLEN LEFT SCHOOL.
HERE'S THE LATEST. NOT QUITE THREE WEEKS AGO.
KEEP OUT
KILL ARCADE

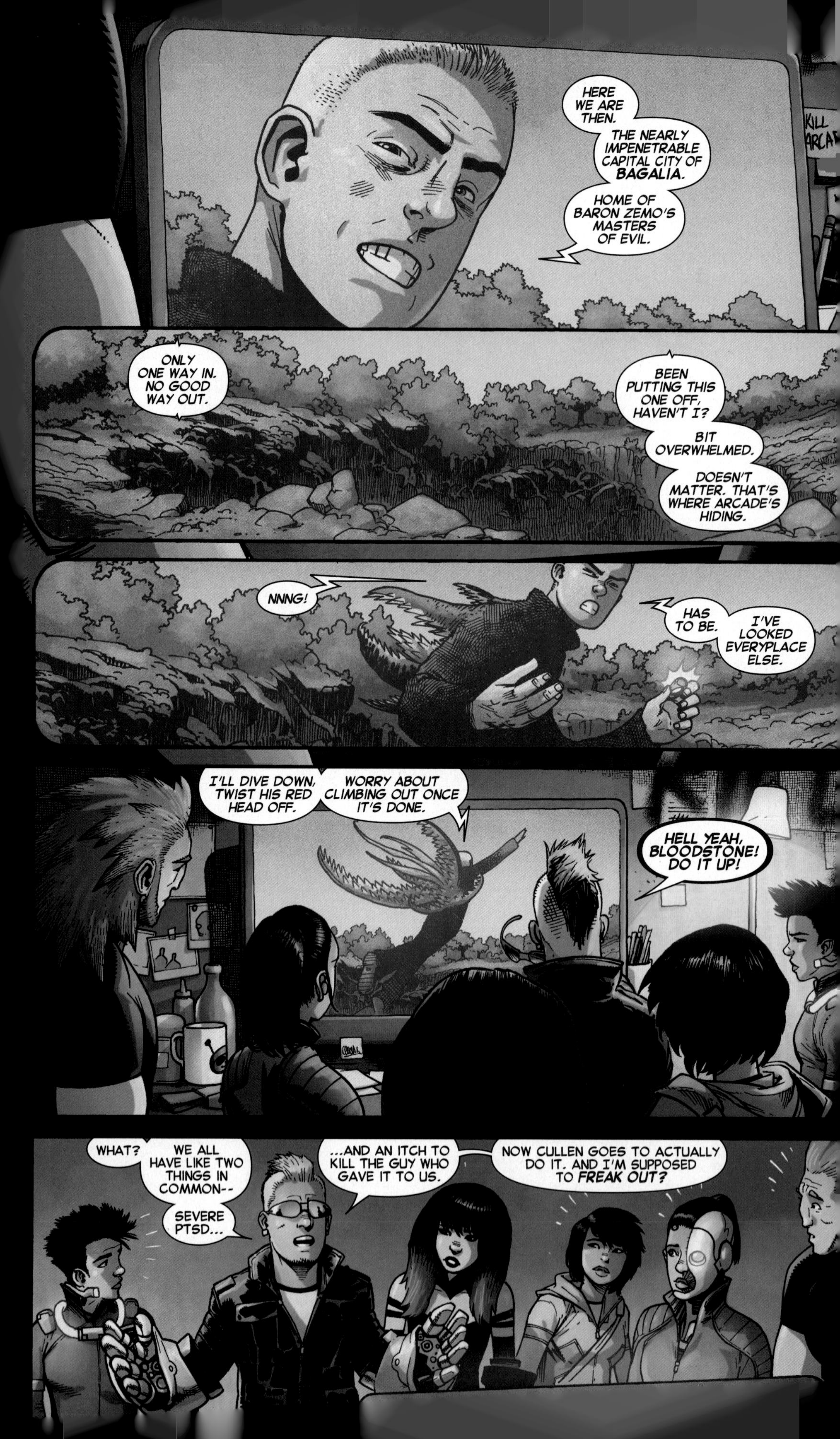
HERE WE ARE THEN.
THE NEARLY IMPENETRABLE CAPITAL CITY OF BAGALIA.
HOME OF BARON ZEMO'S MASTERS OF EVIL.
ONLY ONE WAY IN. NO GOOD WAY OUT.
BEEN PUTTING THIS ONE OFF, HAVEN'T I?
BIT OVERWHELMED.
DOESN'T MATTER. THAT'S WHERE ARCADE'S HIDING.
NNNG!
HAS TO BE.
I'VE LOOKED EVERYPLACE ELSE.
I'LL DIVE DOWN, TWIST HIS RED HEAD OFF.
WORRY ABOUT CLIMBING OUT ONCE IT'S DONE.
HELL YEAH, BLOODSTONE! DO IT UP!
WHAT?
WE ALL HAVE LIKE TWO THINGS IN COMMON--
SEVERE PTSD...
...AND AN ITCH TO KILL THE GUY WHO GAVE IT TO US.
NOW CULLEN GOES TO ACTUALLY DO IT. AND I'M SUPPOSED TO FREAK OUT?

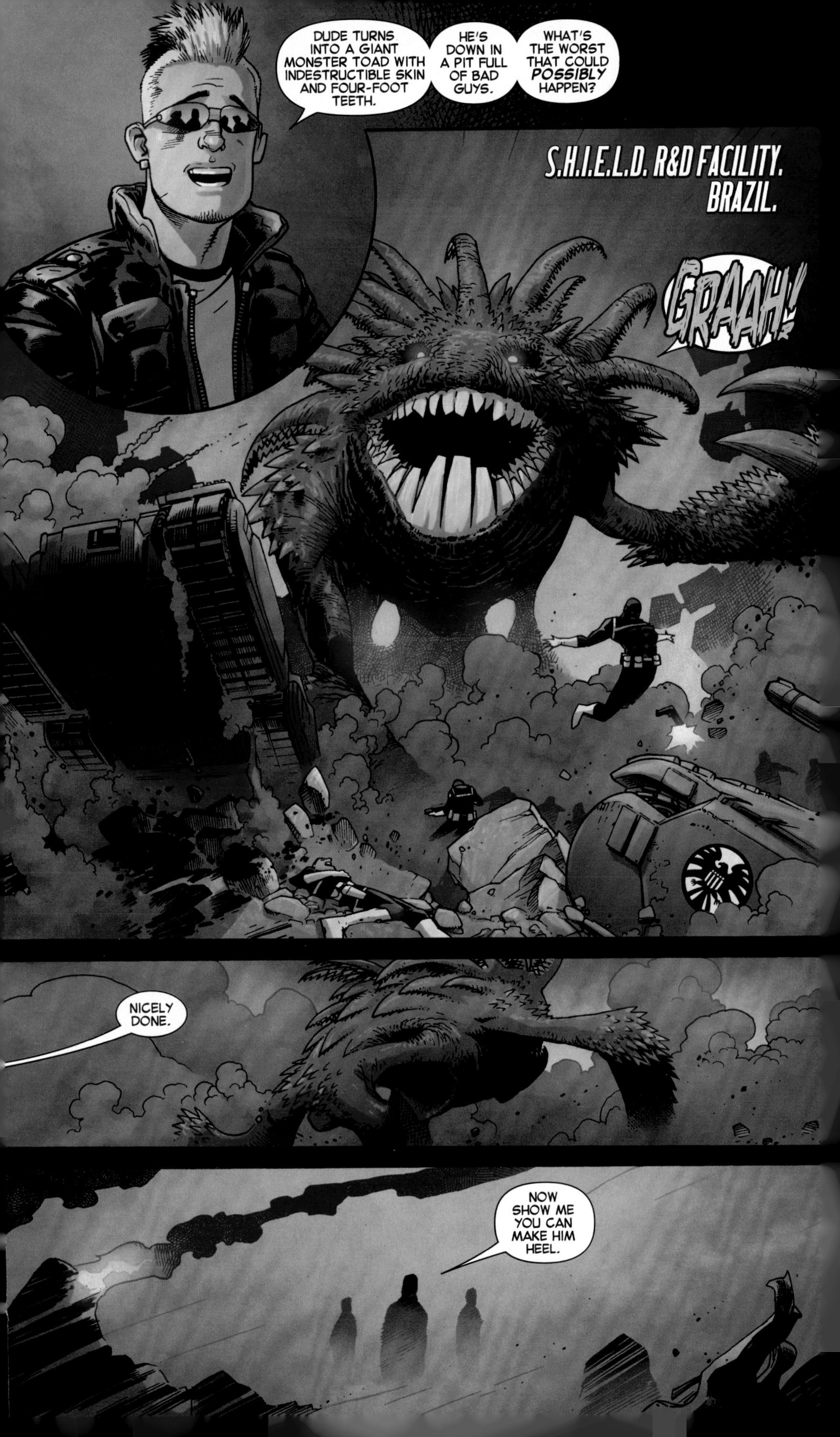
DUDE TURNS INTO A GIANT MONSTER TOAD WITH INDESTRUCTIBLE SKIN AND FOUR-FOOT TEETH.
HE'S DOWN IN A PIT FULL OF BAD GUYS.
WHAT'S THE WORST THAT COULD *POSSIBLY* HAPPEN?
S.H.I.E.L.D. R&D FACILITY. BRAZIL.
GRAAH!
NICELY DONE.
NOW SHOW ME YOU CAN MAKE HIM HEEL.

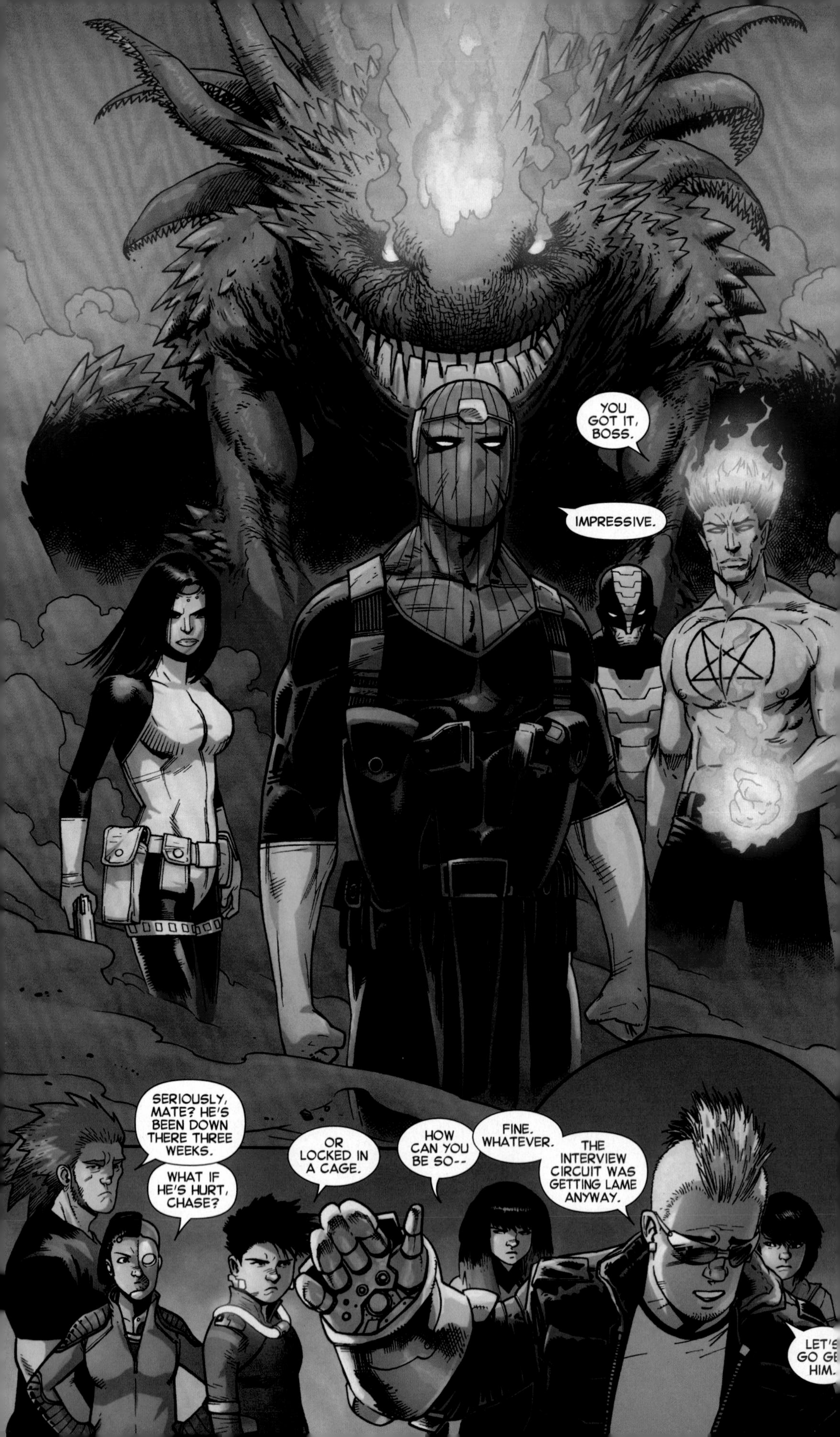
YOU GOT IT, BOSS.
IMPRESSIVE.
SERIOUSLY, MATE? HE'S BEEN DOWN THERE THREE WEEKS.
WHAT IF HE'S HURT, CHASE?
OR LOCKED IN A CAGE.
HOW CAN YOU BE SO--
FINE. WHATEVER.
THE INTERVIEW CIRCUIT WAS GETTING LAME ANYWAY.

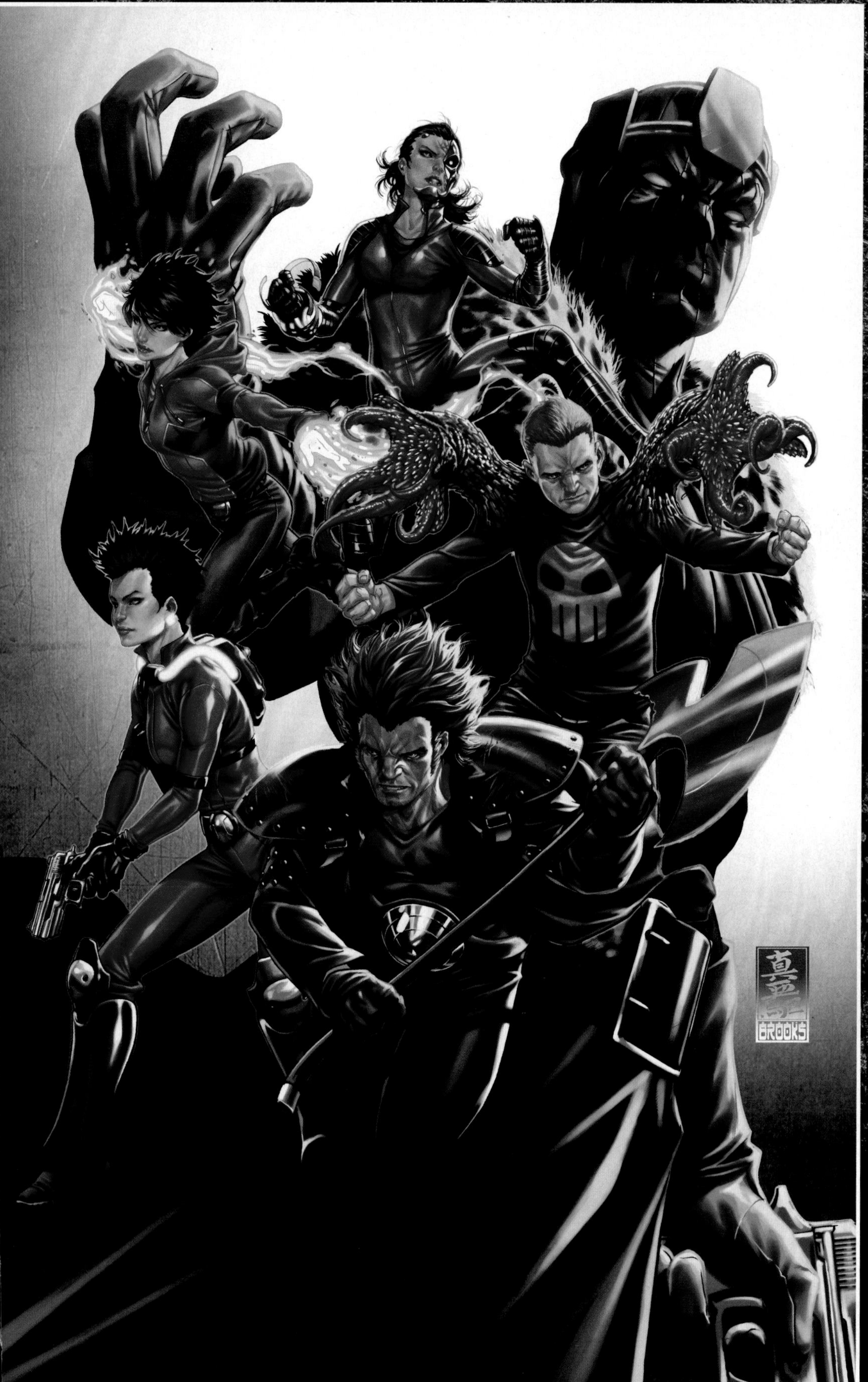
BROOKS

#1 VARIANT BY MARK BROOKS

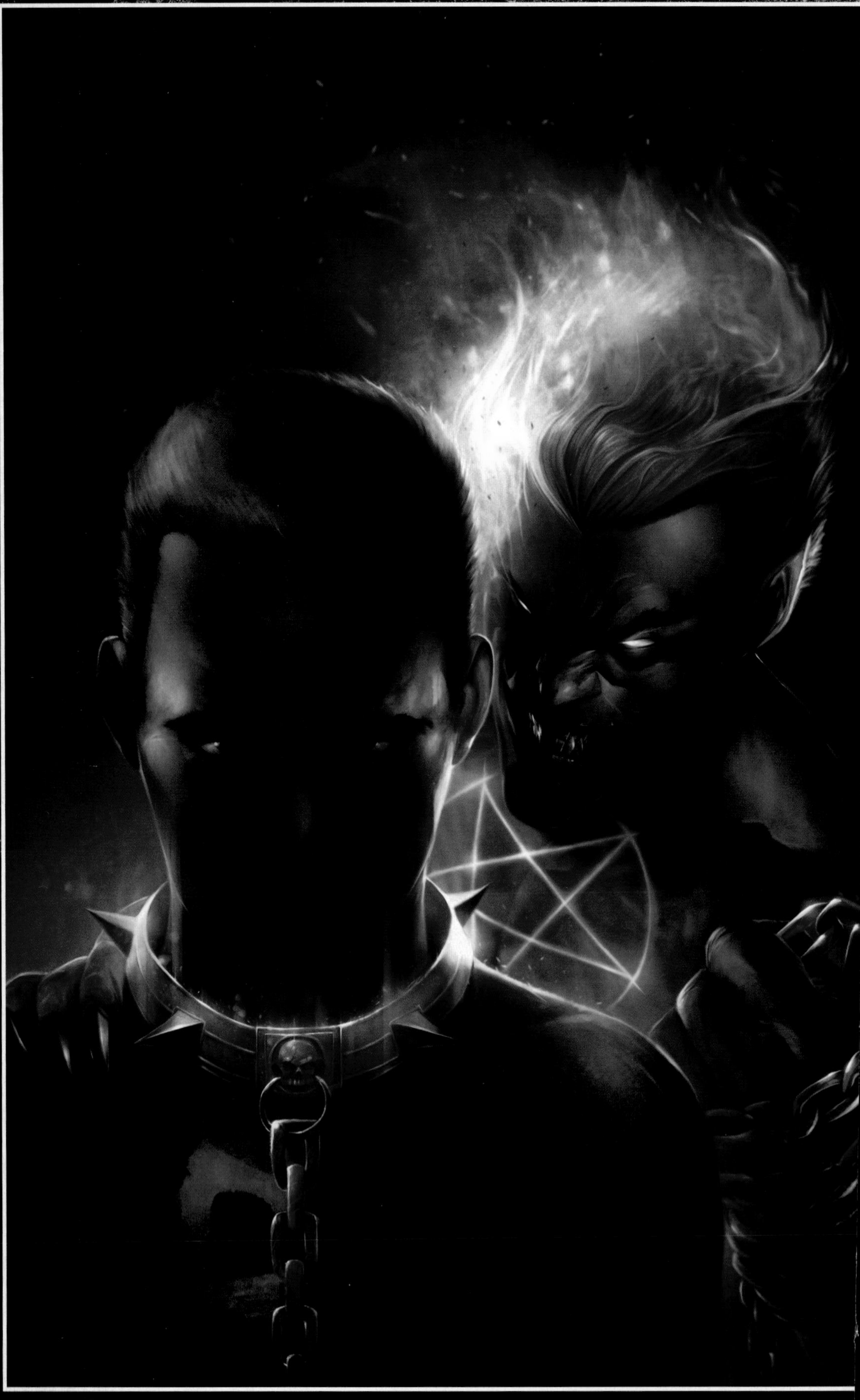

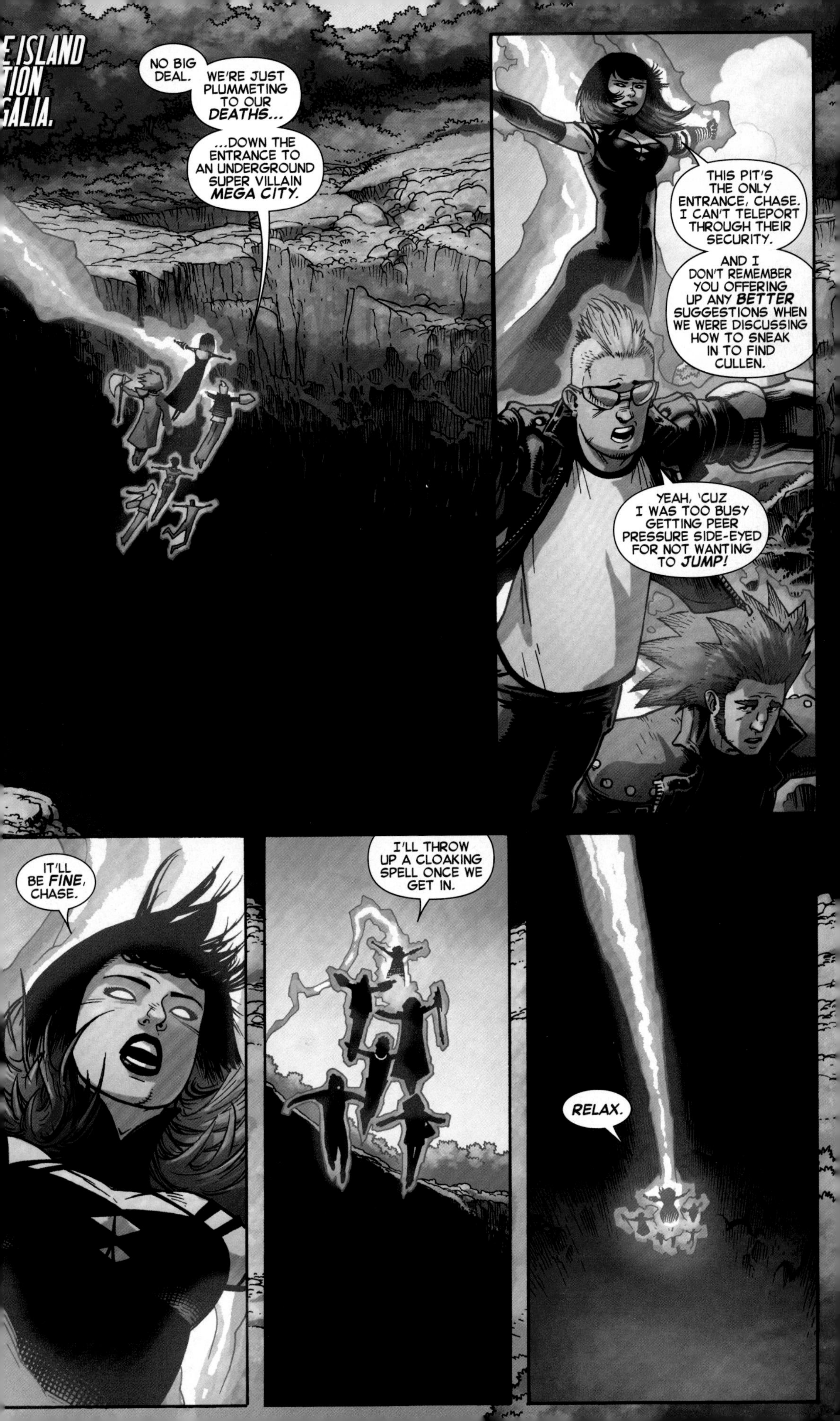
E ISLAND
TION
GALIA.
NO BIG DEAL.
WE'RE JUST PLUMMETING TO OUR DEATHS...
...DOWN THE ENTRANCE TO AN UNDERGROUND SUPER VILLAIN MEGA CITY.
THIS PIT'S THE ONLY ENTRANCE, CHASE. I CAN'T TELEPORT THROUGH THEIR SECURITY.
AND I DON'T REMEMBER YOU OFFERING UP ANY BETTER SUGGESTIONS WHEN WE WERE DISCUSSING HOW TO SNEAK IN TO FIND CULLEN.
YEAH, 'CUZ I WAS TOO BUSY GETTING PEER PRESSURE SIDE-EYED FOR NOT WANTING TO JUMP!
IT'LL BE FINE, CHASE.
I'LL THROW UP A CLOAKING SPELL ONCE WE GET IN.
RELAX.

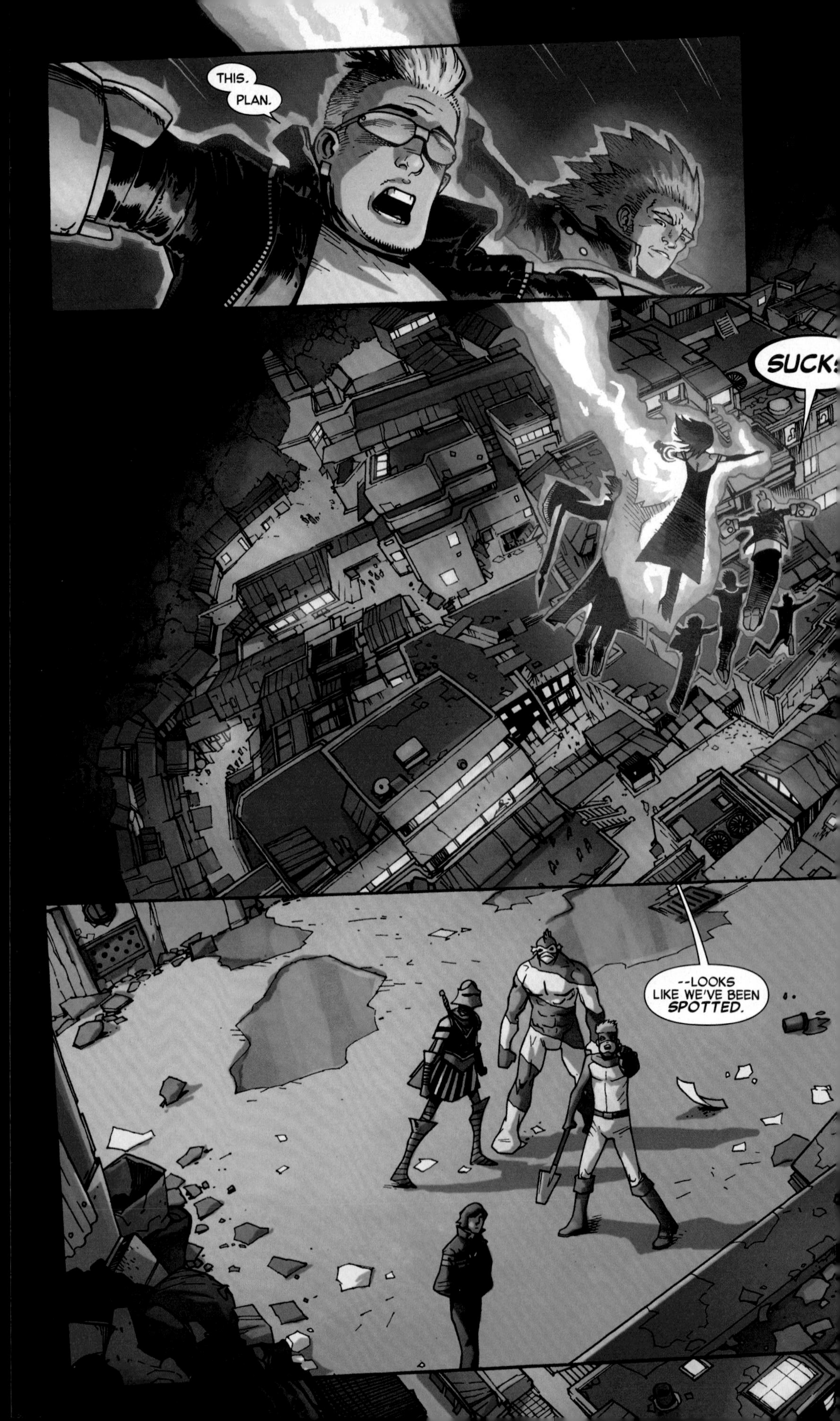
THIS. PLAN.
SUCK:
--LOOKS LIKE WE'VE BEEN SPOTTED.

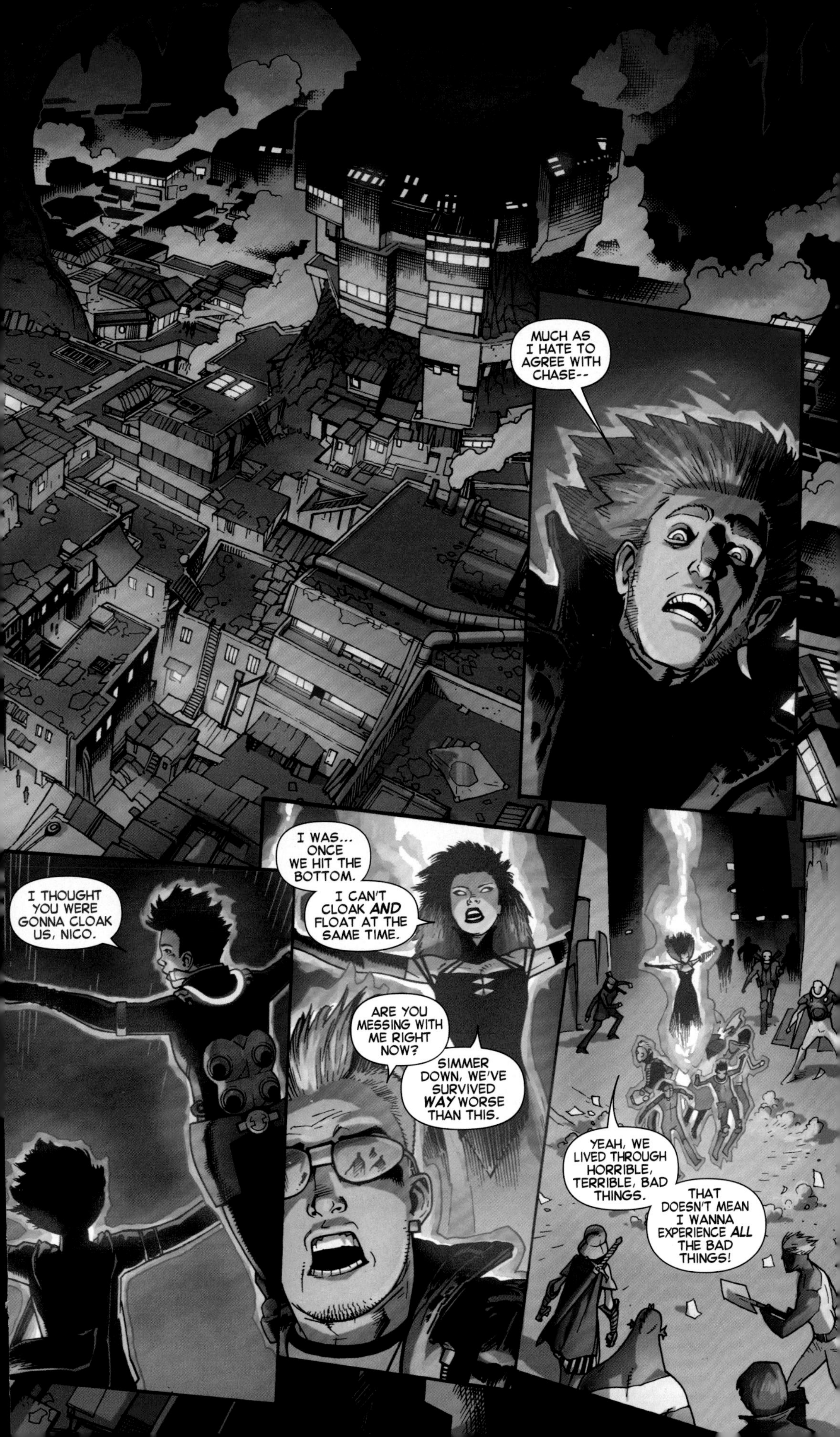

MUCH AS I HATE TO AGREE WITH CHASE--
I THOUGHT YOU WERE GONNA CLOAK US, NICO.
I WAS... ONCE WE HIT THE BOTTOM.
I CAN'T CLOAK AND FLOAT AT THE SAME TIME.
ARE YOU MESSING WITH ME RIGHT NOW?
SIMMER DOWN, WE'VE SURVIVED WAY WORSE THAN THIS.
YEAH, WE LIVED THROUGH HORRIBLE, TERRIBLE, BAD THINGS.
THAT DOESN'T MEAN I WANNA EXPERIENCE ALL THE BAD THINGS!

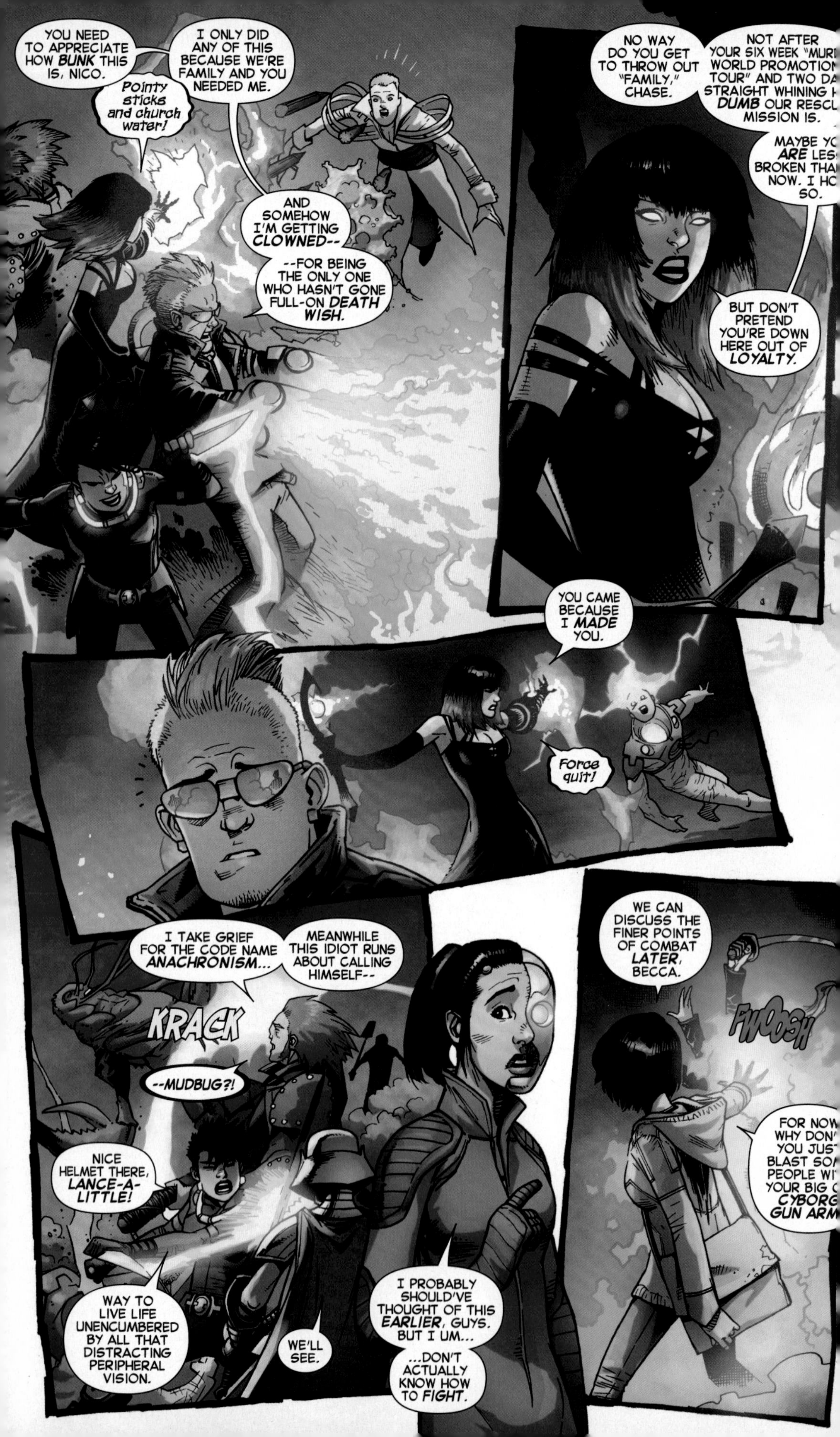
YOU NEED TO APPRECIATE HOW BUNK THIS IS, NICO.
I ONLY DID ANY OF THIS BECAUSE WE'RE FAMILY AND YOU NEEDED ME.
Pointy sticks and church water!
AND SOMEHOW I'M GETTING CLOWNED--
--FOR BEING THE ONLY ONE WHO HASN'T GONE FULL-ON DEATH WISH.
NO WAY DO YOU GET TO THROW OUT "FAMILY," CHASE.
NOT AFTER YOUR SIX WEEK "MURI WORLD PROMOTION TOUR" AND TWO DA STRAIGHT WHINING H DUMB OUR RESCU MISSION IS.
MAYBE YO ARE LES BROKEN THA NOW. I HO SO.
BUT DON'T PRETEND YOU'RE DOWN HERE OUT OF LOYALTY.
YOU CAME BECAUSE I MADE YOU.
Force quit!
I TAKE GRIEF FOR THE CODE NAME ANACHRONISM...
MEANWHILE THIS IDIOT RUNS ABOUT CALLING HIMSELF--
KRACK
--MUDBUG?!
NICE HELMET THERE, LANCE-A-LITTLE!
WAY TO LIVE LIFE UNENCUMBERED BY ALL THAT DISTRACTING PERIPHERAL VISION.
WE'LL SEE.
I PROBABLY SHOULD'VE THOUGHT OF THIS EARLIER, GUYS. BUT I UM...
...DON'T ACTUALLY KNOW HOW TO FIGHT.
WE CAN DISCUSS THE FINER POINTS OF COMBAT LATER, BECCA.
FWOOSH
FOR NOW WHY DON' YOU JUST BLAST SO PEOPLE WI YOUR BIG CYBORG GUN ARM

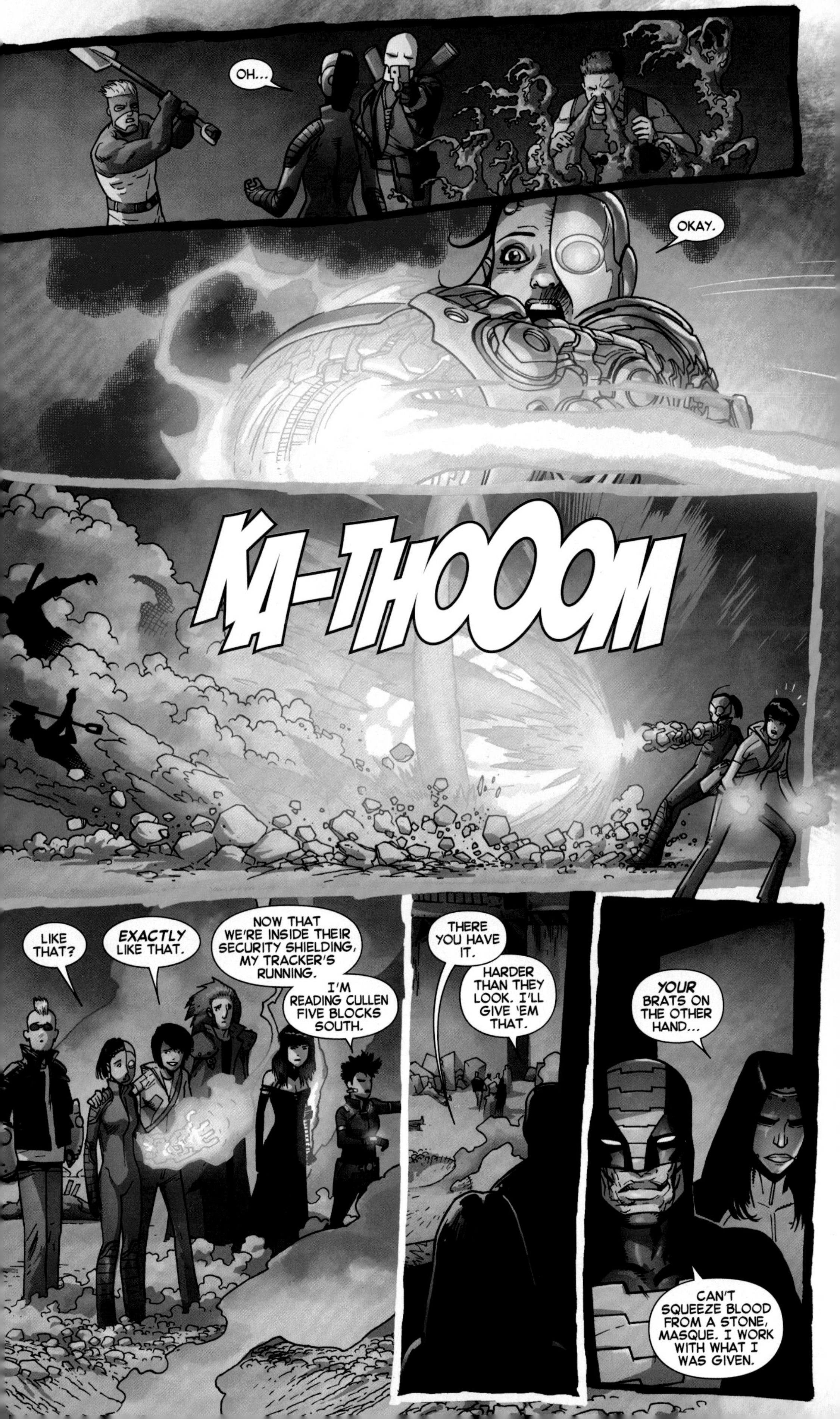
OH...
OKAY.
KA-THOOOM
LIKE THAT?
EXACTLY LIKE THAT.
NOW THAT WE'RE INSIDE THEIR SECURITY SHIELDING, MY TRACKER'S RUNNING.
I'M READING CULLEN FIVE BLOCKS SOUTH.
THERE YOU HAVE IT.
HARDER THAN THEY LOOK. I'LL GIVE 'EM THAT.
YOUR BRATS ON THE OTHER HAND...
CAN'T SQUEEZE BLOOD FROM A STONE, MASQUE. I WORK WITH WHAT I WAS GIVEN.

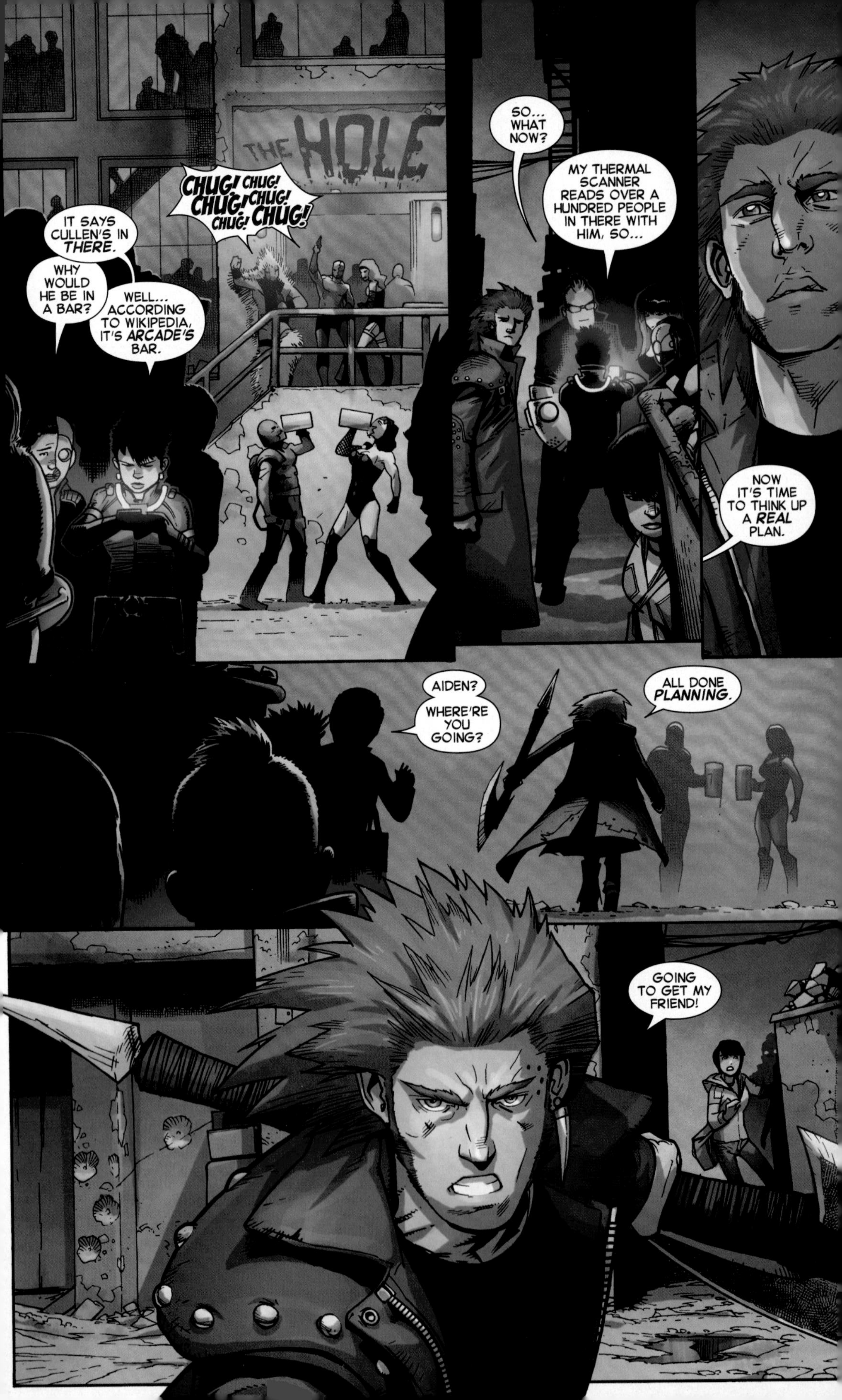

IT SAYS CULLEN'S IN THERE.
WHY WOULD HE BE IN A BAR?
WELL... ACCORDING TO WIKIPEDIA, IT'S ARCADE'S BAR.
THE HOLE
CHUG! CHUG! CHUG! CHUG! CHUG! CHUG!
SO... WHAT NOW?
MY THERMAL SCANNER READS OVER A HUNDRED PEOPLE IN THERE WITH HIM, SO...
NOW IT'S TIME TO THINK UP A REAL PLAN.
AIDEN?
WHERE'RE YOU GOING?
ALL DONE PLANNING.
GOING TO GET MY FRIEND!

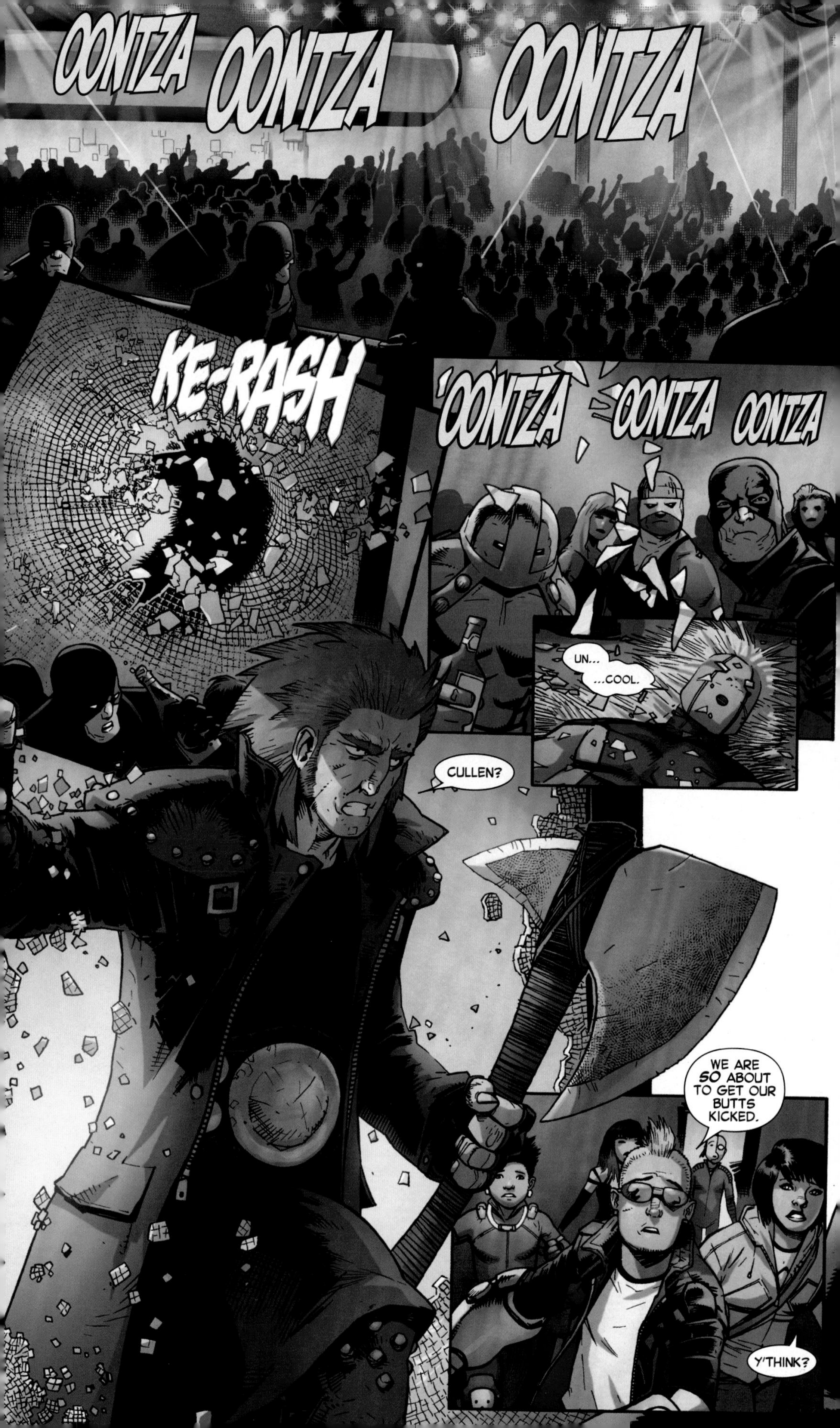
OONTZA OONTZA OONTZA
KE-RASH
'OONTZA OONTZA OONTZA
UN...
...COOL.
CULLEN?
WE ARE SO ABOUT TO GET OUR BUTTS KICKED.
Y'THINK?

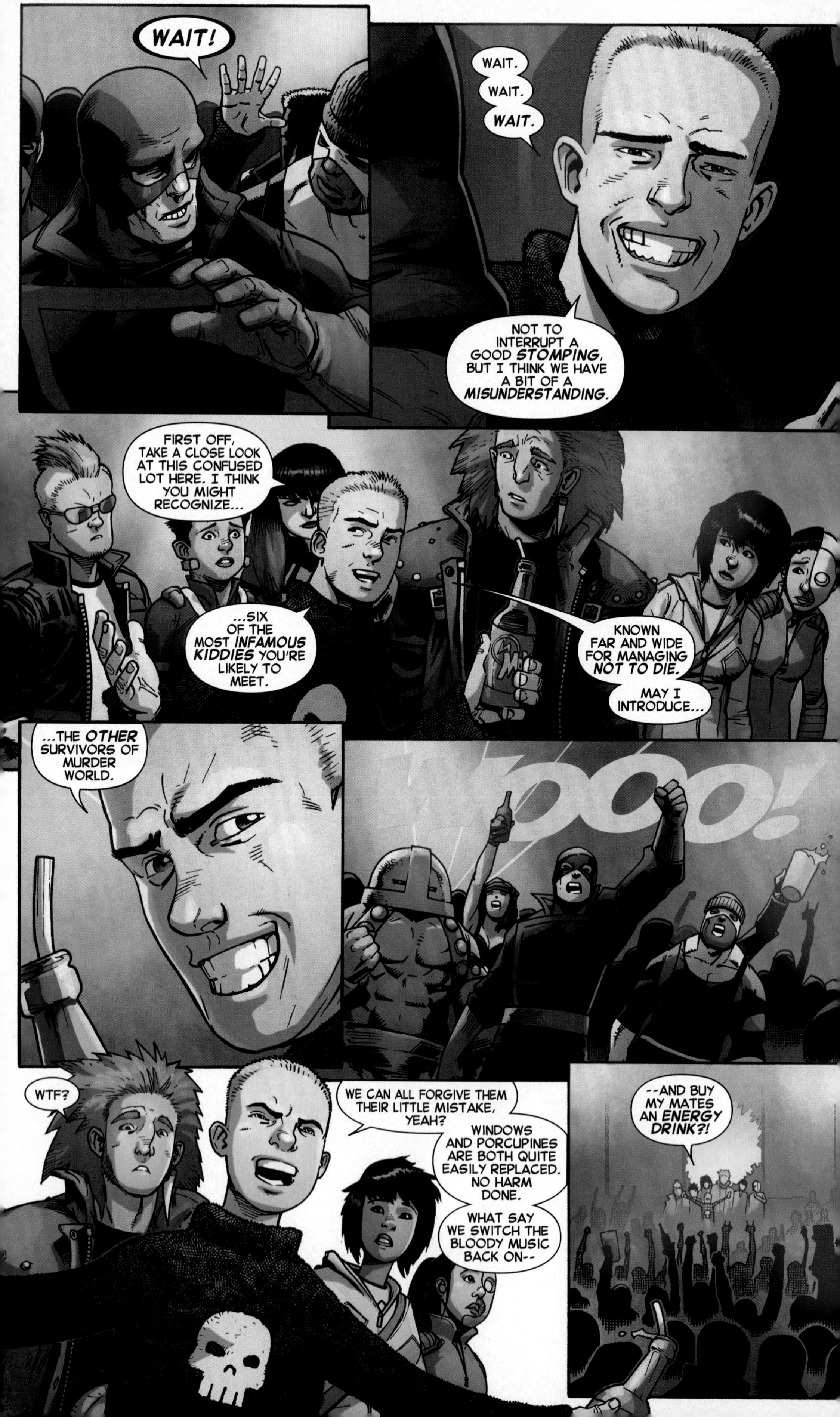
WAIT!
WAIT.
WAIT.
WAIT.
NOT TO INTERRUPT A GOOD STOMPING, BUT I THINK WE HAVE A BIT OF A MISUNDERSTANDING.
FIRST OFF, TAKE A CLOSE LOOK AT THIS CONFUSED LOT HERE. I THINK YOU MIGHT RECOGNIZE...
...SIX OF THE MOST INFAMOUS KIDDIES YOU'RE LIKELY TO MEET.
KNOWN FAR AND WIDE FOR MANAGING NOT TO DIE.
MAY I INTRODUCE...
...THE OTHER SURVIVORS OF MURDER WORLD.
WOOO!
WTF?
WE CAN ALL FORGIVE THEM THEIR LITTLE MISTAKE, YEAH?
WINDOWS AND PORCUPINES ARE BOTH QUITE EASILY REPLACED. NO HARM DONE.
WHAT SAY WE SWITCH THE BLOODY MUSIC BACK ON--
--AND BUY MY MATES AN ENERGY DRINK?!

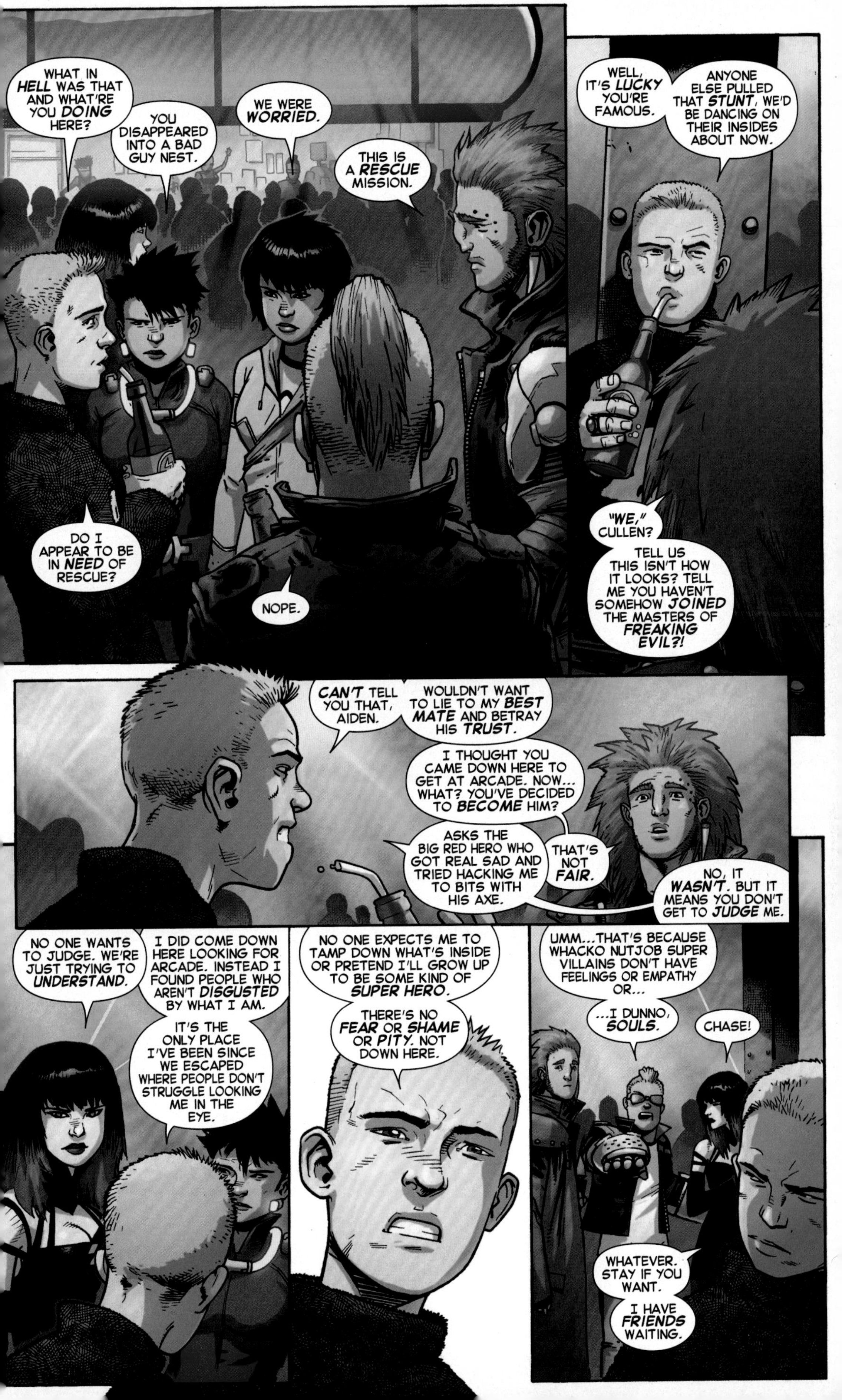
WHAT IN HELL WAS THAT AND WHAT'RE YOU DOING HERE?
YOU DISAPPEARED INTO A BAD GUY NEST.
WE WERE WORRIED.
THIS IS A RESCUE MISSION.
DO I APPEAR TO BE IN NEED OF RESCUE?
NOPE.
WELL, IT'S LUCKY YOU'RE FAMOUS.
ANYONE ELSE PULLED THAT STUNT, WE'D BE DANCING ON THEIR INSIDES ABOUT NOW.
"WE," CULLEN?
TELL US THIS ISN'T HOW IT LOOKS? TELL ME YOU HAVEN'T SOMEHOW JOINED THE MASTERS OF FREAKING EVIL?!
CAN'T TELL YOU THAT, AIDEN.
WOULDN'T WANT TO LIE TO MY BEST MATE AND BETRAY HIS TRUST.
I THOUGHT YOU CAME DOWN HERE TO GET AT ARCADE. NOW... WHAT? YOU'VE DECIDED TO BECOME HIM?
ASKS THE BIG RED HERO WHO GOT REAL SAD AND TRIED HACKING ME TO BITS WITH HIS AXE.
THAT'S NOT FAIR.
NO, IT WASN'T. BUT IT MEANS YOU DON'T GET TO JUDGE ME.
NO ONE WANTS TO JUDGE. WE'RE JUST TRYING TO UNDERSTAND.
I DID COME DOWN HERE LOOKING FOR ARCADE. INSTEAD I FOUND PEOPLE WHO AREN'T DISGUSTED BY WHAT I AM.
IT'S THE ONLY PLACE I'VE BEEN SINCE WE ESCAPED WHERE PEOPLE DON'T STRUGGLE LOOKING ME IN THE EYE.
NO ONE EXPECTS ME TO TAMP DOWN WHAT'S INSIDE OR PRETEND I'LL GROW UP TO BE SOME KIND OF SUPER HERO.
THERE'S NO FEAR OR SHAME OR PITY. NOT DOWN HERE.
UMM...THAT'S BECAUSE WHACKO NUTJOB SUPER VILLAINS DON'T HAVE FEELINGS OR EMPATHY OR...
...I DUNNO, SOULS.
CHASE!
WHATEVER. STAY IF YOU WANT.
I HAVE FRIENDS WAITING.

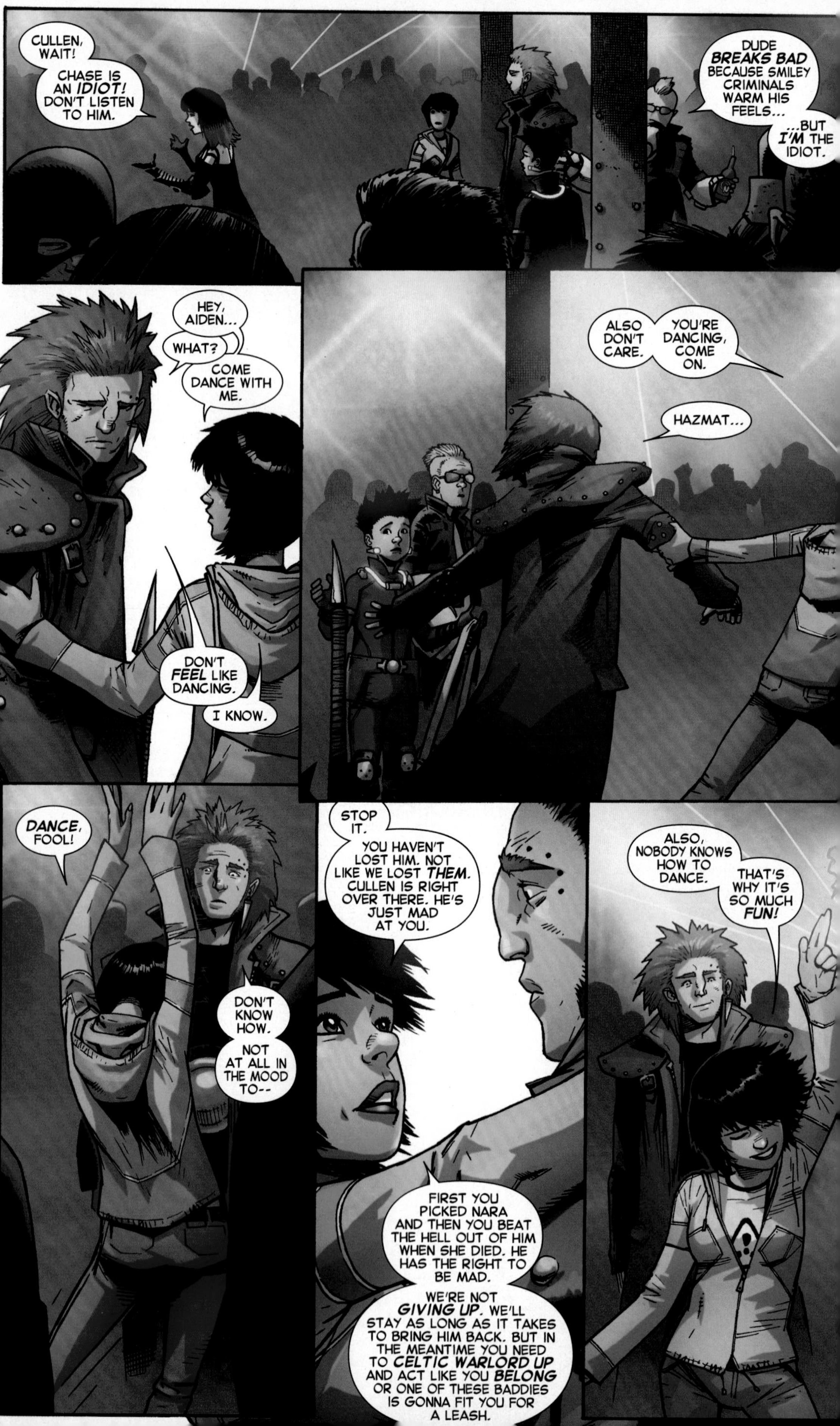
CULLEN, WAIT!
CHASE IS AN IDIOT! DON'T LISTEN TO HIM.
DUDE BREAKS BAD BECAUSE SMILEY CRIMINALS WARM HIS FEELS...
...BUT I'M THE IDIOT.
HEY, AIDEN...
WHAT?
COME DANCE WITH ME.
DON'T FEEL LIKE DANCING.
I KNOW.
ALSO DON'T CARE.
YOU'RE DANCING, COME ON.
HAZMAT...
DANCE, FOOL!
DON'T KNOW HOW.
NOT AT ALL IN THE MOOD TO--
STOP IT.
YOU HAVEN'T LOST HIM. NOT LIKE WE LOST THEM. CULLEN IS RIGHT OVER THERE. HE'S JUST MAD AT YOU.
FIRST YOU PICKED NARA AND THEN YOU BEAT THE HELL OUT OF HIM WHEN SHE DIED. HE HAS THE RIGHT TO BE MAD.
WE'RE NOT GIVING UP. WE'LL STAY AS LONG AS IT TAKES TO BRING HIM BACK. BUT IN THE MEANTIME YOU NEED TO CELTIC WARLORD UP AND ACT LIKE YOU BELONG OR ONE OF THESE BADDIES IS GONNA FIT YOU FOR A LEASH.
ALSO, NOBODY KNOWS HOW TO DANCE.
THAT'S WHY IT'S SO MUCH FUN!

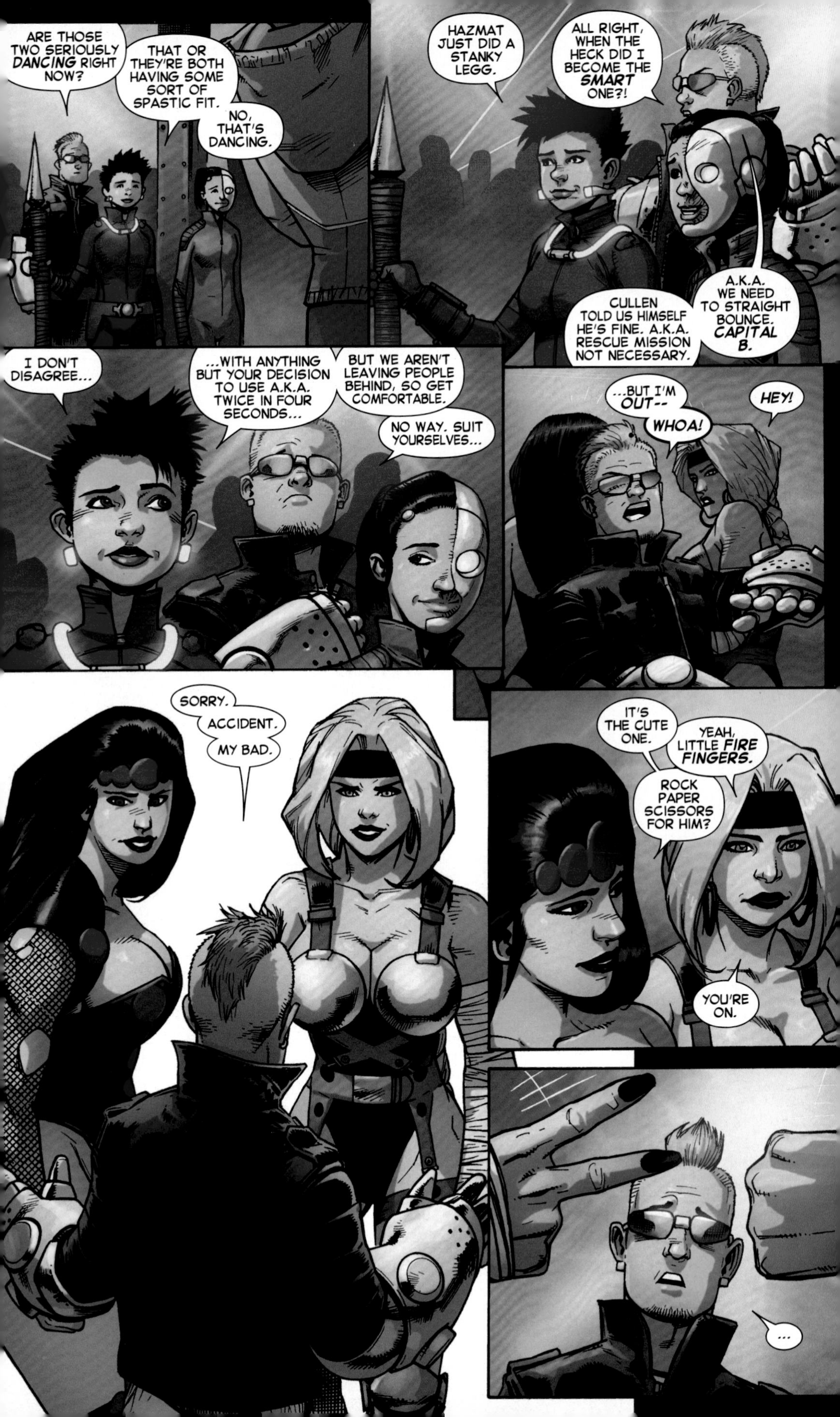
ARE THOSE TWO SERIOUSLY DANCING RIGHT NOW?
THAT OR THEY'RE BOTH HAVING SOME SORT OF SPASTIC FIT.
NO, THAT'S DANCING.
HAZMAT JUST DID A STANKY LEGG.
ALL RIGHT, WHEN THE HECK DID I BECOME THE SMART ONE?!
CULLEN TOLD US HIMSELF HE'S FINE. A.K.A. RESCUE MISSION NOT NECESSARY.
A.K.A. WE NEED TO STRAIGHT BOUNCE. CAPITAL B.
I DON'T DISAGREE...
...WITH ANYTHING BUT YOUR DECISION TO USE A.K.A. TWICE IN FOUR SECONDS...
BUT WE AREN'T LEAVING PEOPLE BEHIND, SO GET COMFORTABLE.
NO WAY. SUIT YOURSELVES...
...BUT I'M OUT--
WHOA!
HEY!
SORRY.
ACCIDENT.
MY BAD.
IT'S THE CUTE ONE.
YEAH, LITTLE FIRE FINGERS.
ROCK PAPER SCISSORS FOR HIM?
YOU'RE ON.
...

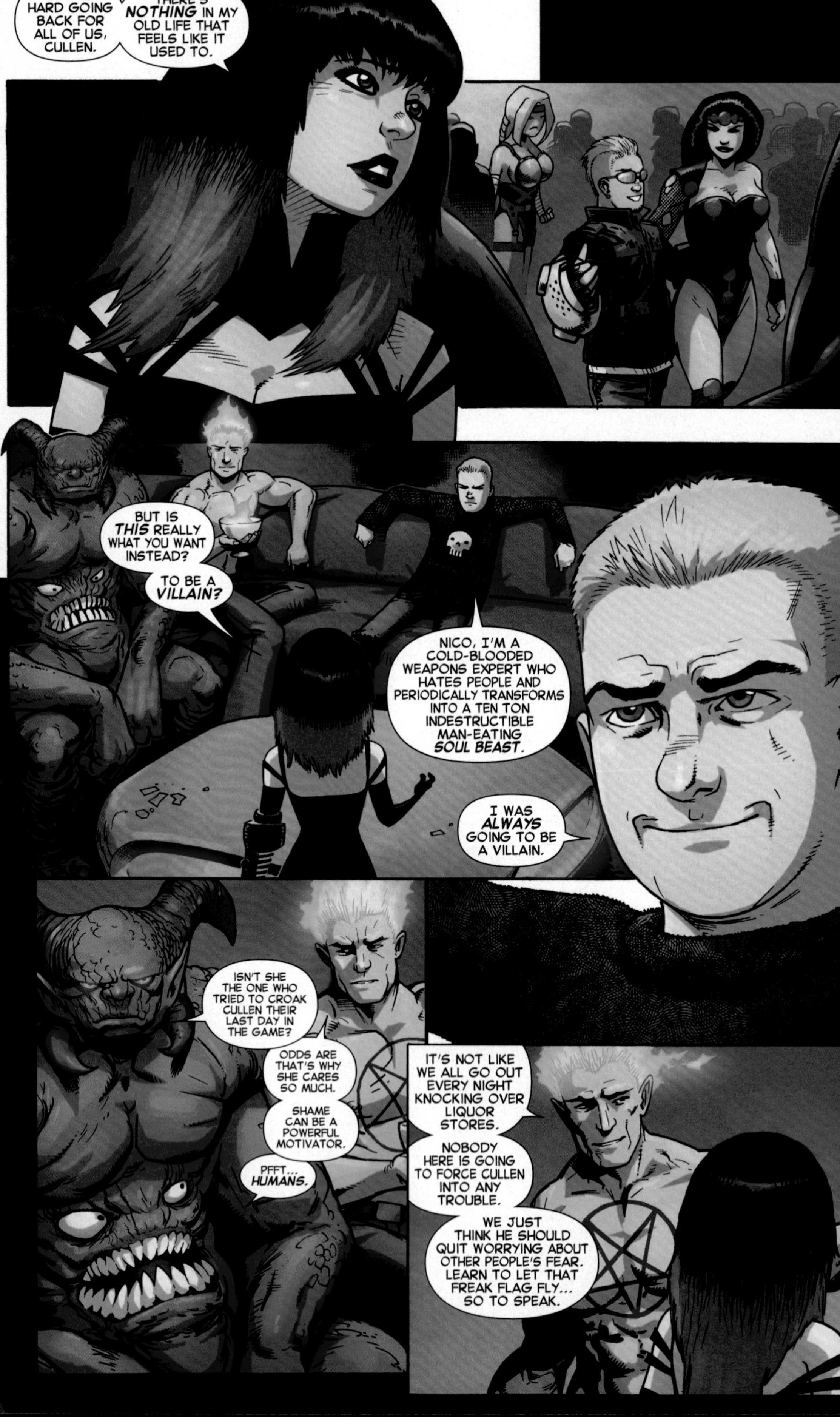
HARD GOING BACK FOR ALL OF US, CULLEN.
NOTHING IN MY OLD LIFE THAT FEELS LIKE IT USED TO.
BUT IS THIS REALLY WHAT YOU WANT INSTEAD?
TO BE A VILLAIN?
NICO, I'M A COLD-BLOODED WEAPONS EXPERT WHO HATES PEOPLE AND PERIODICALLY TRANSFORMS INTO A TEN TON INDESTRUCTIBLE MAN-EATING SOUL BEAST.
I WAS ALWAYS GOING TO BE A VILLAIN.
ISN'T SHE THE ONE WHO TRIED TO CROAK CULLEN THEIR LAST DAY IN THE GAME?
ODDS ARE THAT'S WHY SHE CARES SO MUCH.
SHAME CAN BE A POWERFUL MOTIVATOR.
PFFT... HUMANS.
IT'S NOT LIKE WE ALL GO OUT EVERY NIGHT KNOCKING OVER LIQUOR STORES.
NOBODY HERE IS GOING TO FORCE CULLEN INTO ANY TROUBLE.
WE JUST THINK HE SHOULD QUIT WORRYING ABOUT OTHER PEOPLE'S FEAR. LEARN TO LET THAT FREAK FLAG FLY... SO TO SPEAK.

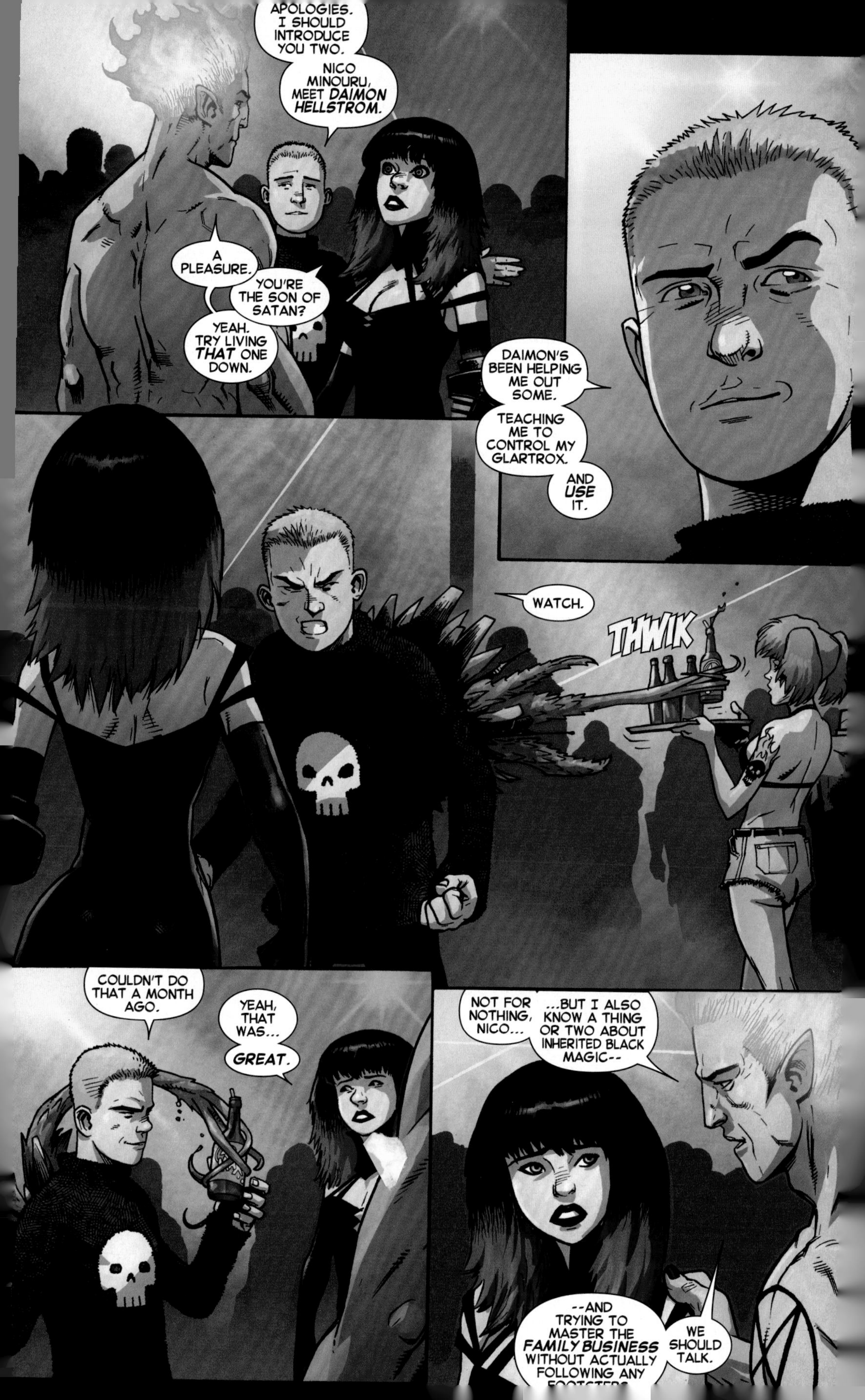
APOLOGIES. I SHOULD INTRODUCE YOU TWO.
NICO MINOURU, MEET DAIMON HELLSTROM.
A PLEASURE.
YOU'RE THE SON OF SATAN?
YEAH. TRY LIVING THAT ONE DOWN.
DAIMON'S BEEN HELPING ME OUT SOME.
TEACHING ME TO CONTROL MY GLARTROX.
AND USE IT.
WATCH.
THWIK
COULDN'T DO THAT A MONTH AGO.
YEAH, THAT WAS...
GREAT.
NOT FOR NOTHING, NICO...
...BUT I ALSO KNOW A THING OR TWO ABOUT INHERITED BLACK MAGIC--
--AND TRYING TO MASTER THE FAMILY BUSINESS WITHOUT ACTUALLY FOLLOWING ANY
WE SHOULD TALK.

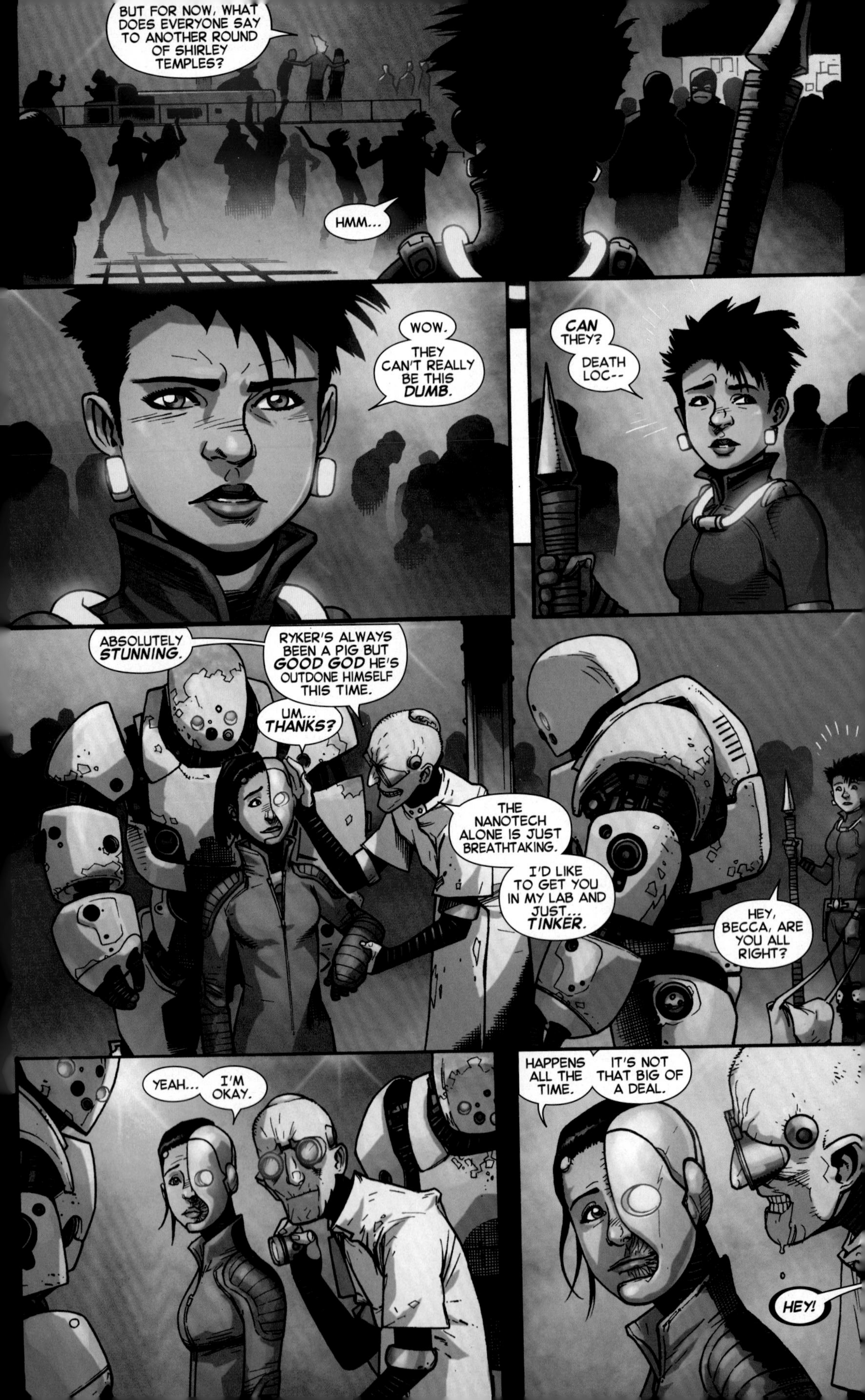
BUT FOR NOW, WHAT DOES EVERYONE SAY TO ANOTHER ROUND OF SHIRLEY TEMPLES?
HMM...
WOW.
THEY CAN'T REALLY BE THIS DUMB.
CAN THEY?
DEATH LOC--
ABSOLUTELY STUNNING.
RYKER'S ALWAYS BEEN A PIG BUT GOOD GOD HE'S OUTDONE HIMSELF THIS TIME.
UM... THANKS?
THE NANOTECH ALONE IS JUST BREATHTAKING.
I'D LIKE TO GET YOU IN MY LAB AND JUST... TINKER.
HEY, BECCA, ARE YOU ALL RIGHT?
YEAH...
I'M OKAY.
HAPPENS ALL THE TIME.
IT'S NOT THAT BIG OF A DEAL.
HEY!

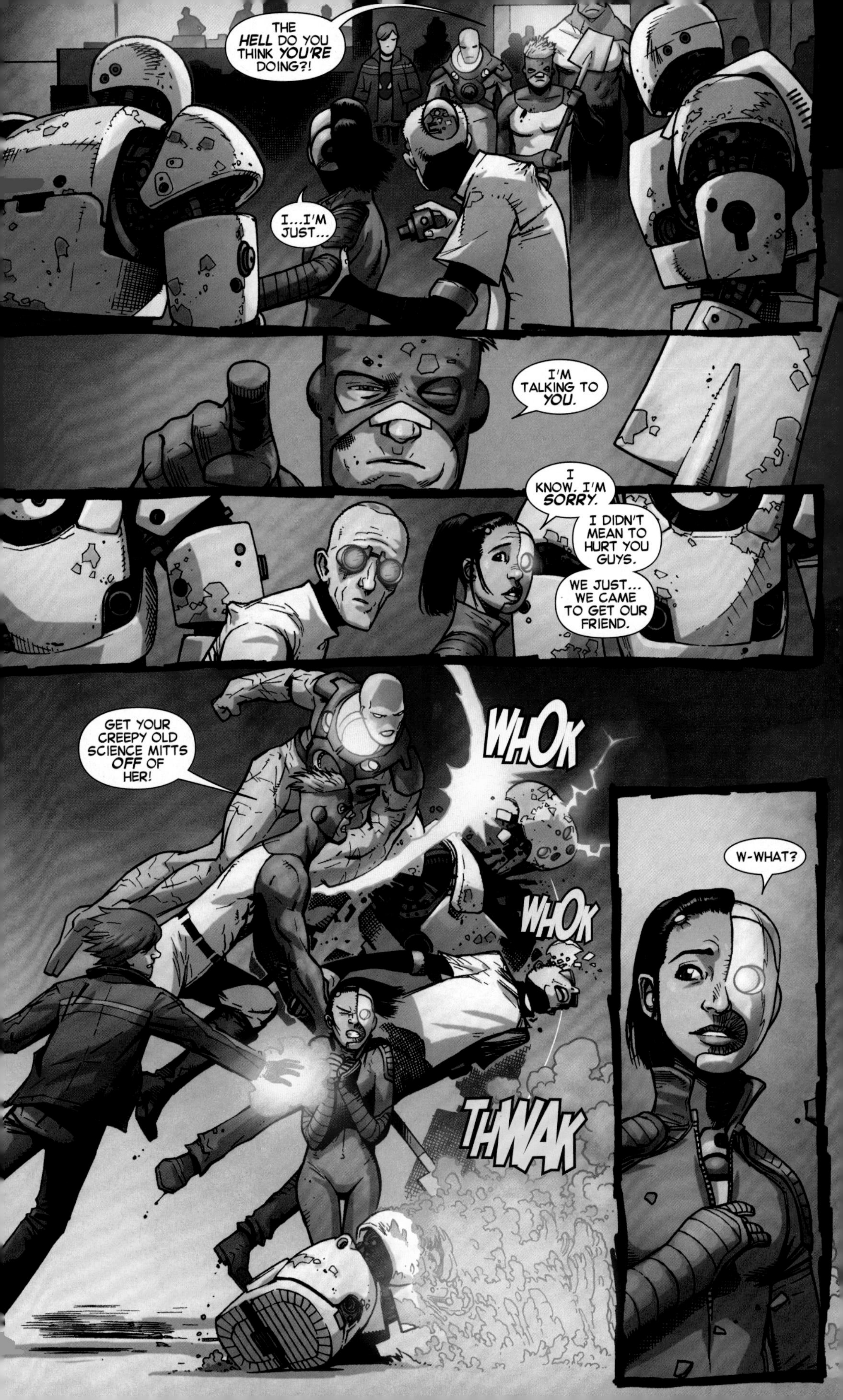
THE HELL DO YOU THINK YOU'RE DOING?!
I...I'M JUST...
I'M TALKING TO YOU.
I KNOW. I'M SORRY.
I DIDN'T MEAN TO HURT YOU GUYS.
WE JUST... WE CAME TO GET OUR FRIEND.
GET YOUR CREEPY OLD SCIENCE MITTS OFF OF HER!
WHOK
WHOK
THWAK
W-WHAT?

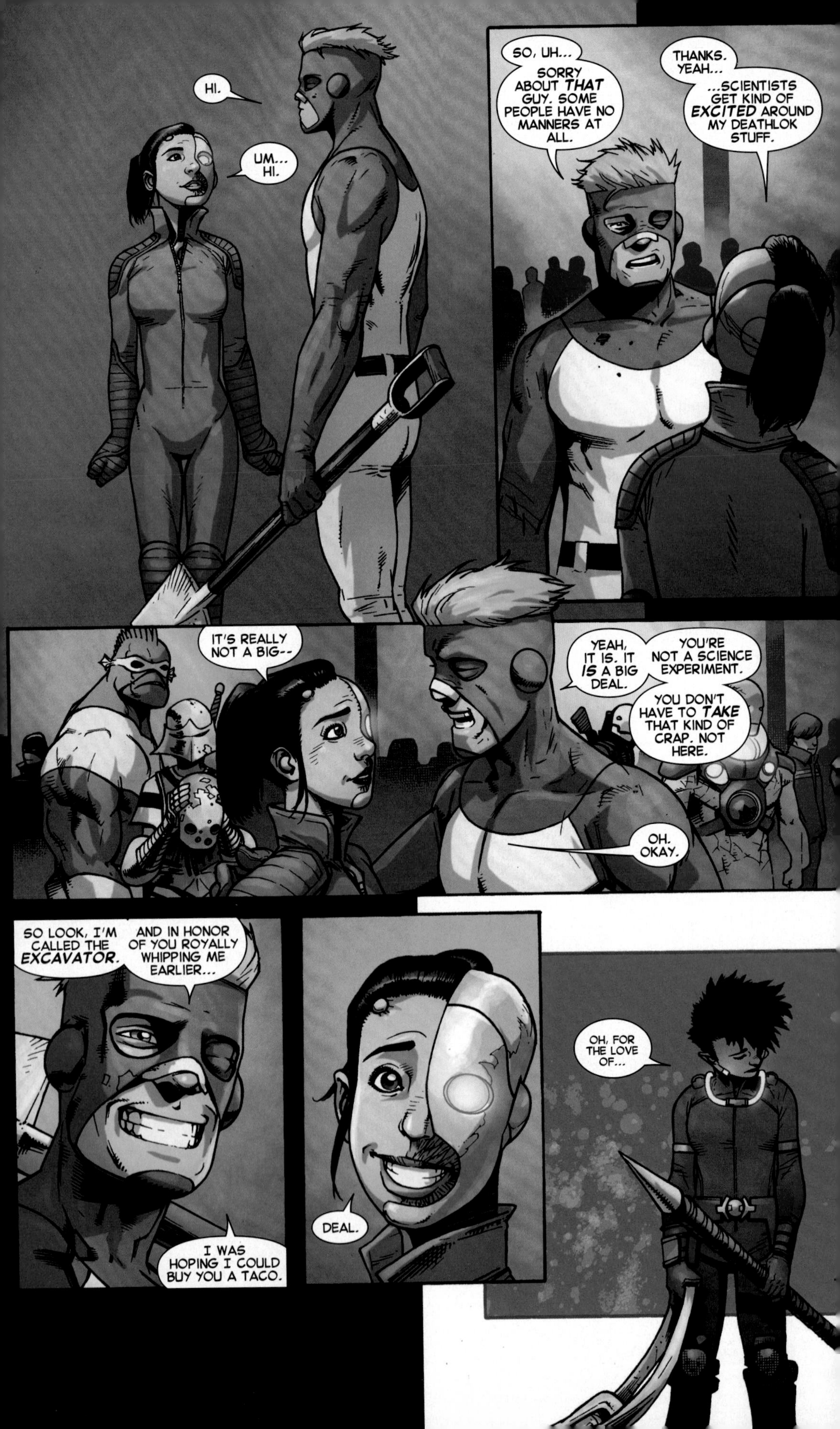
HI.
UM... HI.
SO, UH...
SORRY ABOUT THAT GUY. SOME PEOPLE HAVE NO MANNERS AT ALL.
THANKS. YEAH...
...SCIENTISTS GET KIND OF EXCITED AROUND MY DEATHLOK STUFF.
IT'S REALLY NOT A BIG--
YEAH, IT IS. IT IS A BIG DEAL.
YOU'RE NOT A SCIENCE EXPERIMENT.
YOU DON'T HAVE TO TAKE THAT KIND OF CRAP. NOT HERE.
OH. OKAY.
SO LOOK, I'M CALLED THE EXCAVATOR.
AND IN HONOR OF YOU ROYALLY WHIPPING ME EARLIER...
I WAS HOPING I COULD BUY YOU A TACO.
DEAL.
OH, FOR THE LOVE OF...

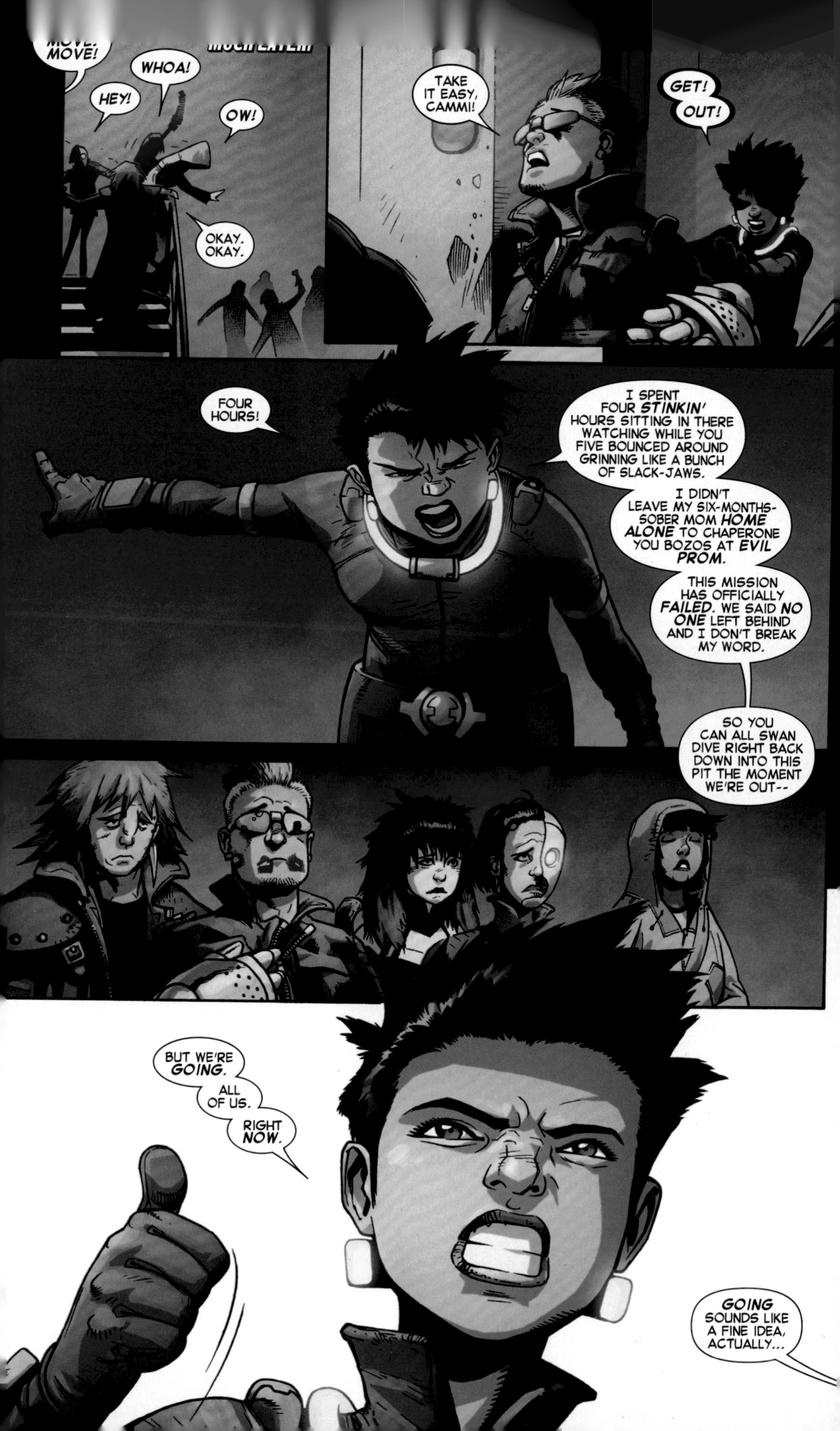
MOVE!
HEY!
WHOA!
OW!
OKAY. OKAY.
TAKE IT EASY, CAMMI!
GET! OUT!
FOUR HOURS!
I SPENT FOUR STINKIN' HOURS SITTING IN THERE WATCHING WHILE YOU FIVE BOUNCED AROUND GRINNING LIKE A BUNCH OF SLACK-JAWS.
I DIDN'T LEAVE MY SIX-MONTHS-SOBER MOM HOME ALONE TO CHAPERONE YOU BOZOS AT EVIL PROM.
THIS MISSION HAS OFFICIALLY FAILED. WE SAID NO ONE LEFT BEHIND AND I DON'T BREAK MY WORD.
SO YOU CAN ALL SWAN DIVE RIGHT BACK DOWN INTO THIS PIT THE MOMENT WE'RE OUT--
BUT WE'RE GOING.
ALL OF US.
RIGHT NOW.
GOING SOUNDS LIKE A FINE IDEA, ACTUALLY...

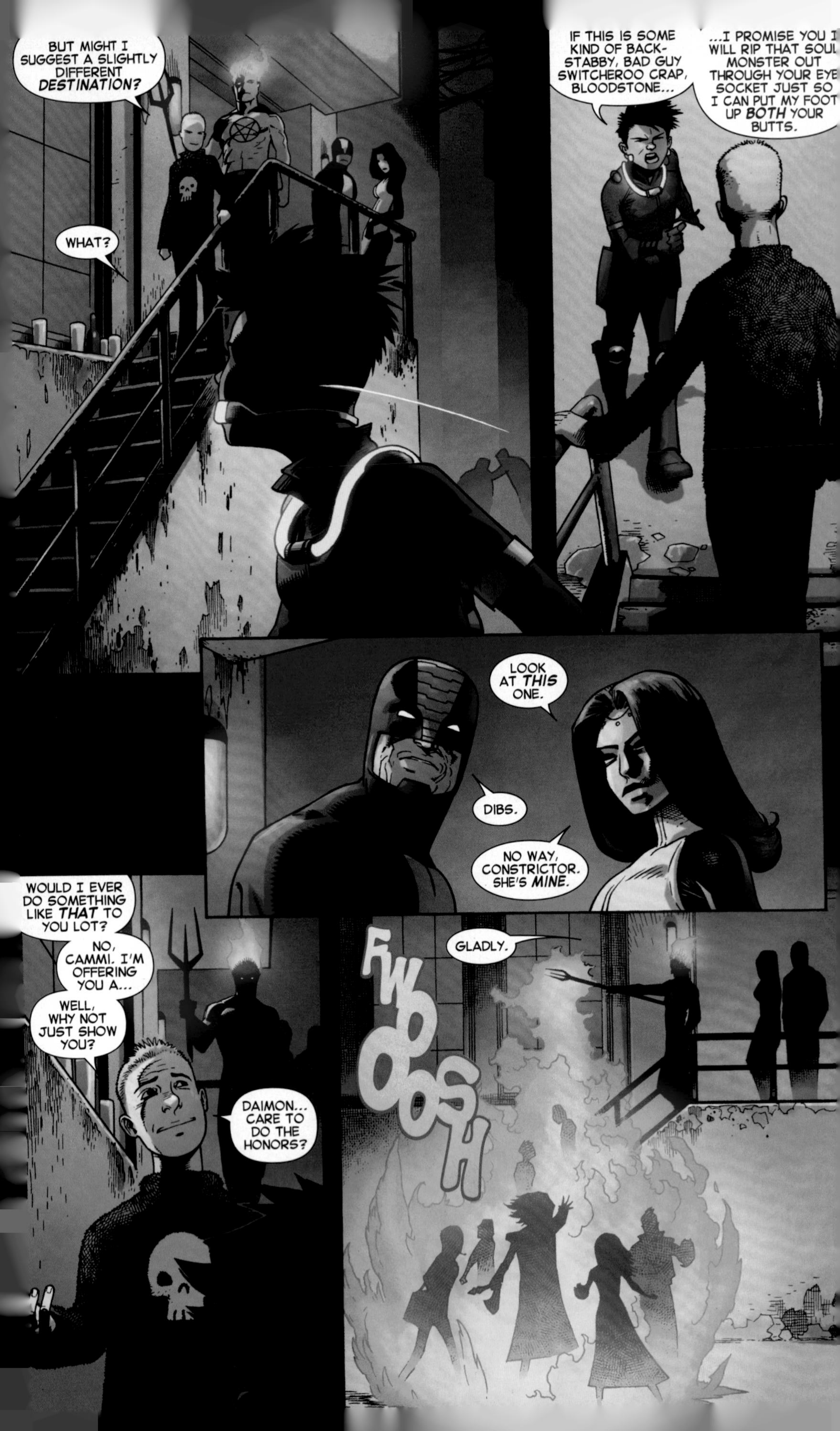
BUT MIGHT I SUGGEST A SLIGHTLY DIFFERENT DESTINATION?
WHAT?
IF THIS IS SOME KIND OF BACK-STABBY, BAD GUY SWITCHEROO CRAP, BLOODSTONE...
...I PROMISE YOU I WILL RIP THAT SOUL MONSTER OUT THROUGH YOUR EYE SOCKET JUST SO I CAN PUT MY FOOT UP BOTH YOUR BUTTS.
LOOK AT THIS ONE.
DIBS.
NO WAY, CONSTRICTOR. SHE'S MINE.
WOULD I EVER DO SOMETHING LIKE THAT TO YOU LOT?
NO, CAMMI. I'M OFFERING YOU A...
WELL, WHY NOT JUST SHOW YOU?
DAIMON... CARE TO DO THE HONORS?
GLADLY.
FWOOOSH

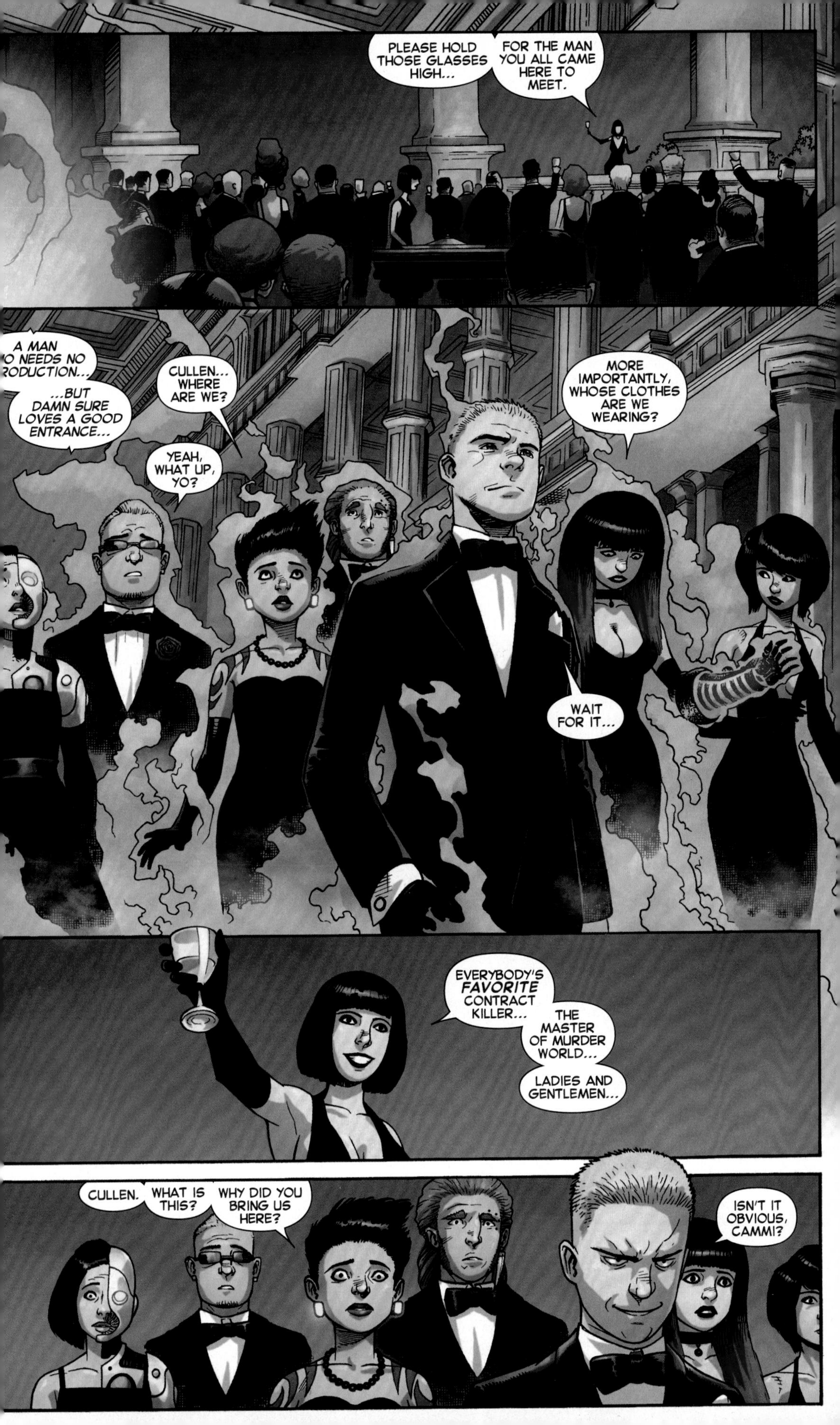
PLEASE HOLD THOSE GLASSES HIGH...
FOR THE MAN YOU ALL CAME HERE TO MEET.
A MAN O NEEDS NO RODUCTION...
...BUT DAMN SURE LOVES A GOOD ENTRANCE...
CULLEN... WHERE ARE WE?
YEAH, WHAT UP, YO?
MORE IMPORTANTLY, WHOSE CLOTHES ARE WE WEARING?
WAIT FOR IT...
EVERYBODY'S *FAVORITE* CONTRACT KILLER...
THE MASTER OF MURDER WORLD...
LADIES AND GENTLEMEN...
CULLEN.
WHAT IS THIS?
WHY DID YOU BRING US HERE?
ISN'T IT OBVIOUS, CAMMI?

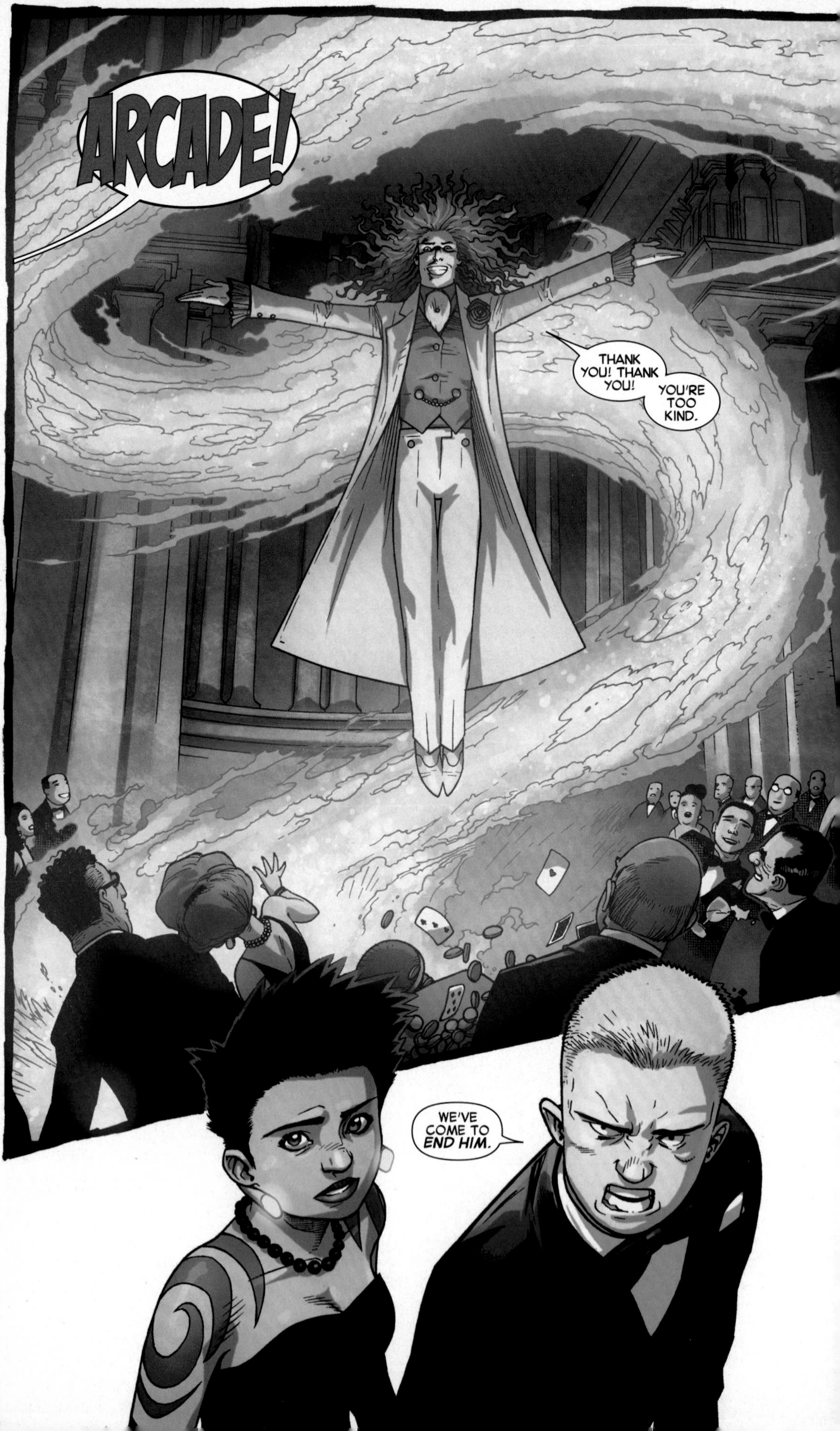
ARCADE!
THANK YOU! THANK YOU!
YOU'RE TOO KIND.
WE'VE COME TO END HIM.

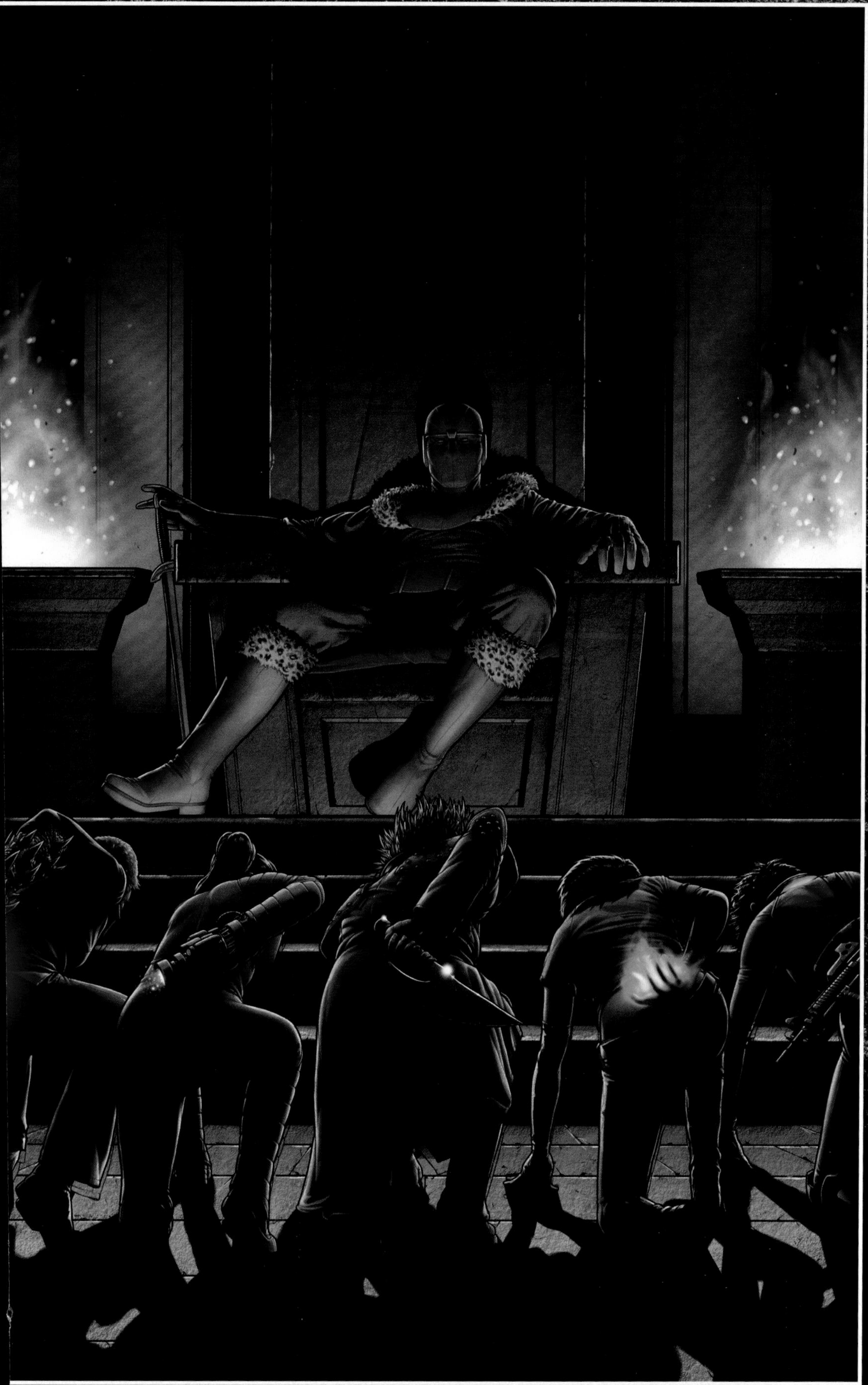

#2 VARIANT BY JOHN TYLER CHRISTOPHER

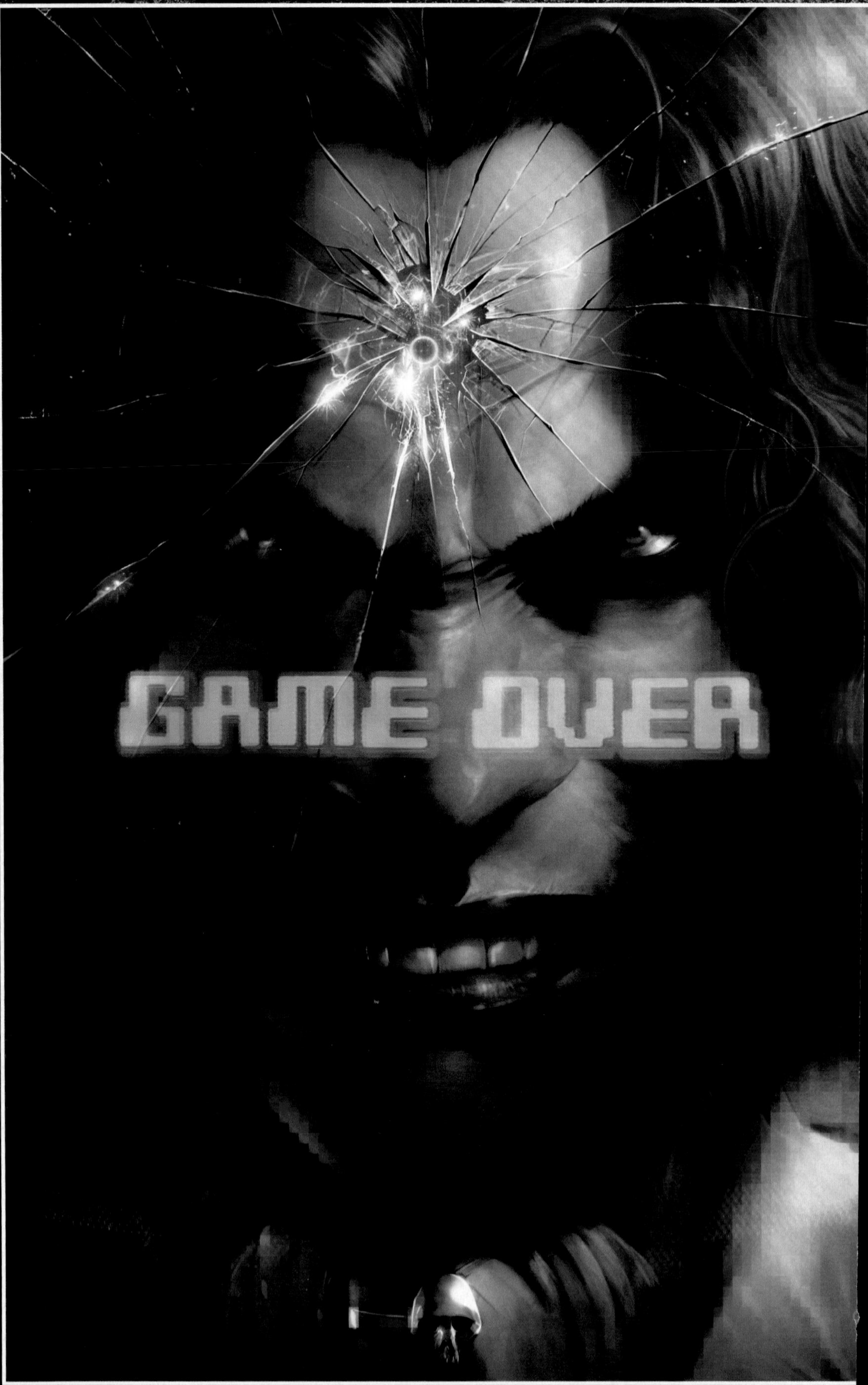
GAME OVER

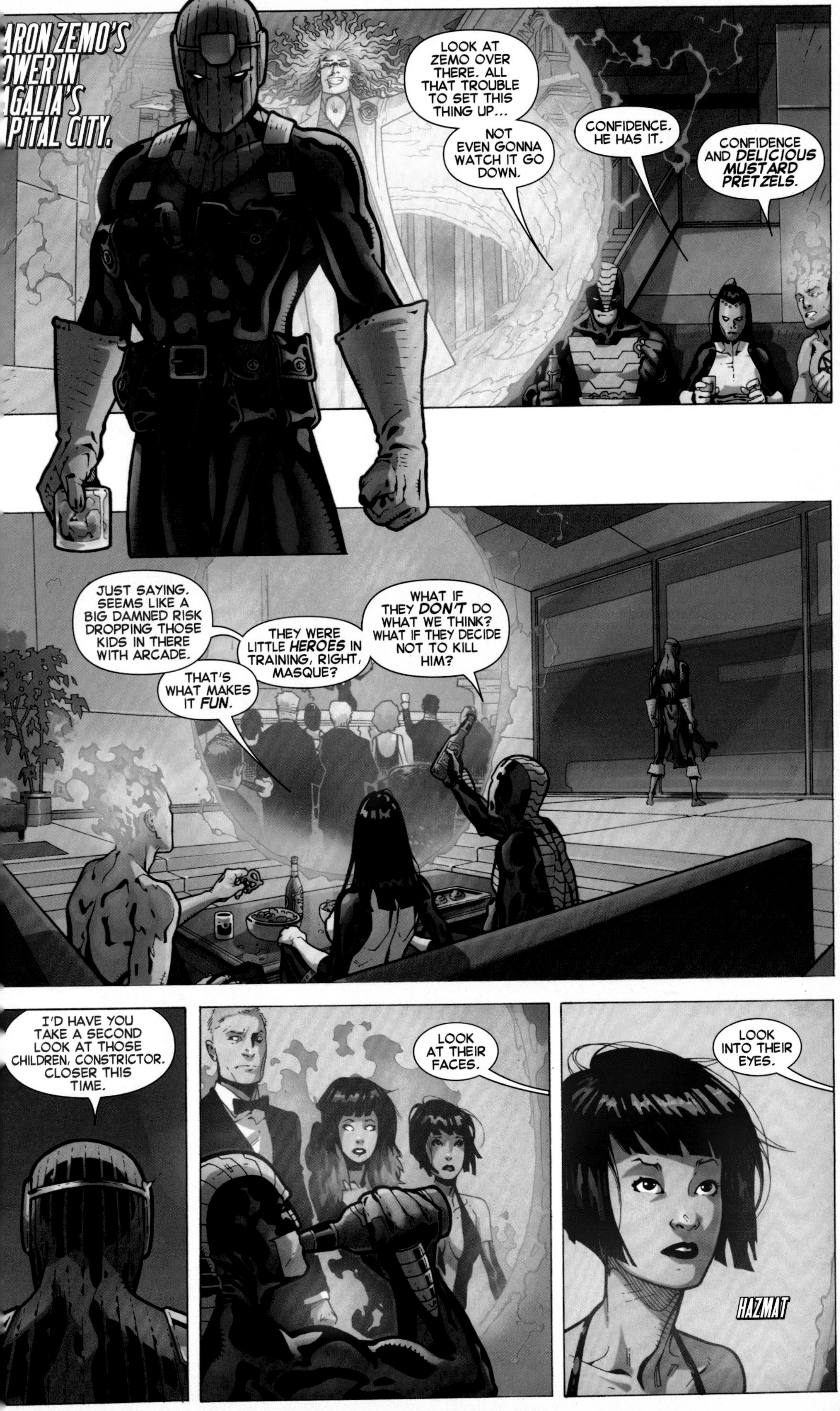
ARON ZEMO'S
OWER IN
AGALIA'S
PITAL CITY.
LOOK AT ZEMO OVER THERE. ALL THAT TROUBLE TO SET THIS THING UP...
NOT EVEN GONNA WATCH IT GO DOWN.
CONFIDENCE. HE HAS IT.
CONFIDENCE AND DELICIOUS MUSTARD PRETZELS.
JUST SAYING. SEEMS LIKE A BIG DAMNED RISK DROPPING THOSE KIDS IN THERE WITH ARCADE.
THEY WERE LITTLE HEROES IN TRAINING, RIGHT, MASQUE?
WHAT IF THEY DON'T DO WHAT WE THINK? WHAT IF THEY DECIDE NOT TO KILL HIM?
THAT'S WHAT MAKES IT FUN.
I'D HAVE YOU TAKE A SECOND LOOK AT THOSE CHILDREN, CONSTRICTOR. CLOSER THIS TIME.
LOOK AT THEIR FACES.
LOOK INTO THEIR EYES.
HAZMAT

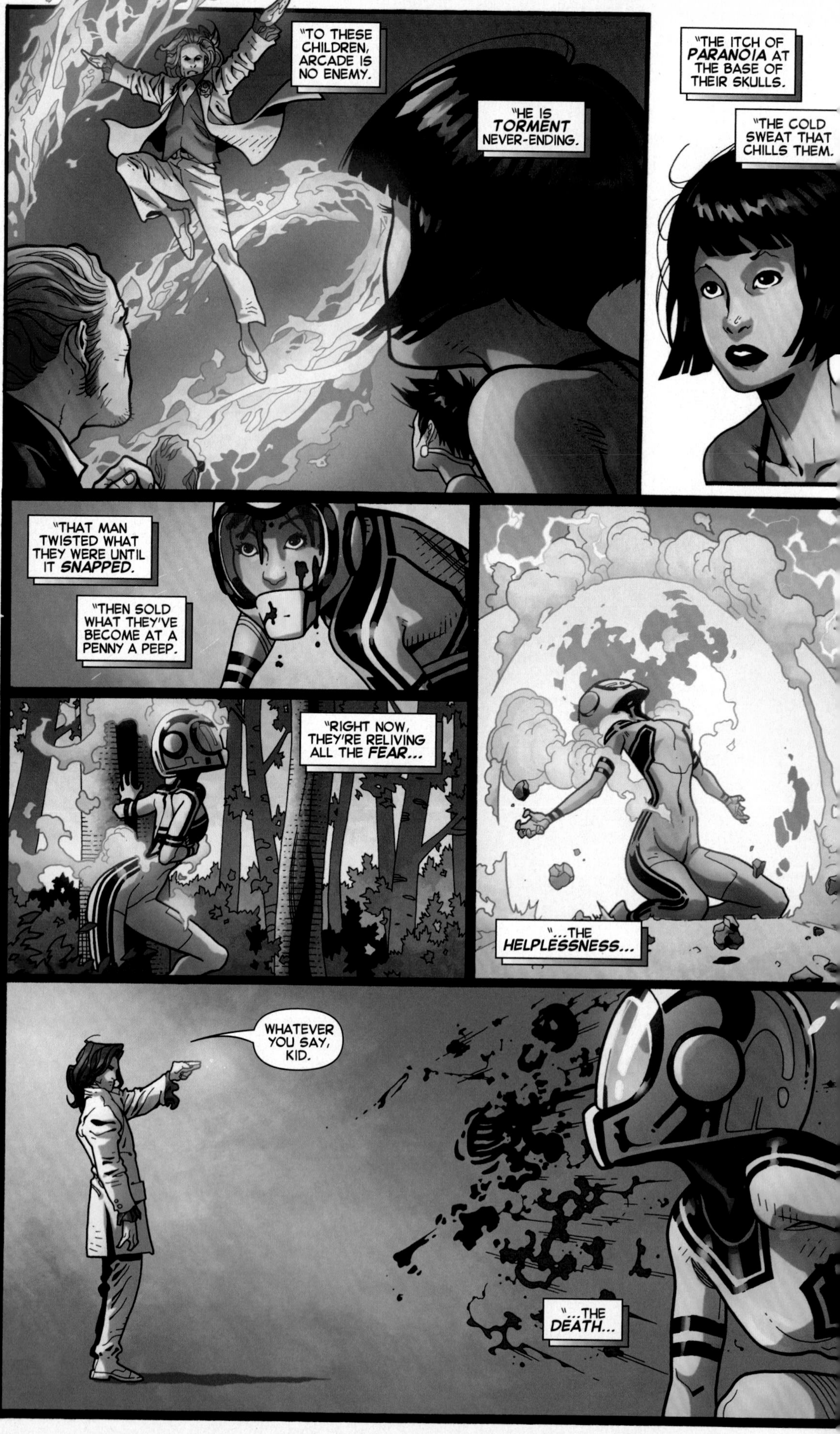
"TO THESE CHILDREN, ARCADE IS NO ENEMY.
"HE IS TORMENT NEVER-ENDING.
"THE ITCH OF PARANOIA AT THE BASE OF THEIR SKULLS.
"THE COLD SWEAT THAT CHILLS THEM.
"THAT MAN TWISTED WHAT THEY WERE UNTIL IT SNAPPED.
"THEN SOLD WHAT THEY'VE BECOME AT A PENNY A PEEP.
"RIGHT NOW, THEY'RE RELIVING ALL THE FEAR...
"...THE HELPLESSNESS...
WHATEVER YOU SAY, KID.
"...THE DEATH...

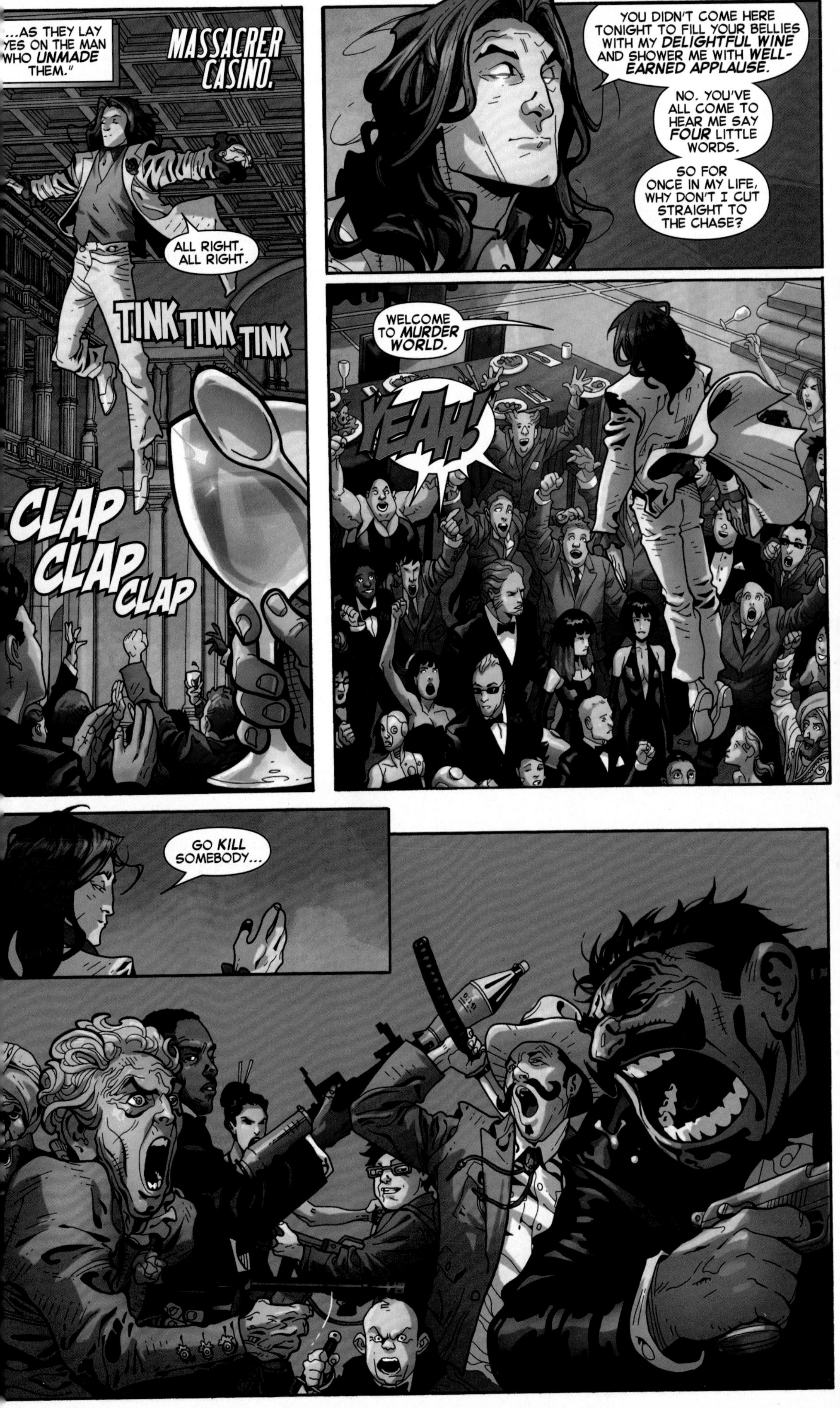

...AS THEY LAY
YES ON THE MAN
WHO UNMADE
THEM."
MASSACRER CASINO.
ALL RIGHT. ALL RIGHT.
TINK TINK TINK
CLAP CLAP CLAP
YOU DIDN'T COME HERE TONIGHT TO FILL YOUR BELLIES WITH MY DELIGHTFUL WINE AND SHOWER ME WITH WELL-EARNED APPLAUSE.
NO. YOU'VE ALL COME TO HEAR ME SAY FOUR LITTLE WORDS.
SO FOR ONCE IN MY LIFE, WHY DON'T I CUT STRAIGHT TO THE CHASE?
WELCOME TO MURDER WORLD.
YEAH!
GO KILL SOMEBODY...

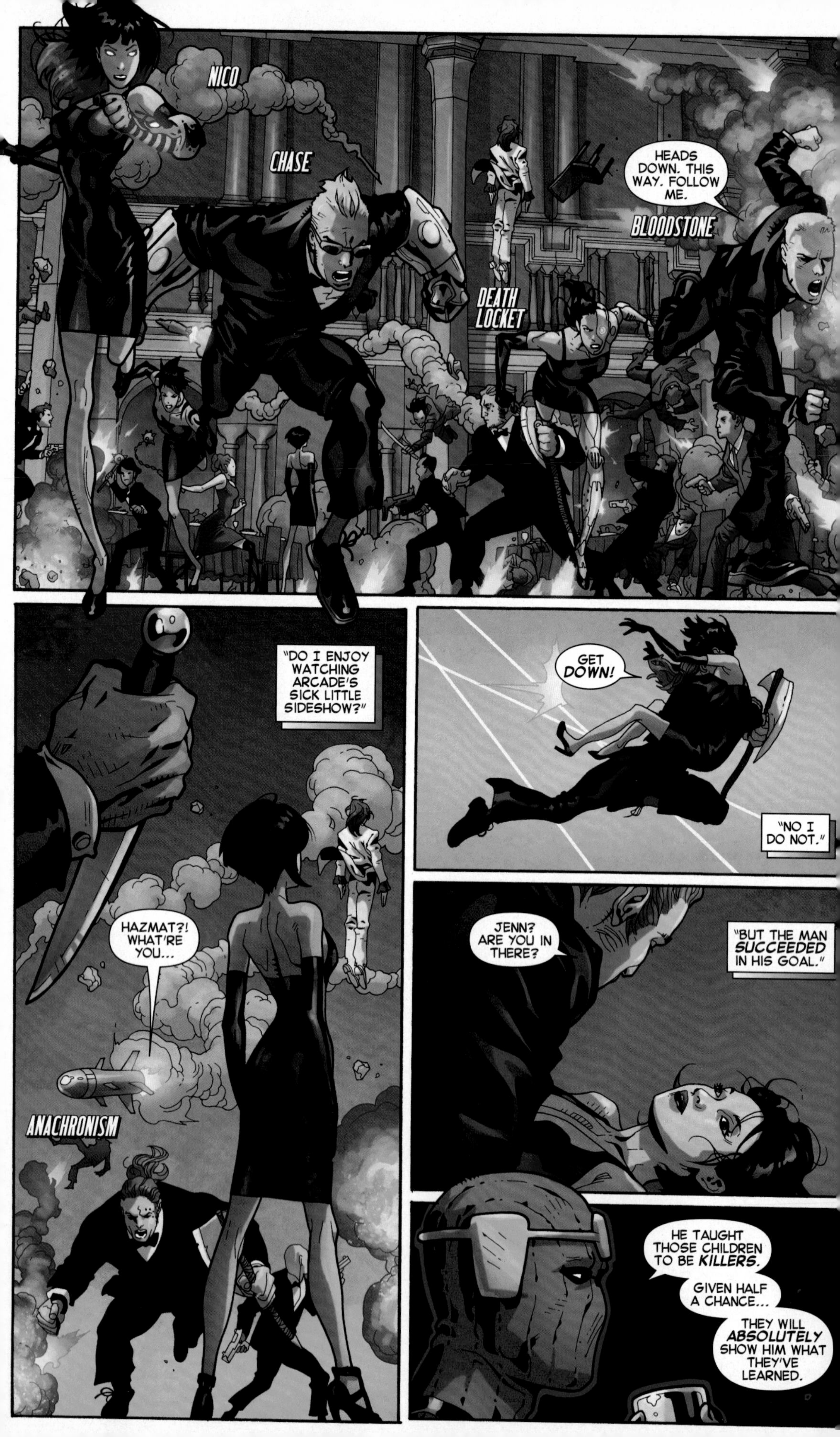
NICO
CHASE
HEADS DOWN. THIS WAY. FOLLOW ME.
BLOODSTONE
DEATH LOCKET
"DO I ENJOY WATCHING ARCADE'S SICK LITTLE SIDESHOW?"
HAZMAT?! WHAT'RE YOU...
ANACHRONISM
GET DOWN!
"NO I DO NOT."
JENN? ARE YOU IN THERE?
"BUT THE MAN SUCCEEDED IN HIS GOAL."
HE TAUGHT THOSE CHILDREN TO BE KILLERS.
GIVEN HALF A CHANCE...
THEY WILL ABSOLUTELY SHOW HIM WHAT THEY'VE LEARNED.

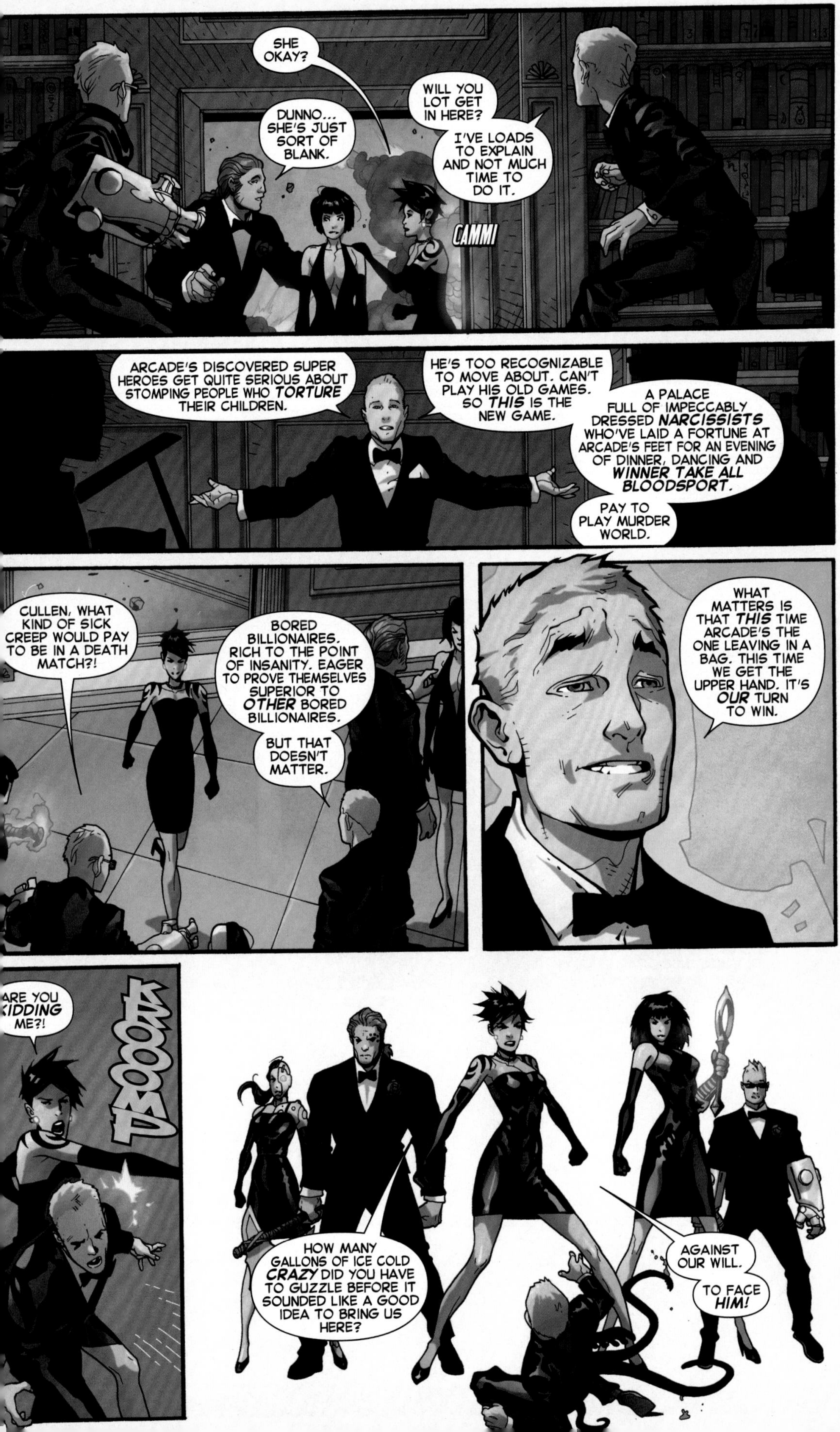

SHE OKAY?
DUNNO... SHE'S JUST SORT OF BLANK.
WILL YOU LOT GET IN HERE?
I'VE LOADS TO EXPLAIN AND NOT MUCH TIME TO DO IT.
CAMMI
ARCADE'S DISCOVERED SUPER HEROES GET QUITE SERIOUS ABOUT STOMPING PEOPLE WHO TORTURE THEIR CHILDREN.
HE'S TOO RECOGNIZABLE TO MOVE ABOUT. CAN'T PLAY HIS OLD GAMES. SO THIS IS THE NEW GAME.
A PALACE FULL OF IMPECCABLY DRESSED NARCISSISTS WHO'VE LAID A FORTUNE AT ARCADE'S FEET FOR AN EVENING OF DINNER, DANCING AND WINNER TAKE ALL BLOODSPORT.
PAY TO PLAY MURDER WORLD.
CULLEN, WHAT KIND OF SICK CREEP WOULD PAY TO BE IN A DEATH MATCH?!
BORED BILLIONAIRES. RICH TO THE POINT OF INSANITY. EAGER TO PROVE THEMSELVES SUPERIOR TO OTHER BORED BILLIONAIRES.
BUT THAT DOESN'T MATTER.
WHAT MATTERS IS THAT THIS TIME ARCADE'S THE ONE LEAVING IN A BAG. THIS TIME WE GET THE UPPER HAND. IT'S OUR TURN TO WIN.
ARE YOU KIDDING ME?!
KLOOOOMP
HOW MANY GALLONS OF ICE COLD CRAZY DID YOU HAVE TO GUZZLE BEFORE IT SOUNDED LIKE A GOOD IDEA TO BRING US HERE?
AGAINST OUR WILL.
TO FACE HIM!

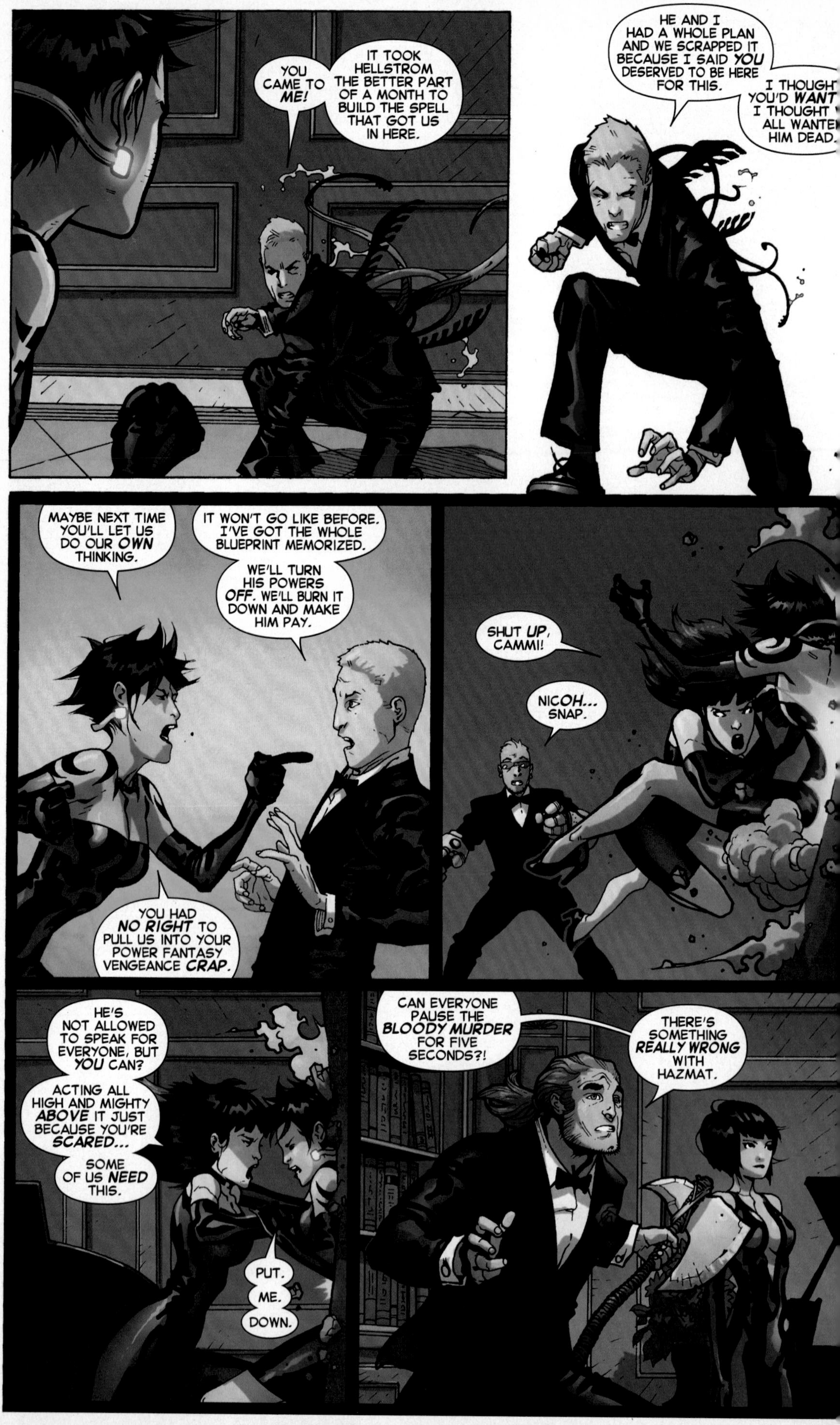
YOU CAME TO ME!
IT TOOK HELLSTROM THE BETTER PART OF A MONTH TO BUILD THE SPELL THAT GOT US IN HERE.
HE AND I HAD A WHOLE PLAN AND WE SCRAPPED IT BECAUSE I SAID YOU DESERVED TO BE HERE FOR THIS.
MAYBE NEXT TIME YOU'LL LET US DO OUR OWN THINKING.
IT WON'T GO LIKE BEFORE. I'VE GOT THE WHOLE BLUEPRINT MEMORIZED.
WE'LL TURN HIS POWERS OFF. WE'LL BURN IT DOWN AND MAKE HIM PAY.
YOU HAD NO RIGHT TO PULL US INTO YOUR POWER FANTASY VENGEANCE CRAP.
SHUT UP, CAMMI!
NICOH... SNAP.
HE'S NOT ALLOWED TO SPEAK FOR EVERYONE, BUT YOU CAN?
ACTING ALL HIGH AND MIGHTY ABOVE IT JUST BECAUSE YOU'RE SCARED...
SOME OF US NEED THIS.
PUT.
ME.
DOWN.
CAN EVERYONE PAUSE THE BLOODY MURDER FOR FIVE SECONDS?!
THERE'S SOMETHING REALLY WRONG WITH HAZMAT.

SHE WON'T TALK. CAN'T GET HER TO LOOK AT ME. JUST THAT DEAD STARE STRAIGHT AHEAD. BARELY BLINKS.

CATATONIC SHOCK.

WHAT?

SORT OF LIKE SCREEN SAVER MODE FOR YOUR BRAIN. HAPPENS SOMETIMES WHEN PEOPLE FREAK *WAY OUT*. THEIR MIND JUST BLINKS OFF FOR A WHILE.

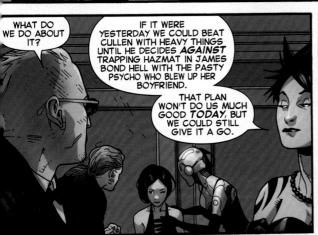

WHAT DO WE DO ABOUT IT?

IF IT WERE YESTERDAY WE COULD BEAT CULLEN WITH HEAVY THINGS UNTIL HE DECIDES *AGAINST* TRAPPING HAZMAT IN JAMES BOND HELL WITH THE PASTY PSYCHO WHO BLEW UP HER BOYFRIEND.

THAT PLAN WON'T DO US MUCH GOOD *TODAY*, BUT WE COULD STILL GIVE IT A GO.

DOES ANYBODY HAVE A *USEFUL* SUGGESTION?

OR ARE WE JUST GONNA STAND HERE LISTENING TO CAMMI'S WITTY INDIGNATION?

YEAH, WHO AM I TO QUESTION SHE-WHO-MUST-NOT-BE-SERIOUS-WITH-THAT-OUTFIT. SHE'S ANGRY AND MAGICAL. THE DARK SIDE *AWAITS*!

ALL RIGHT, LOOK...

I'M SORRY ABOUT HAZMAT. TRULY.

BUT RIGHT THIS MOMENT WE HAVE TO SHUT DOWN HIS SYSTEM. I CAN DO THAT BUT I'LL NEED SOME *HELP*.

I'LL GO.

YEAH, ME TOO!

WHAT?

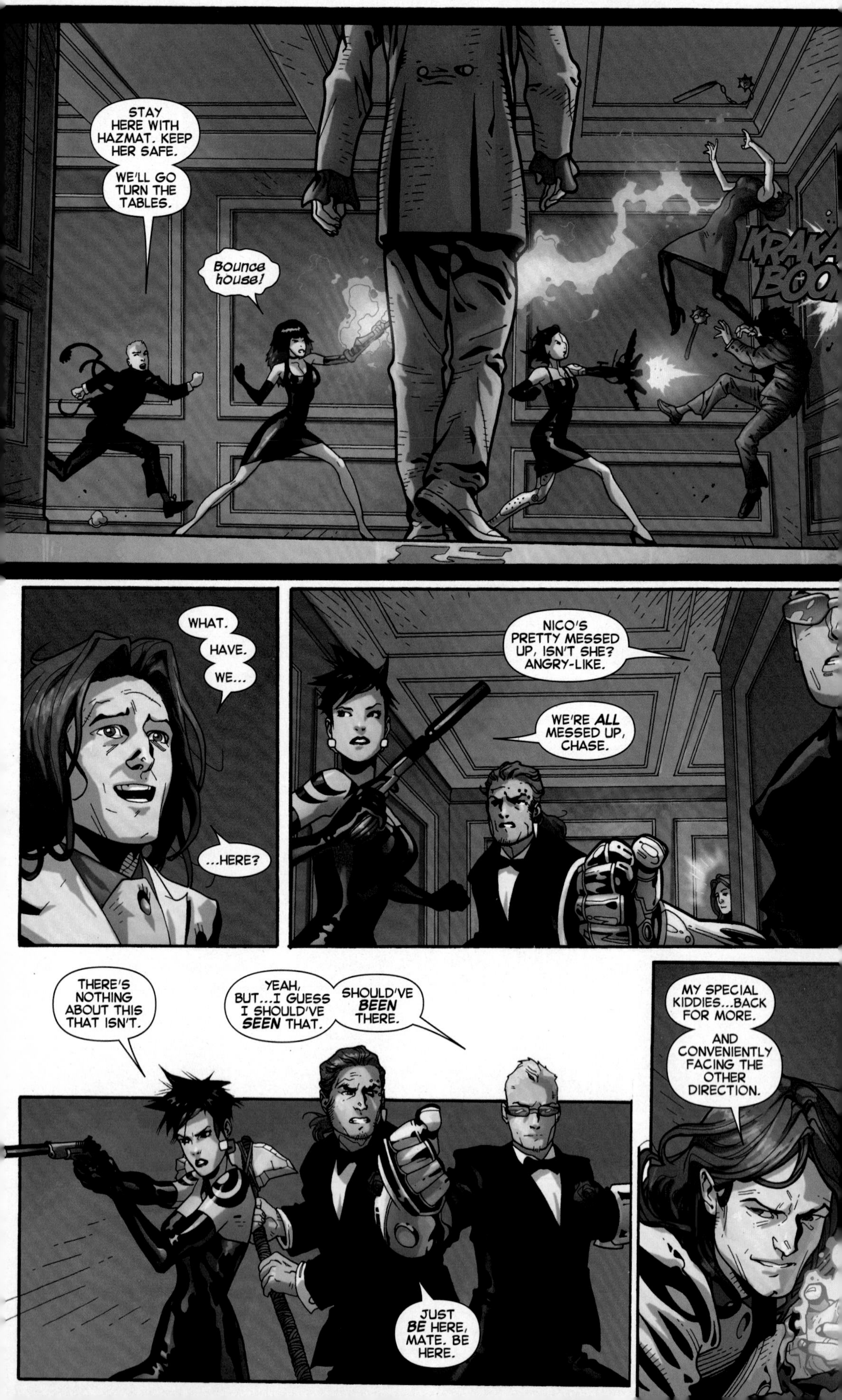

STAY HERE WITH HAZMAT. KEEP HER SAFE.
WE'LL GO TURN THE TABLES.
Bounce house!
WHAT.
HAVE.
WE...
...HERE?
NICO'S PRETTY MESSED UP, ISN'T SHE? ANGRY-LIKE.
WE'RE ALL MESSED UP, CHASE.
THERE'S NOTHING ABOUT THIS THAT ISN'T.
YEAH, BUT...I GUESS I SHOULD'VE SEEN THAT.
SHOULD'VE BEEN THERE.
JUST BE HERE, MATE. BE HERE.
MY SPECIAL KIDDIES...BACK FOR MORE.
AND CONVENIENTLY FACING THE OTHER DIRECTION.

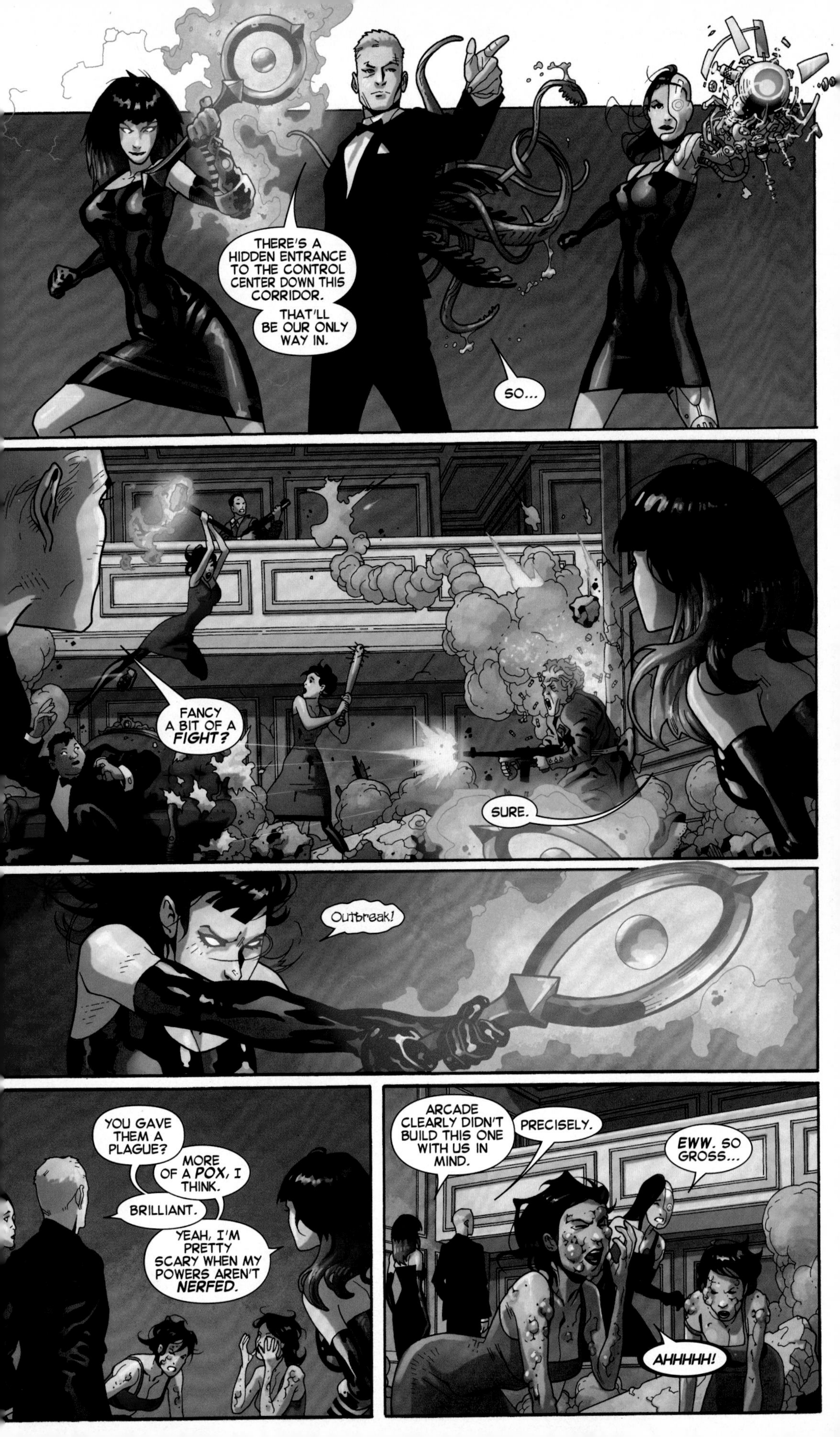
THERE'S A HIDDEN ENTRANCE TO THE CONTROL CENTER DOWN THIS CORRIDOR.
THAT'LL BE OUR ONLY WAY IN.
SO...
FANCY A BIT OF A FIGHT?
SURE.
Outbreak!
YOU GAVE THEM A PLAGUE?
MORE OF A POX, I THINK.
BRILLIANT.
YEAH, I'M PRETTY SCARY WHEN MY POWERS AREN'T NERFED.
ARCADE CLEARLY DIDN'T BUILD THIS ONE WITH US IN MIND.
PRECISELY.
EWW. SO GROSS...
AHHHHH!

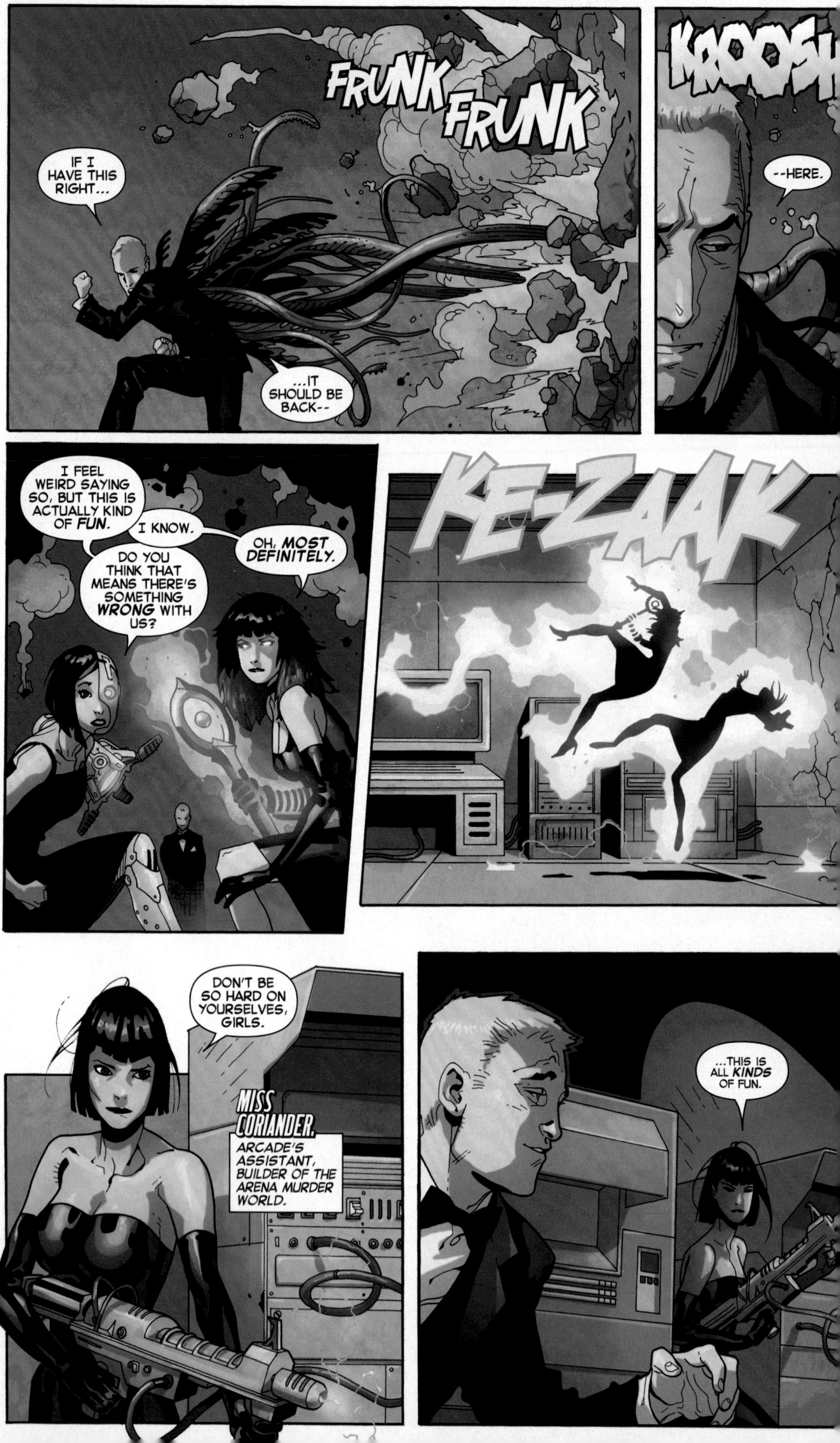
IF I HAVE THIS RIGHT...
FRUNK FRUNK
...IT SHOULD BE BACK--
KROOSH
--HERE.
I FEEL WEIRD SAYING SO, BUT THIS IS ACTUALLY KIND OF FUN.
I KNOW.
DO YOU THINK THAT MEANS THERE'S SOMETHING WRONG WITH US?
OH, MOST DEFINITELY.
KE-ZAAK
DON'T BE SO HARD ON YOURSELVES, GIRLS.
MISS CORIANDER.
ARCADE'S ASSISTANT, BUILDER OF THE ARENA MURDER WORLD.
...THIS IS ALL KINDS OF FUN.

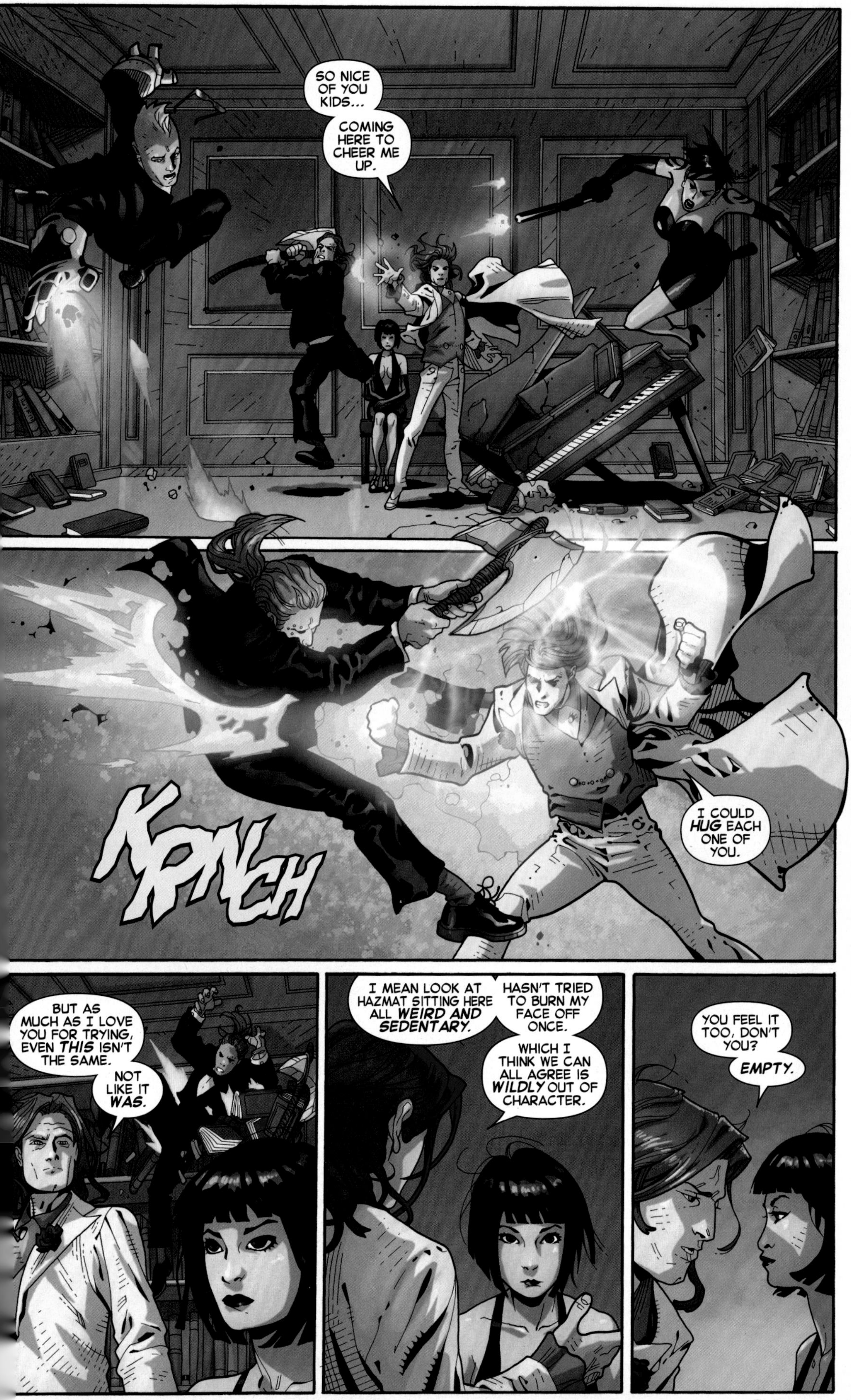
SO NICE OF YOU KIDS...
COMING HERE TO CHEER ME UP.
KRNCH
I COULD HUG EACH ONE OF YOU.
BUT AS MUCH AS I LOVE YOU FOR TRYING, EVEN THIS ISN'T THE SAME.
NOT LIKE IT WAS.
I MEAN LOOK AT HAZMAT SITTING HERE ALL WEIRD AND SEDENTARY.
HASN'T TRIED TO BURN MY FACE OFF ONCE.
WHICH I THINK WE CAN ALL AGREE IS WILDLY OUT OF CHARACTER.
YOU FEEL IT TOO, DON'T YOU?
EMPTY.

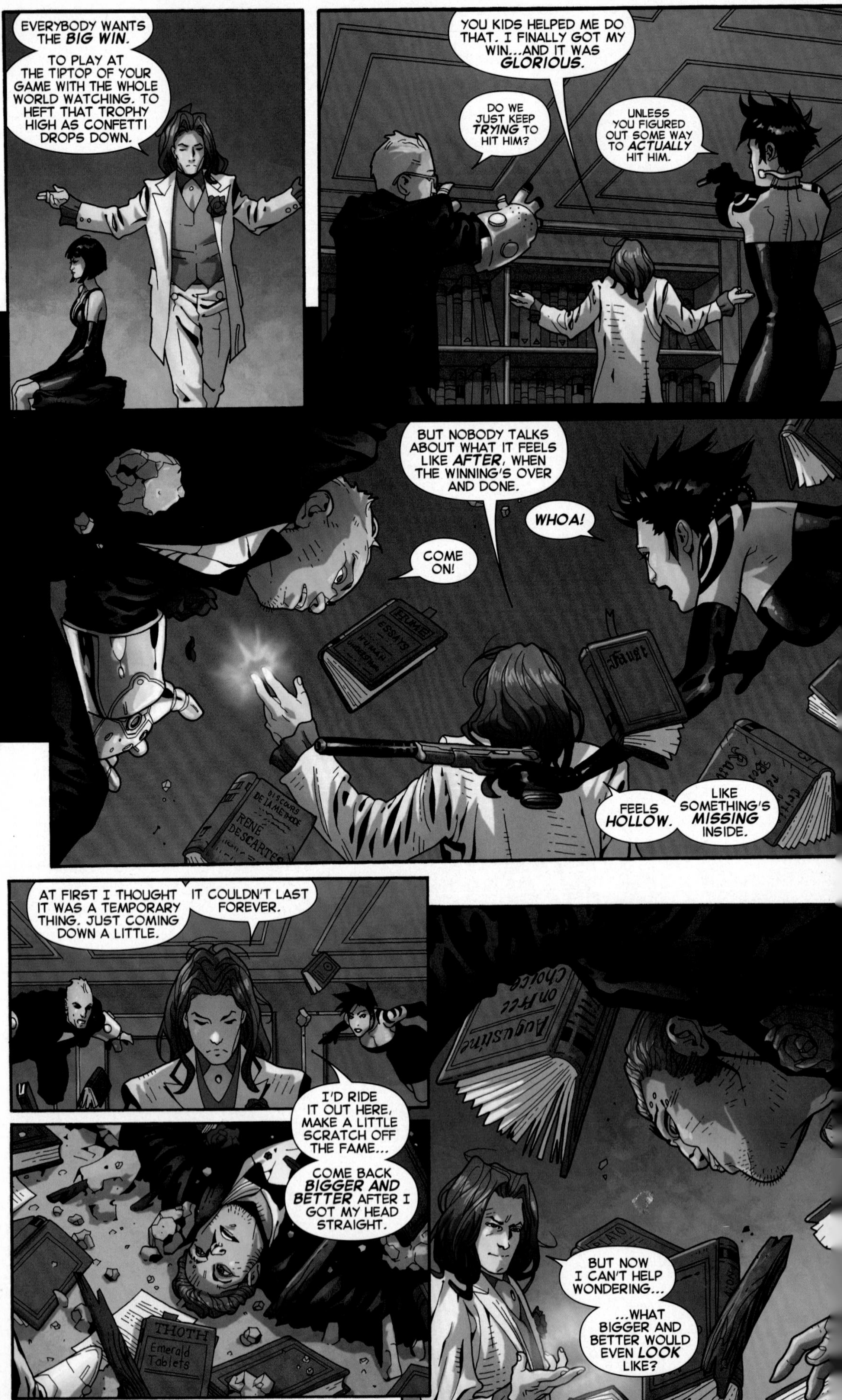

EVERYBODY WANTS THE BIG WIN.
TO PLAY AT THE TIPTOP OF YOUR GAME WITH THE WHOLE WORLD WATCHING. TO HEFT THAT TROPHY HIGH AS CONFETTI DROPS DOWN.
YOU KIDS HELPED ME DO THAT. I FINALLY GOT MY WIN...AND IT WAS GLORIOUS.
DO WE JUST KEEP TRYING TO HIT HIM?
UNLESS YOU FIGURED OUT SOME WAY TO ACTUALLY HIT HIM.
BUT NOBODY TALKS ABOUT WHAT IT FEELS LIKE AFTER, WHEN THE WINNING'S OVER AND DONE.
WHOA!
COME ON!
Faust
RENE DESCARTES
FEELS HOLLOW.
LIKE SOMETHING'S MISSING INSIDE.
AT FIRST I THOUGHT IT WAS A TEMPORARY THING. JUST COMING DOWN A LITTLE.
IT COULDN'T LAST FOREVER.
I'D RIDE IT OUT HERE, MAKE A LITTLE SCRATCH OFF THE FAME...
COME BACK BIGGER AND BETTER AFTER I GOT MY HEAD STRAIGHT.
Augustine on Free Choice
THOTH Emerald Tablets
BUT NOW I CAN'T HELP WONDERING...
...WHAT BIGGER AND BETTER WOULD EVEN LOOK LIKE?

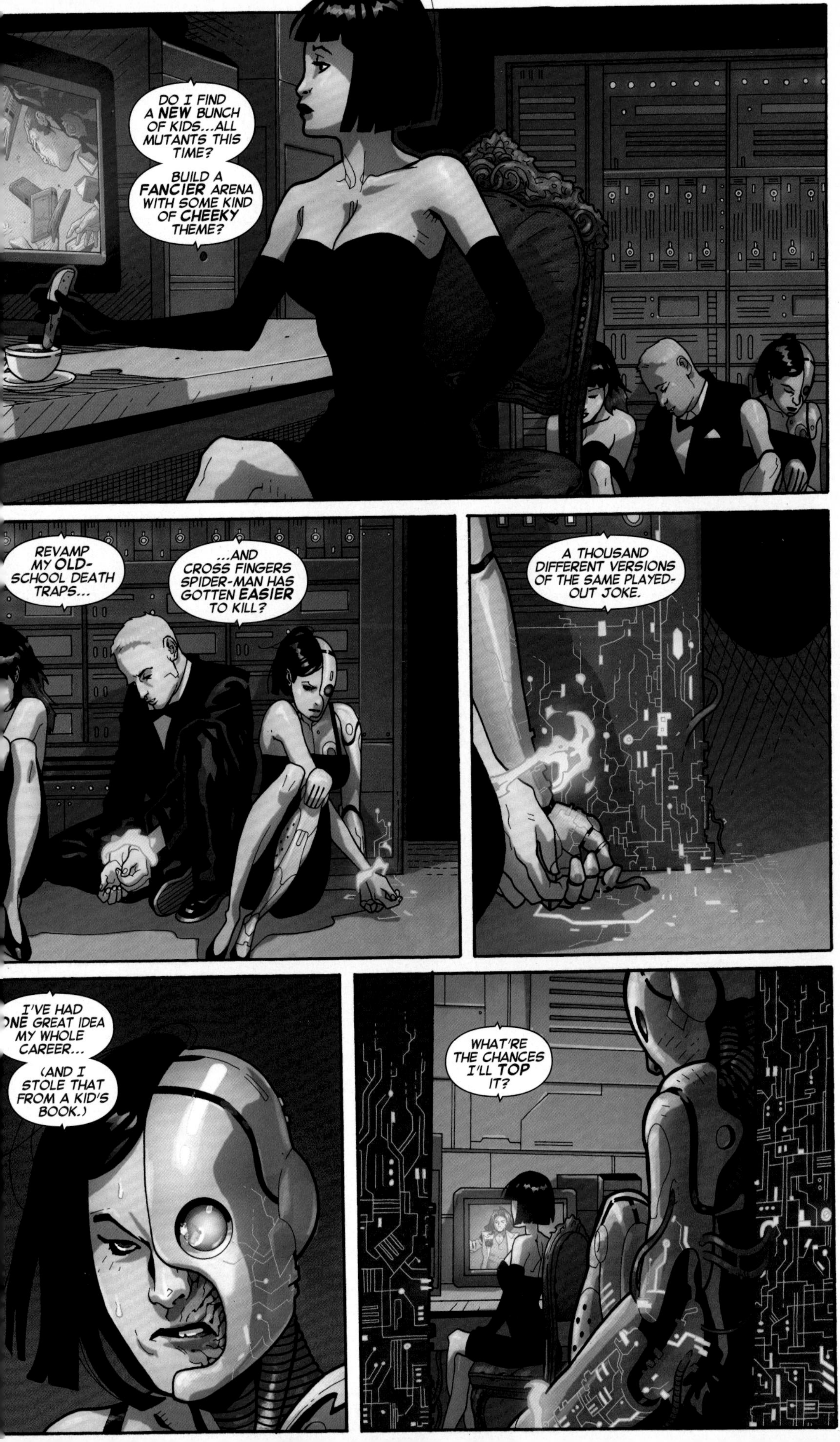
DO I FIND A NEW BUNCH OF KIDS...ALL MUTANTS THIS TIME?
BUILD A FANCIER ARENA WITH SOME KIND OF CHEEKY THEME?
REVAMP MY OLD-SCHOOL DEATH TRAPS...
...AND CROSS FINGERS SPIDER-MAN HAS GOTTEN EASIER TO KILL?
A THOUSAND DIFFERENT VERSIONS OF THE SAME PLAYED-OUT JOKE.
I'VE HAD ONE GREAT IDEA MY WHOLE CAREER...
(AND I STOLE THAT FROM A KID'S BOOK.)
WHAT'RE THE CHANCES I'LL TOP IT?

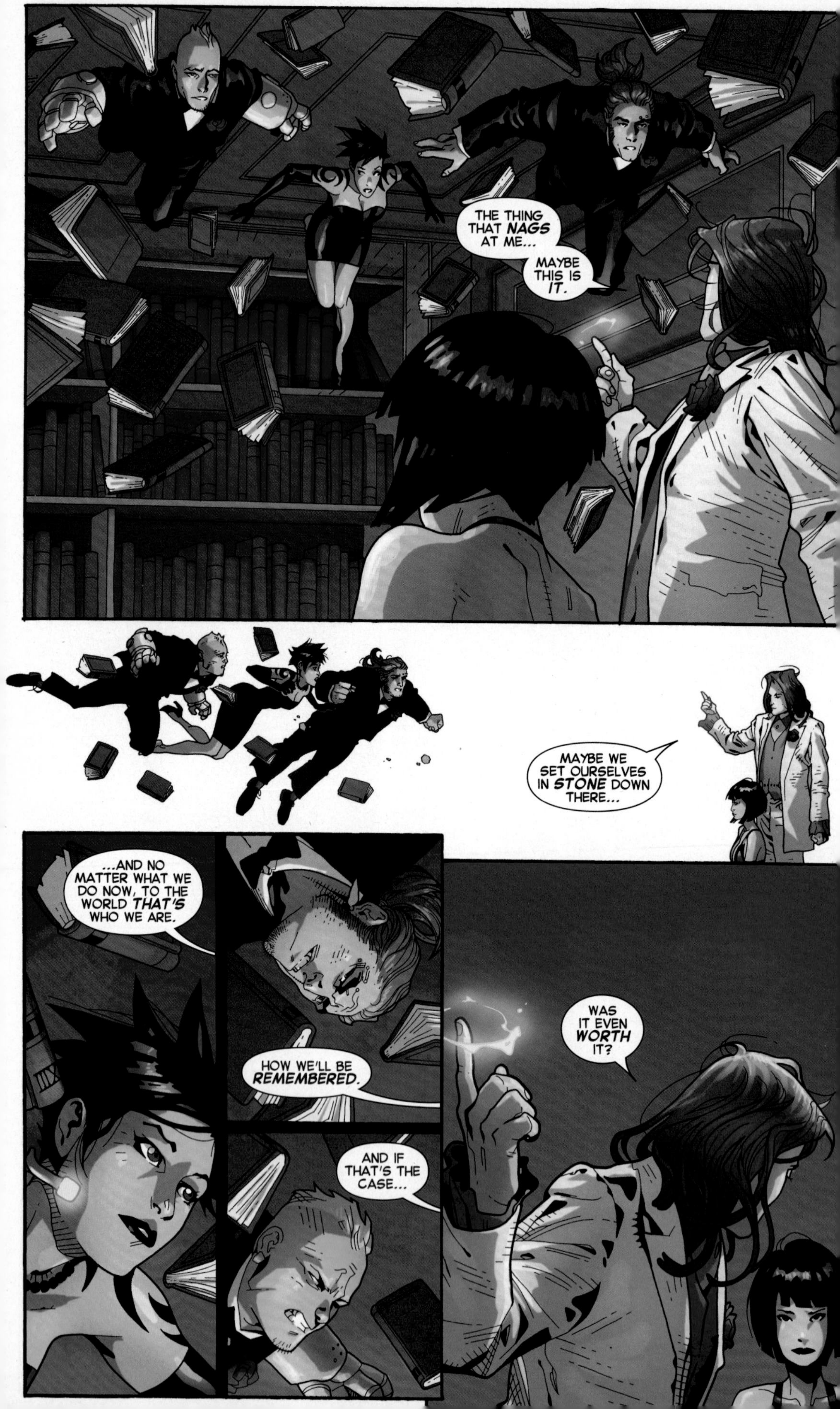
THE THING THAT NAGS AT ME...
MAYBE THIS IS IT.
MAYBE WE SET OURSELVES IN STONE DOWN THERE...
...AND NO MATTER WHAT WE DO NOW, TO THE WORLD THAT'S WHO WE ARE.
HOW WE'LL BE REMEMBERED.
AND IF THAT'S THE CASE...
WAS IT EVEN WORTH IT?

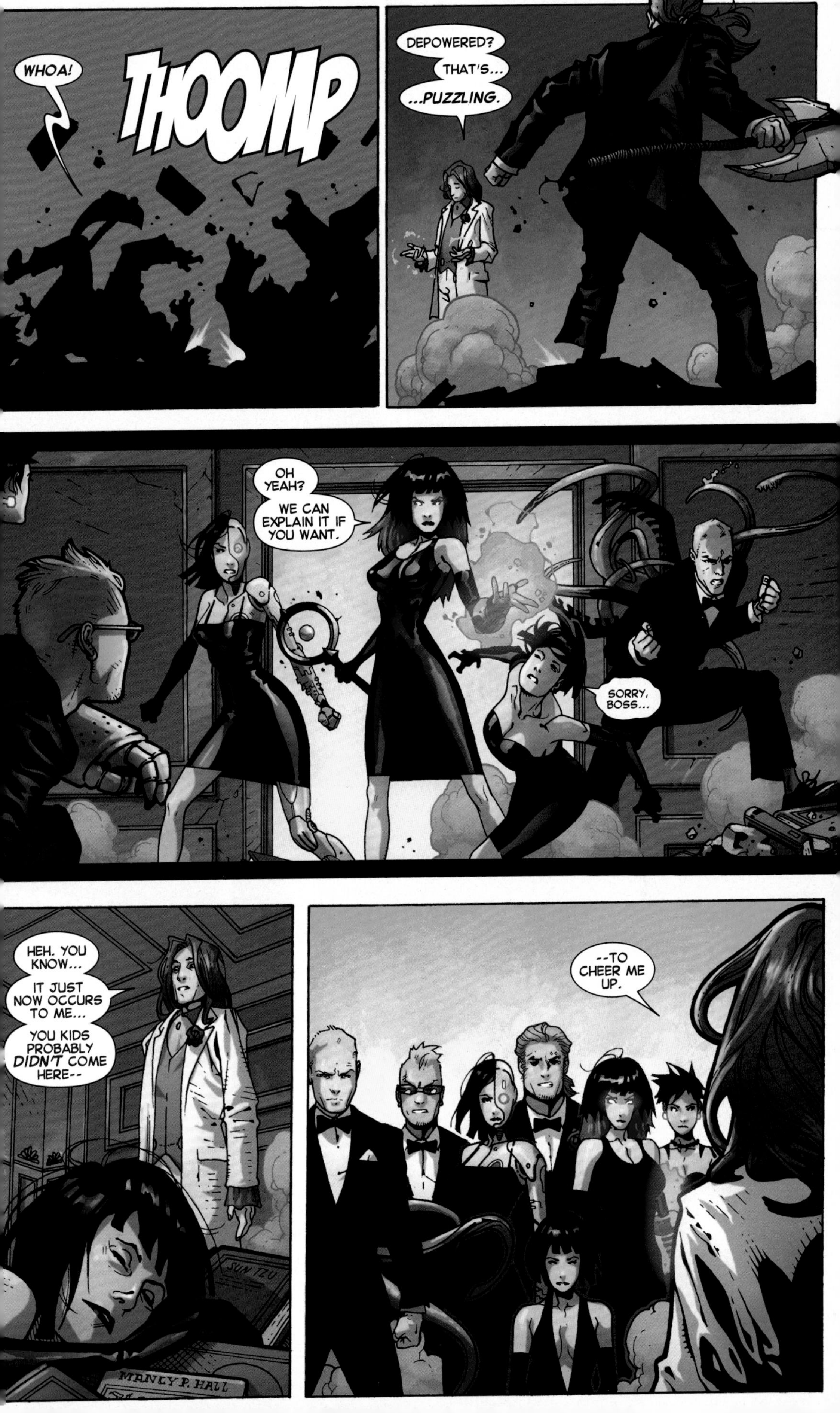
WHOA!
THOOMP
DEPOWERED?
THAT'S...
...PUZZLING.
OH YEAH?
WE CAN EXPLAIN IT IF YOU WANT.
SORRY, BOSS...
HEH. YOU KNOW...
IT JUST NOW OCCURS TO ME...
YOU KIDS PROBABLY *DIDN'T* COME HERE--
--TO CHEER ME UP.
SUN TZU
MANLY P. HALL

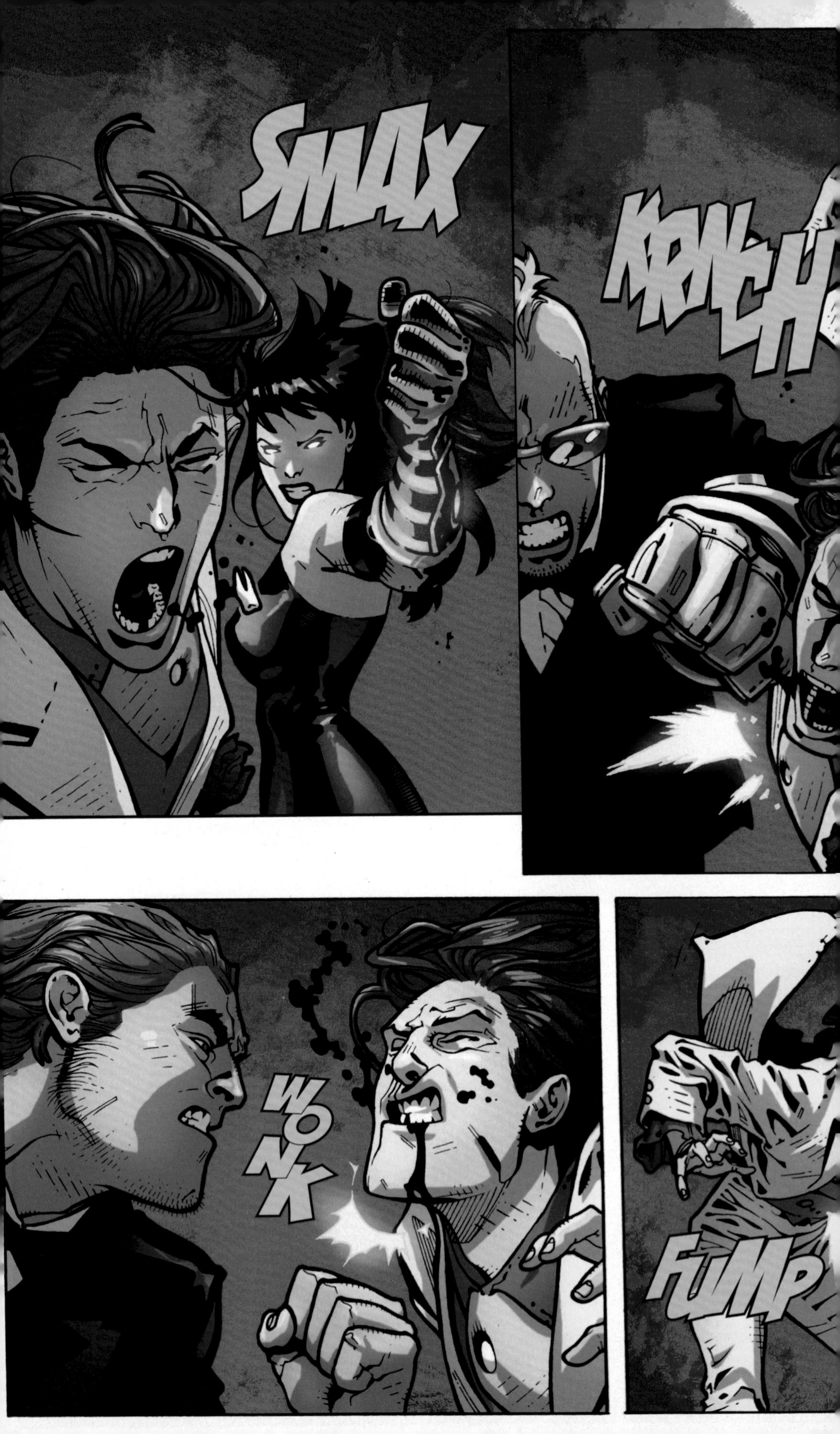
SMAX
KRUNCH
WONK
FUMP

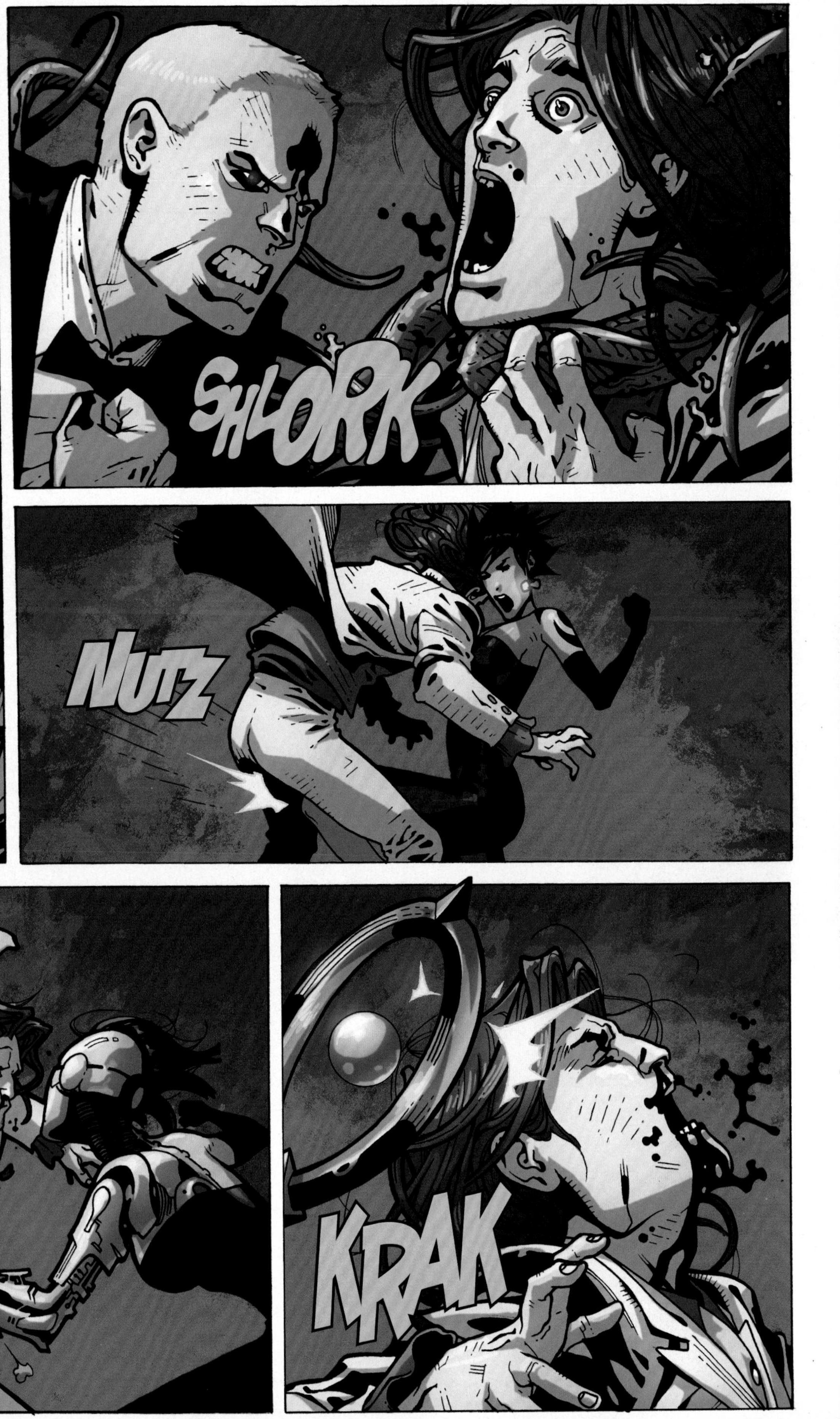
SHLORK
NUTZ
KRAK

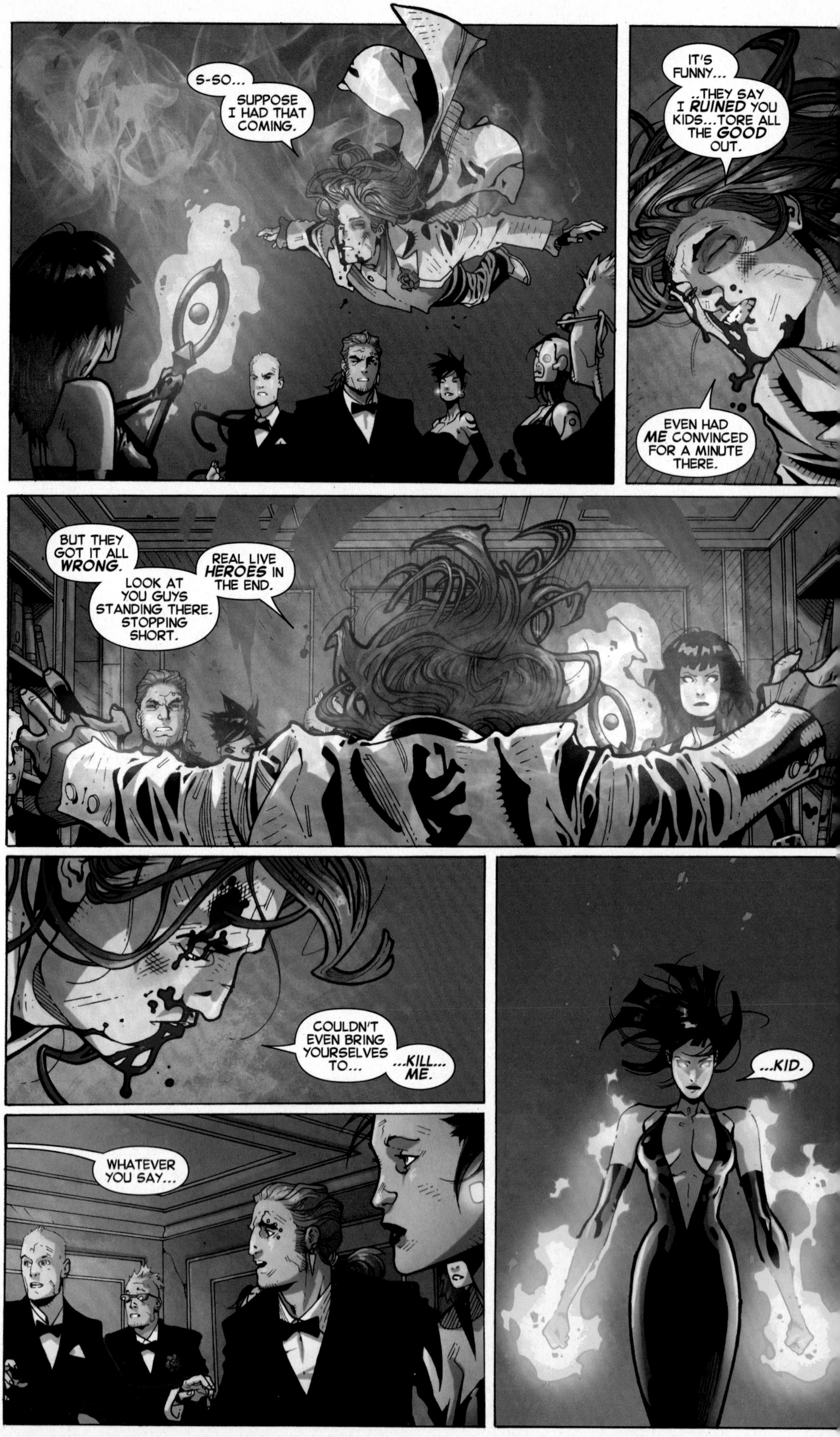
S-SO... SUPPOSE I HAD THAT COMING.
IT'S FUNNY...
..THEY SAY I RUINED YOU KIDS...TORE ALL THE GOOD OUT.
EVEN HAD ME CONVINCED FOR A MINUTE THERE.
BUT THEY GOT IT ALL WRONG.
LOOK AT YOU GUYS STANDING THERE. STOPPING SHORT.
REAL LIVE HEROES IN THE END.
COULDN'T EVEN BRING YOURSELVES TO...
...KILL... ME.
WHATEVER YOU SAY...
...KID.

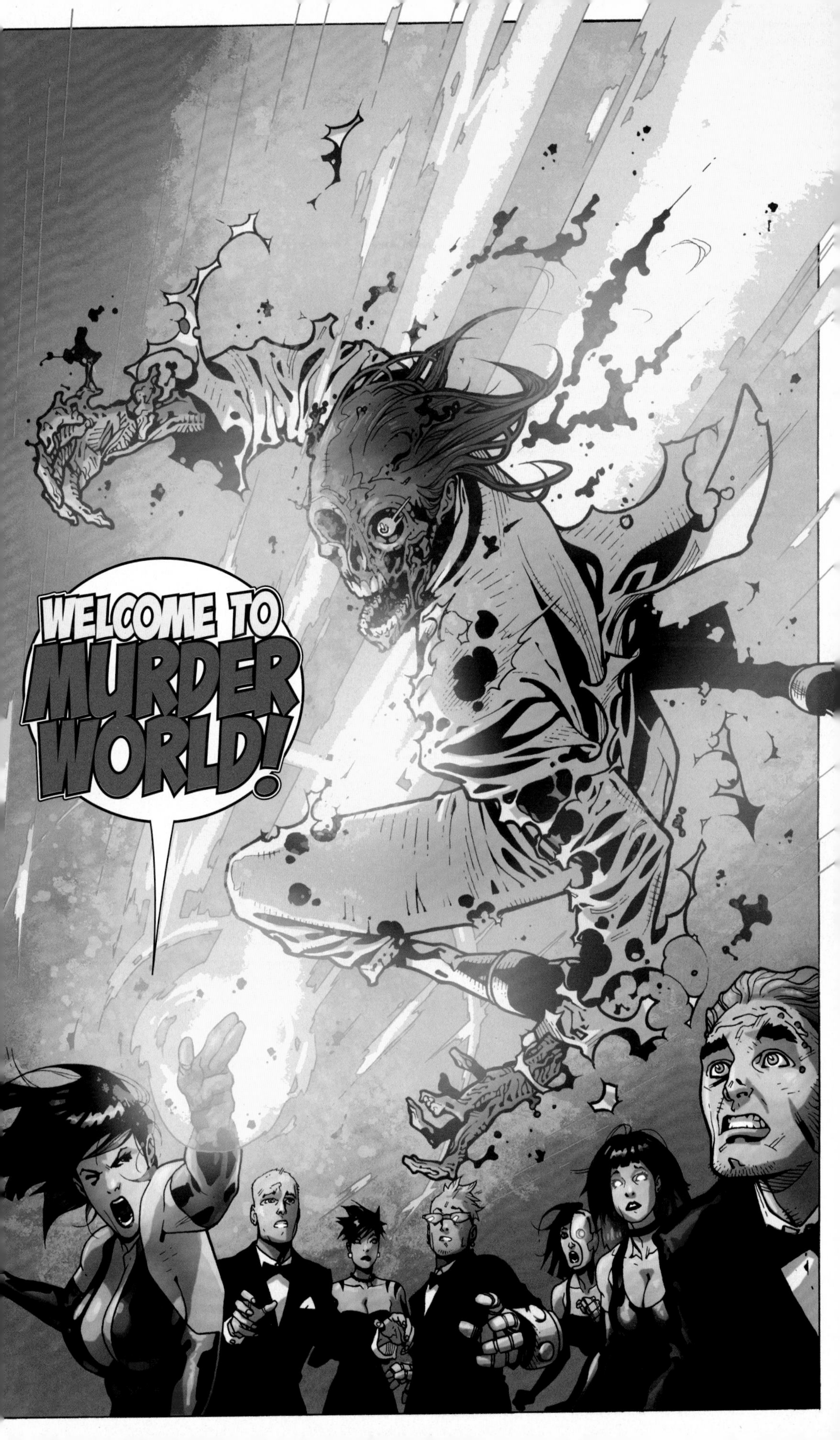
WELCOME TO MURDER WORLD!

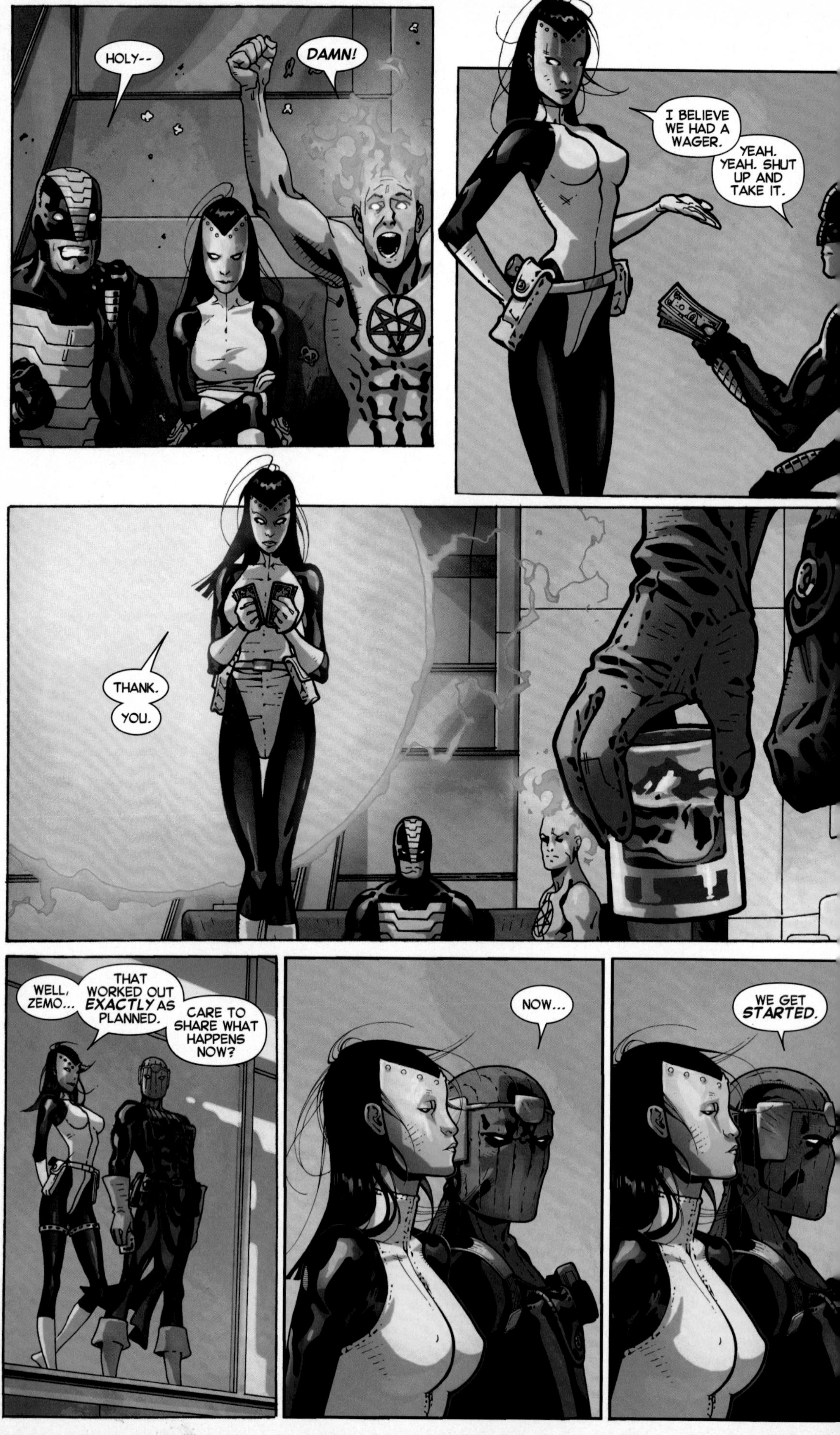
HOLY--
DAMN!
I BELIEVE WE HAD A WAGER.
YEAH. YEAH. SHUT UP AND TAKE IT.
THANK.
YOU.
WELL, ZEMO...
THAT WORKED OUT EXACTLY AS PLANNED.
CARE TO SHARE WHAT HAPPENS NOW?
NOW...
WE GET STARTED.

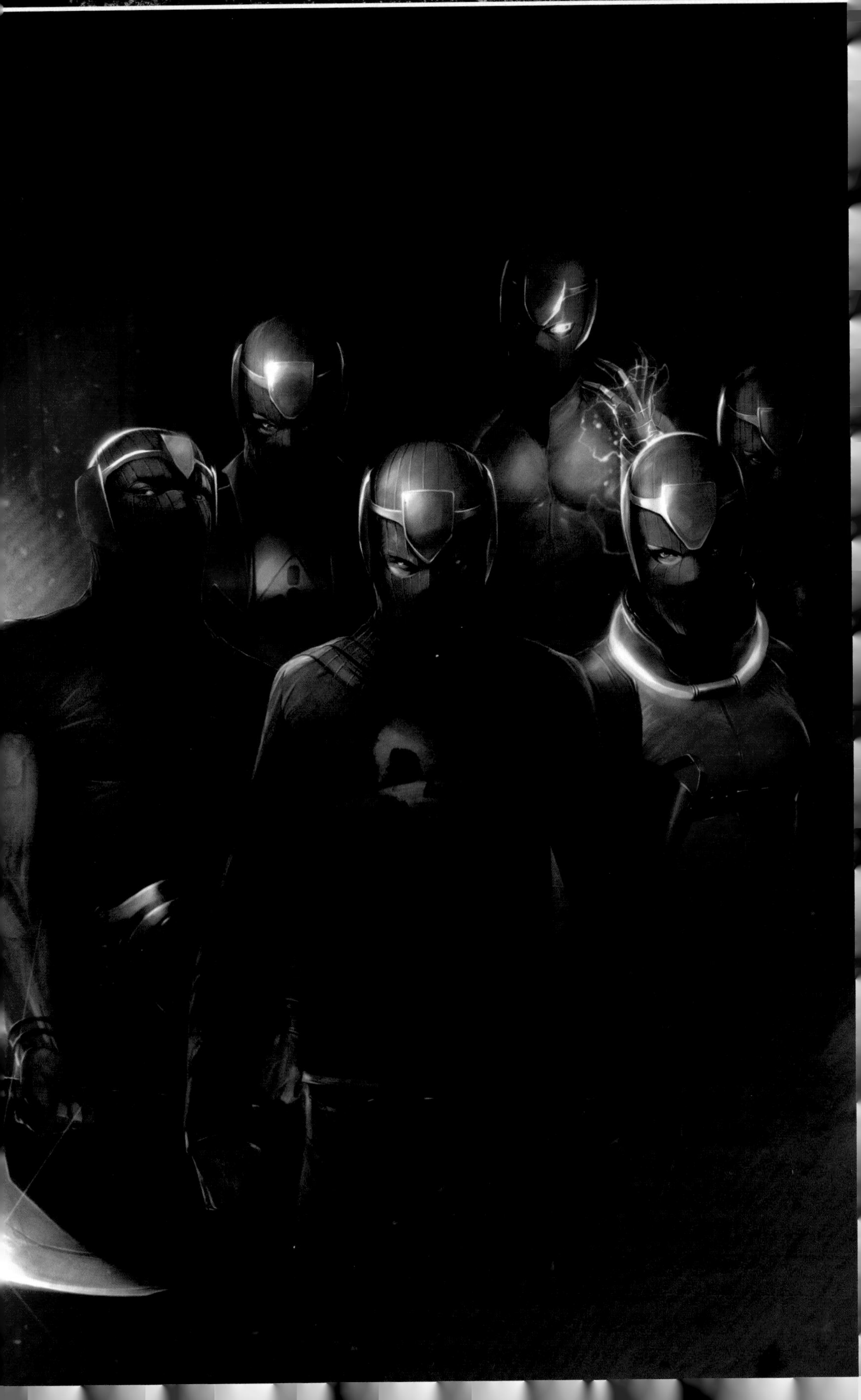

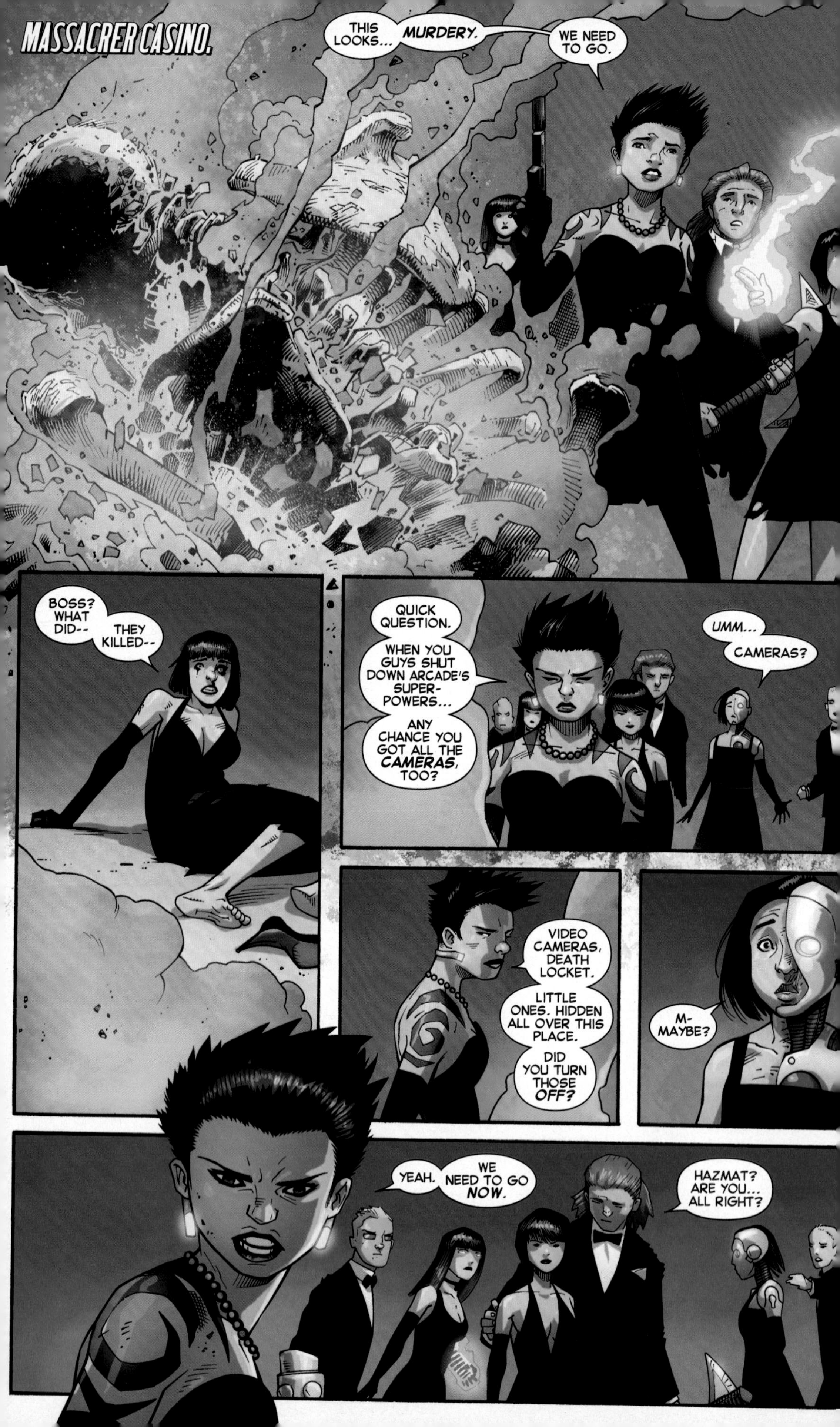
MASSACRER CASINO.
THIS LOOKS... MURDERY.
WE NEED TO GO.
BOSS? WHAT DID--
THEY KILLED--
QUICK QUESTION.
WHEN YOU GUYS SHUT DOWN ARCADE'S SUPER-POWERS...
ANY CHANCE YOU GOT ALL THE CAMERAS, TOO?
UMM...
CAMERAS?
VIDEO CAMERAS, DEATH LOCKET.
LITTLE ONES. HIDDEN ALL OVER THIS PLACE.
DID YOU TURN THOSE OFF?
M-MAYBE?
YEAH.
WE NEED TO GO NOW.
HAZMAT? ARE YOU... ALL RIGHT?

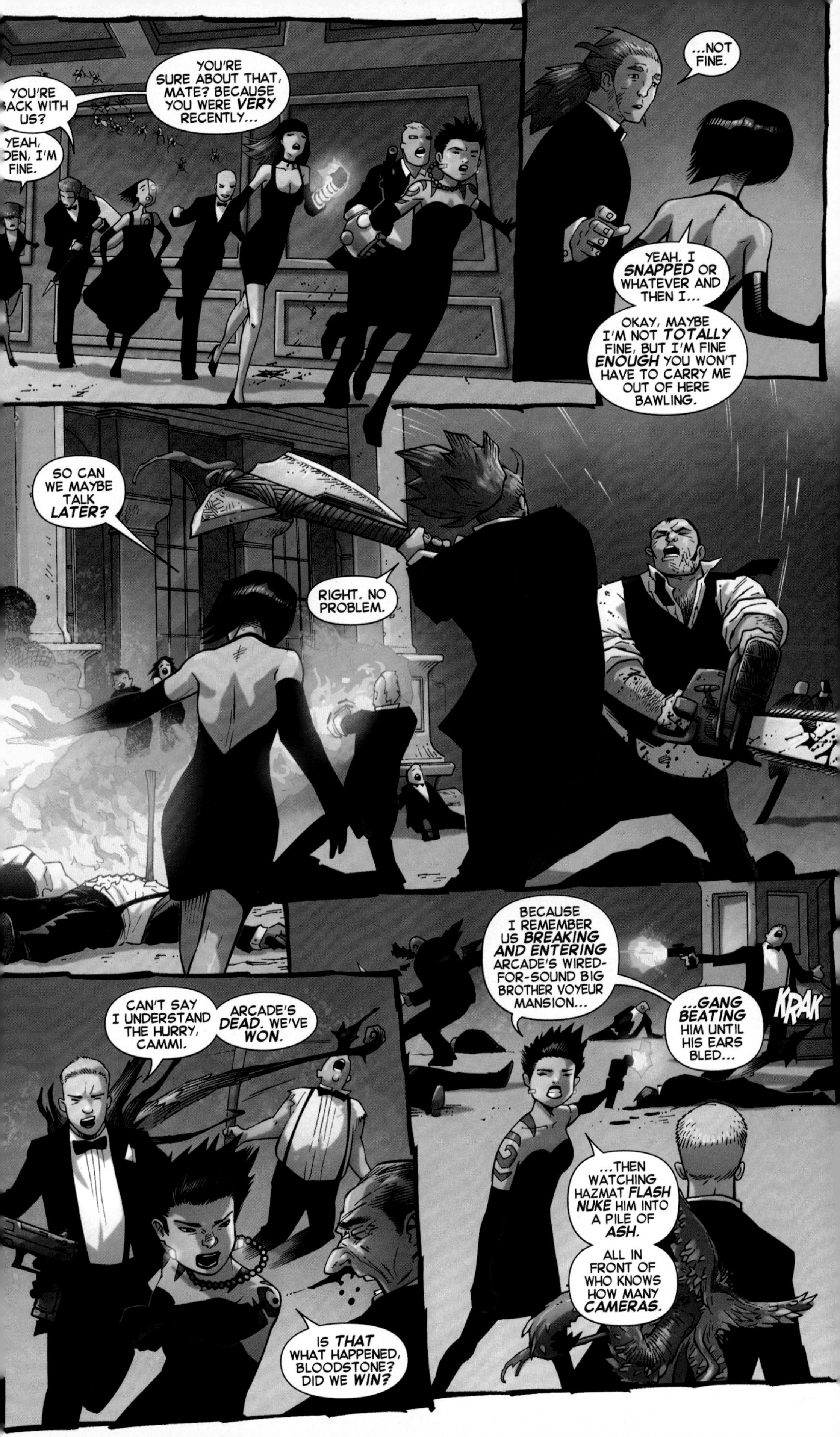
YOU'RE BACK WITH US?
YEAH, DEN, I'M FINE.
YOU'RE SURE ABOUT THAT, MATE? BECAUSE YOU WERE VERY RECENTLY...
...NOT FINE.
YEAH. I SNAPPED OR WHATEVER AND THEN I...
OKAY, MAYBE I'M NOT TOTALLY FINE, BUT I'M FINE ENOUGH YOU WON'T HAVE TO CARRY ME OUT OF HERE BAWLING.
SO CAN WE MAYBE TALK LATER?
RIGHT. NO PROBLEM.
CAN'T SAY I UNDERSTAND THE HURRY, CAMMI.
ARCADE'S DEAD. WE'VE WON.
IS THAT WHAT HAPPENED, BLOODSTONE? DID WE WIN?
BECAUSE I REMEMBER US BREAKING AND ENTERING ARCADE'S WIRED-FOR-SOUND BIG BROTHER VOYEUR MANSION...
...GANG BEATING HIM UNTIL HIS EARS BLED...
KRAK
...THEN WATCHING HAZMAT FLASH NUKE HIM INTO A PILE OF ASH.
ALL IN FRONT OF WHO KNOWS HOW MANY CAMERAS.

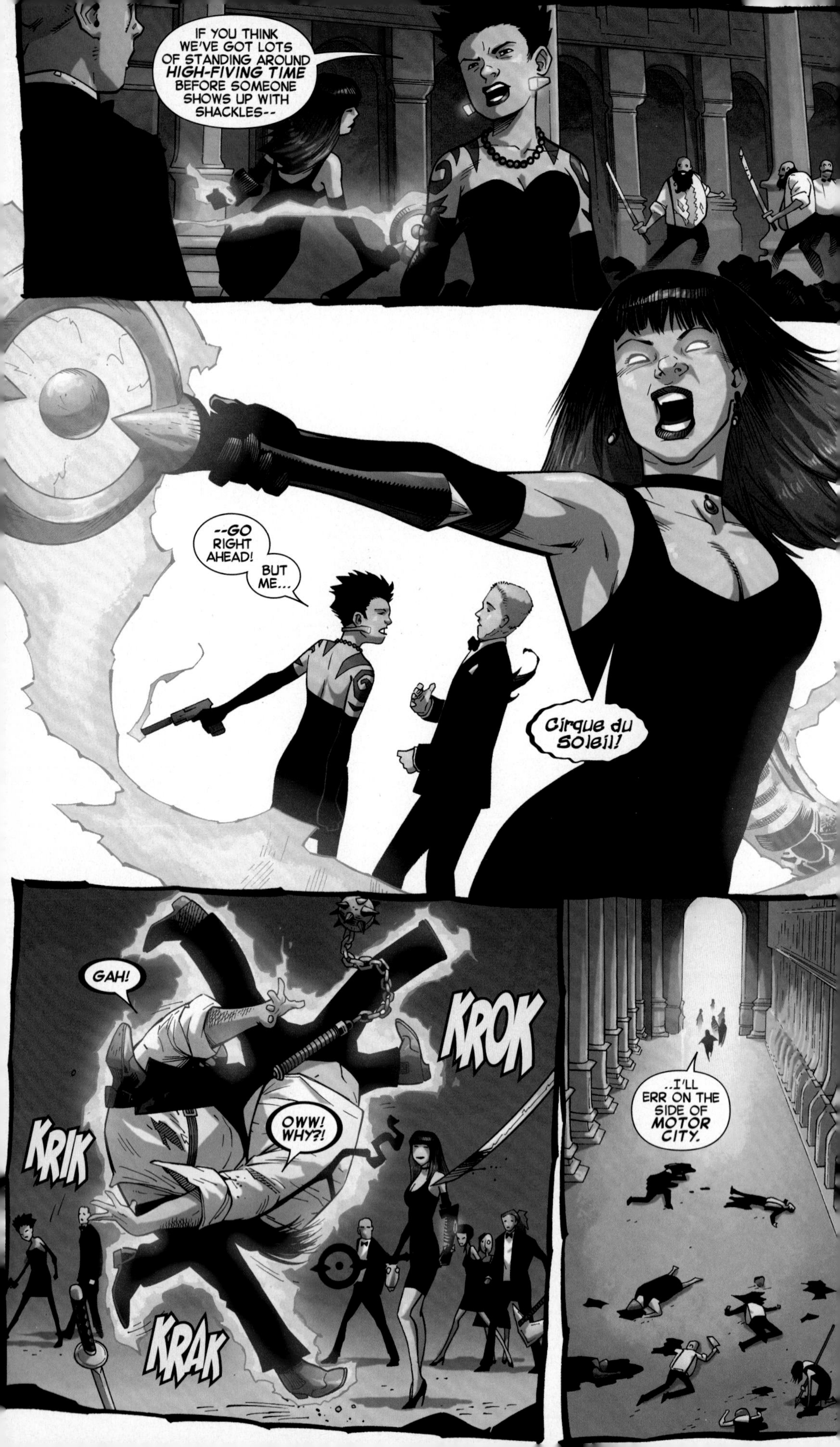
IF YOU THINK WE'VE GOT LOTS OF STANDING AROUND HIGH-FIVING TIME BEFORE SOMEONE SHOWS UP WITH SHACKLES--
--GO RIGHT AHEAD!
BUT ME...
Cirque du Soleil!
GAH!
KROK
KRIK
OWW! WHY?!
KRAK
..I'LL ERR ON THE SIDE OF MOTOR CITY.

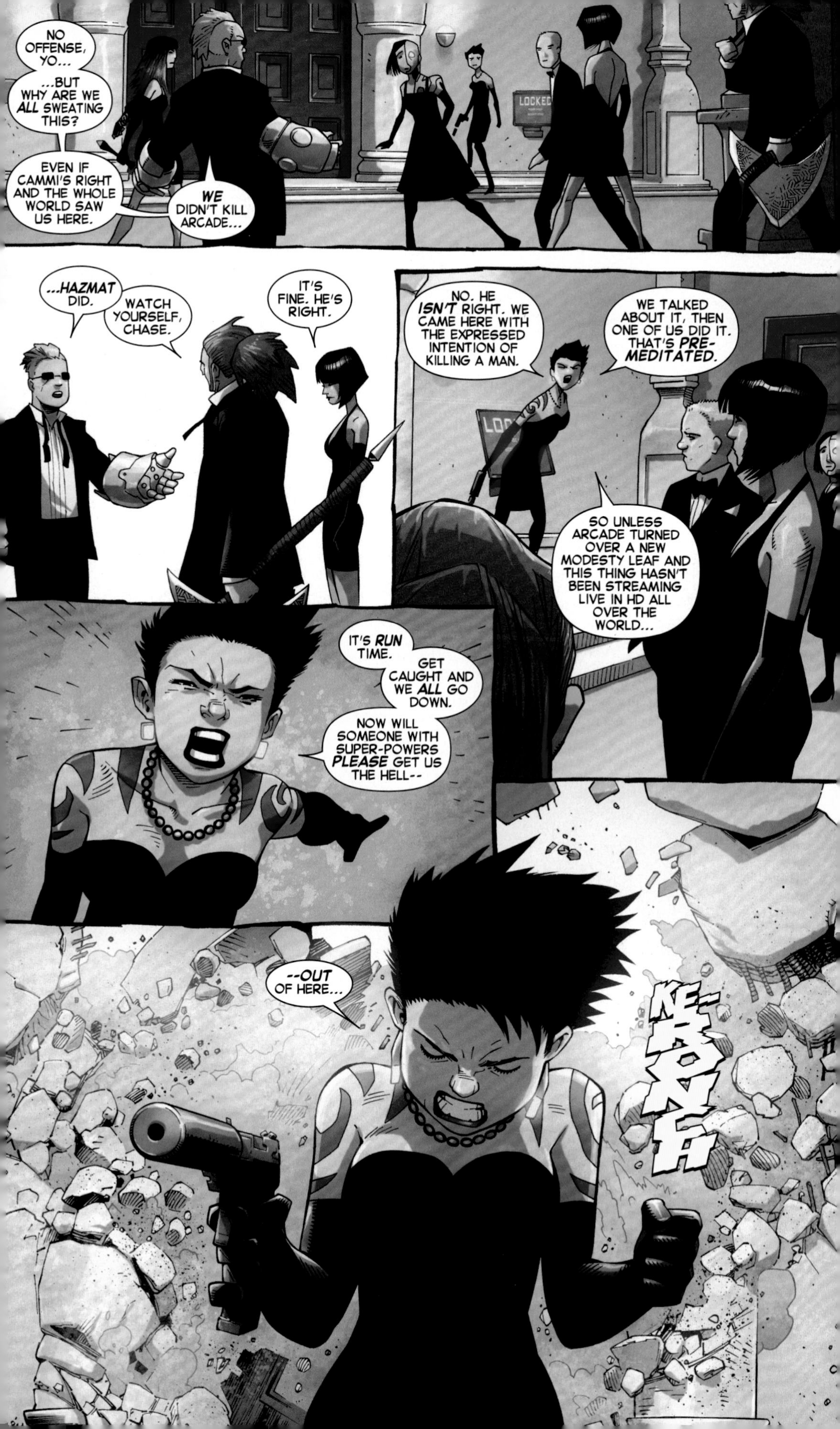
NO OFFENSE, YO...
...BUT WHY ARE WE ALL SWEATING THIS?
EVEN IF CAMMI'S RIGHT AND THE WHOLE WORLD SAW US HERE.
WE DIDN'T KILL ARCADE...
...HAZMAT DID.
WATCH YOURSELF, CHASE.
IT'S FINE. HE'S RIGHT.
NO. HE ISN'T RIGHT. WE CAME HERE WITH THE EXPRESSED INTENTION OF KILLING A MAN.
WE TALKED ABOUT IT, THEN ONE OF US DID IT. THAT'S PRE-MEDITATED.
SO UNLESS ARCADE TURNED OVER A NEW MODESTY LEAF AND THIS THING HASN'T BEEN STREAMING LIVE IN HD ALL OVER THE WORLD...
IT'S RUN TIME.
GET CAUGHT AND WE ALL GO DOWN.
NOW WILL SOMEONE WITH SUPER-POWERS PLEASE GET US THE HELL--
--OUT OF HERE...
KE-RONCH

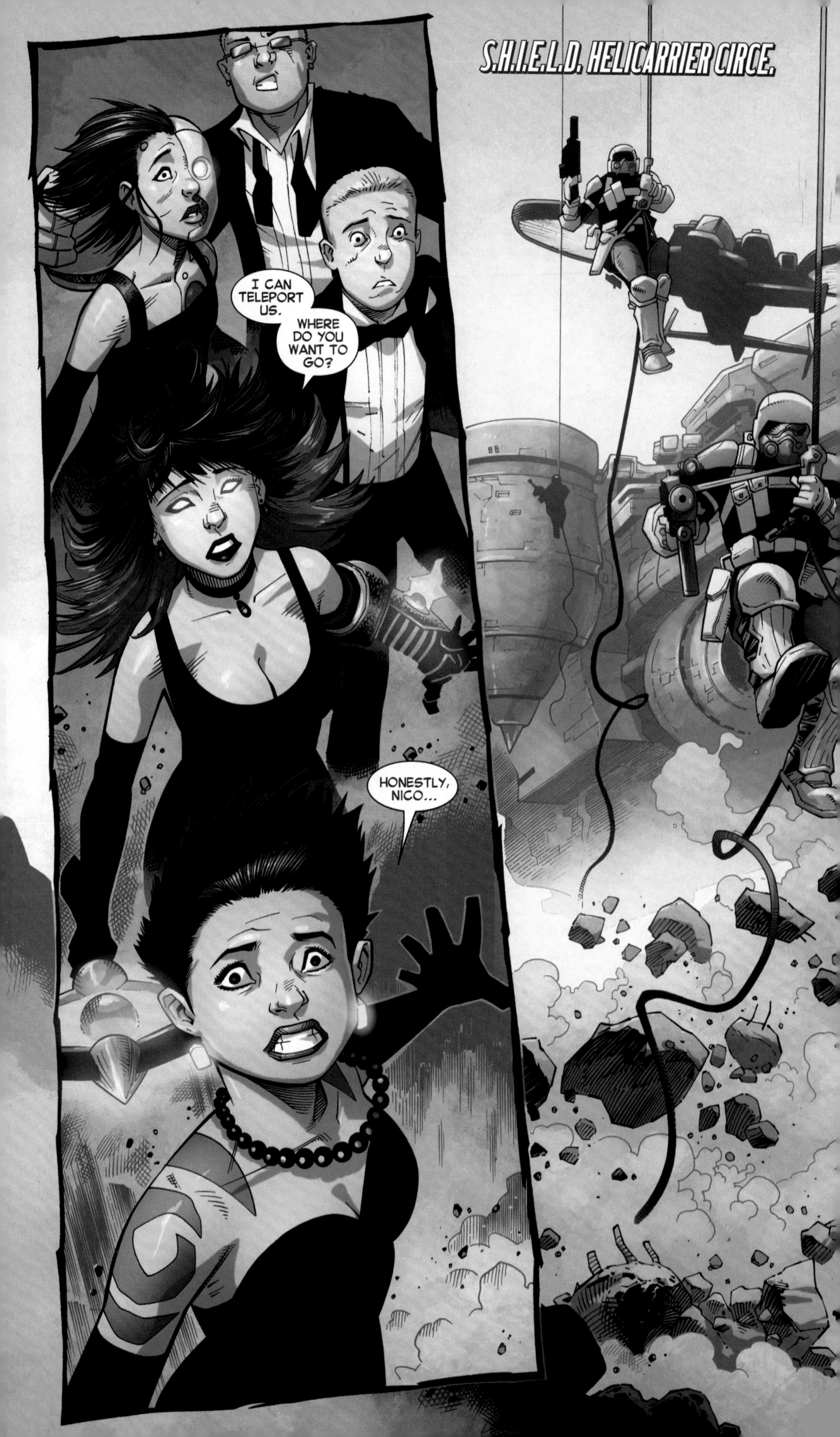
S.H.I.E.L.D. HELICARRIER CIRCE.
I CAN TELEPORT US.
WHERE DO YOU WANT TO GO?
HONESTLY, NICO...

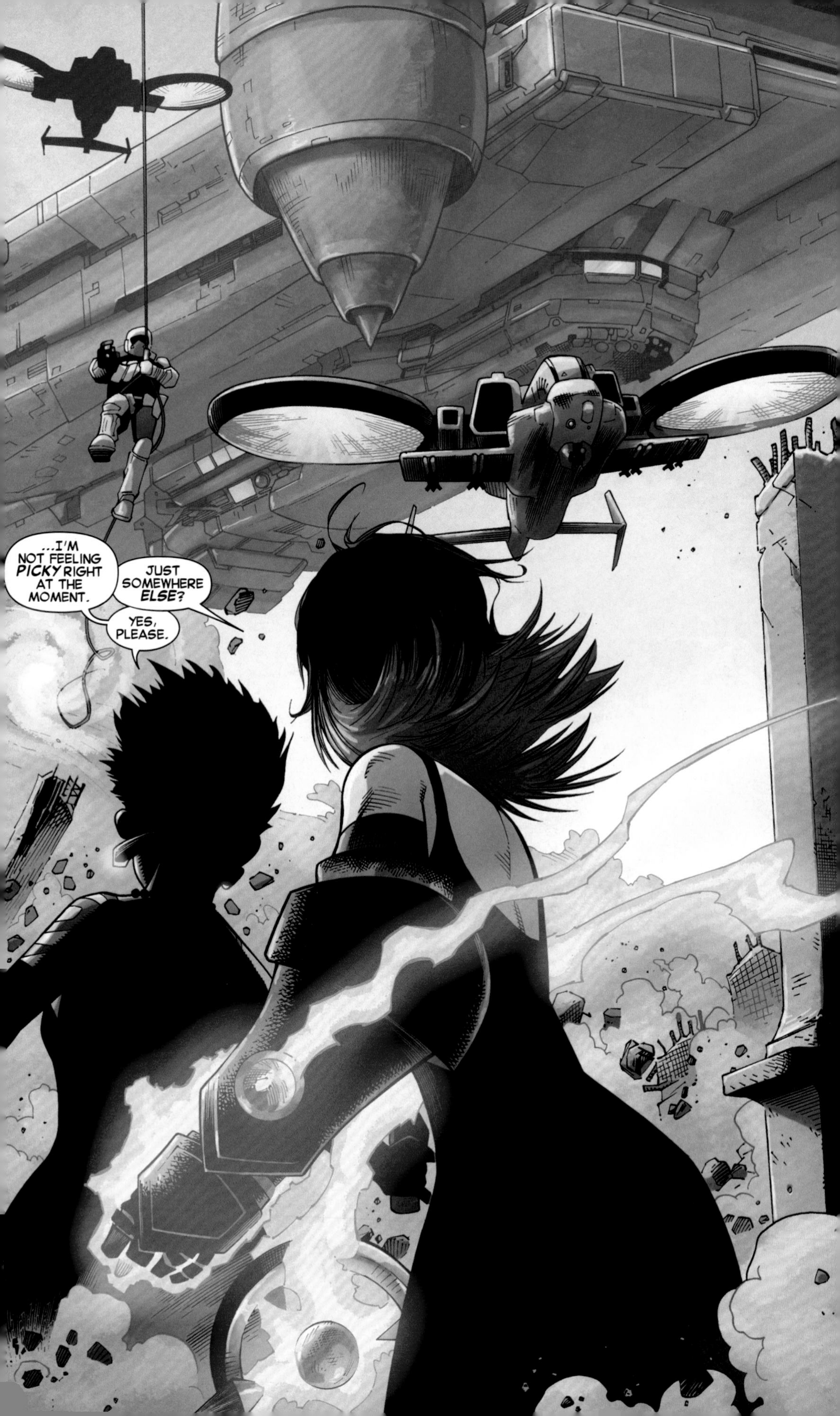
...I'M NOT FEELING PICKY RIGHT AT THE MOMENT.
JUST SOMEWHERE ELSE?
YES, PLEASE.

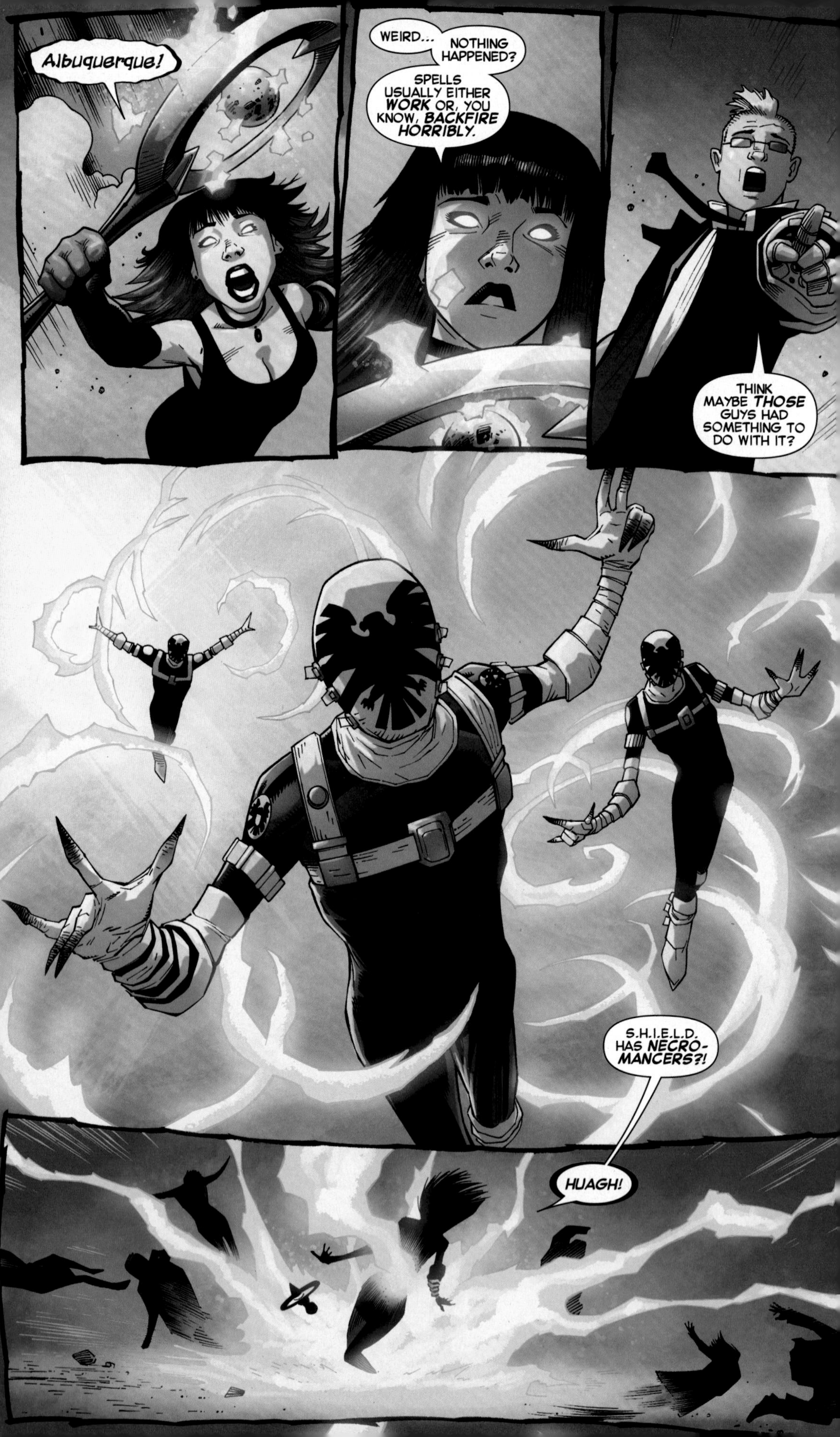
Albuquerque!
WEIRD...
NOTHING HAPPENED?
SPELLS USUALLY EITHER WORK OR, YOU KNOW, BACKFIRE HORRIBLY.
THINK MAYBE THOSE GUYS HAD SOMETHING TO DO WITH IT?
S.H.I.E.L.D. HAS NECRO-MANCERS?!
HUAGH!

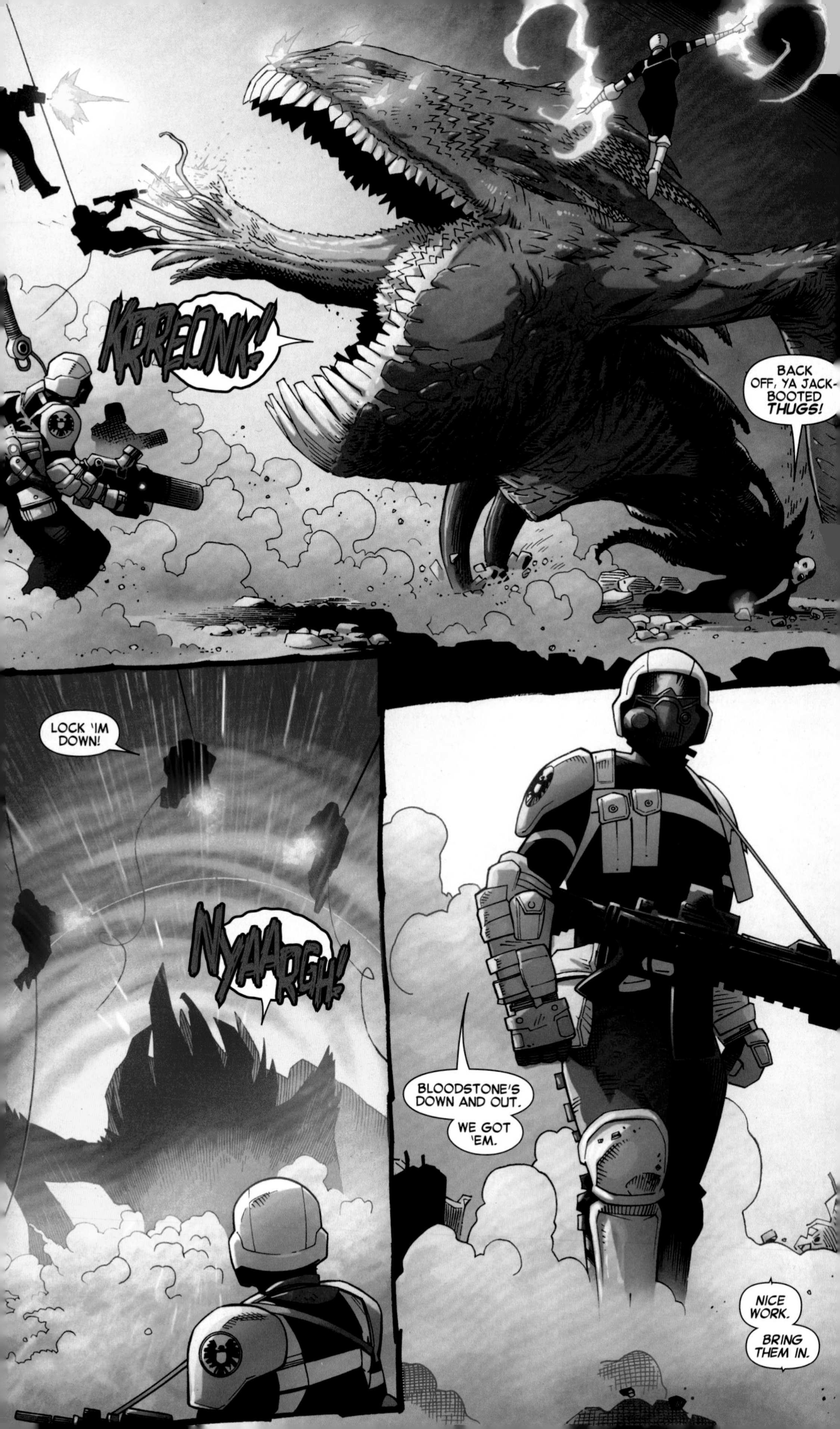

KRREONK!
BACK OFF, YA JACK-BOOTED THUGS!
LOCK 'IM DOWN!
NYAARGH!
BLOODSTONE'S DOWN AND OUT.
WE GOT 'EM.
NICE WORK.
BRING THEM IN.

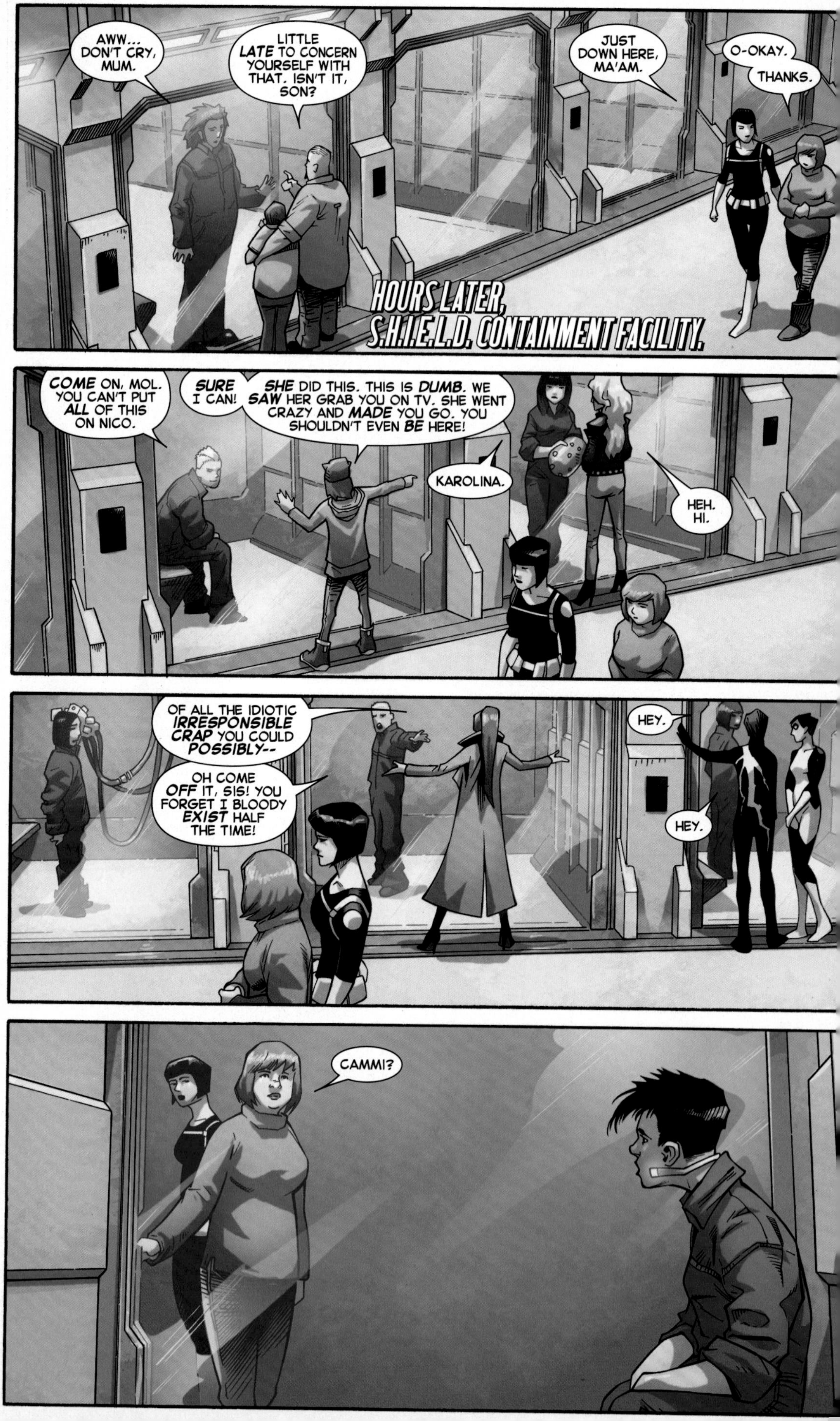
AWW... DON'T CRY, MUM.
LITTLE LATE TO CONCERN YOURSELF WITH THAT. ISN'T IT, SON?
JUST DOWN HERE, MA'AM.
O-OKAY.
THANKS.
HOURS LATER, S.H.I.E.L.D. CONTAINMENT FACILITY.
COME ON, MOL. YOU CAN'T PUT ALL OF THIS ON NICO.
SURE I CAN!
SHE DID THIS. THIS IS DUMB. WE SAW HER GRAB YOU ON TV. SHE WENT CRAZY AND MADE YOU GO. YOU SHOULDN'T EVEN BE HERE!
KAROLINA.
HEH. HI.
OF ALL THE IDIOTIC IRRESPONSIBLE CRAP YOU COULD POSSIBLY--
OH COME OFF IT, SIS! YOU FORGET I BLOODY EXIST HALF THE TIME!
HEY.
HEY.
CAMMI?

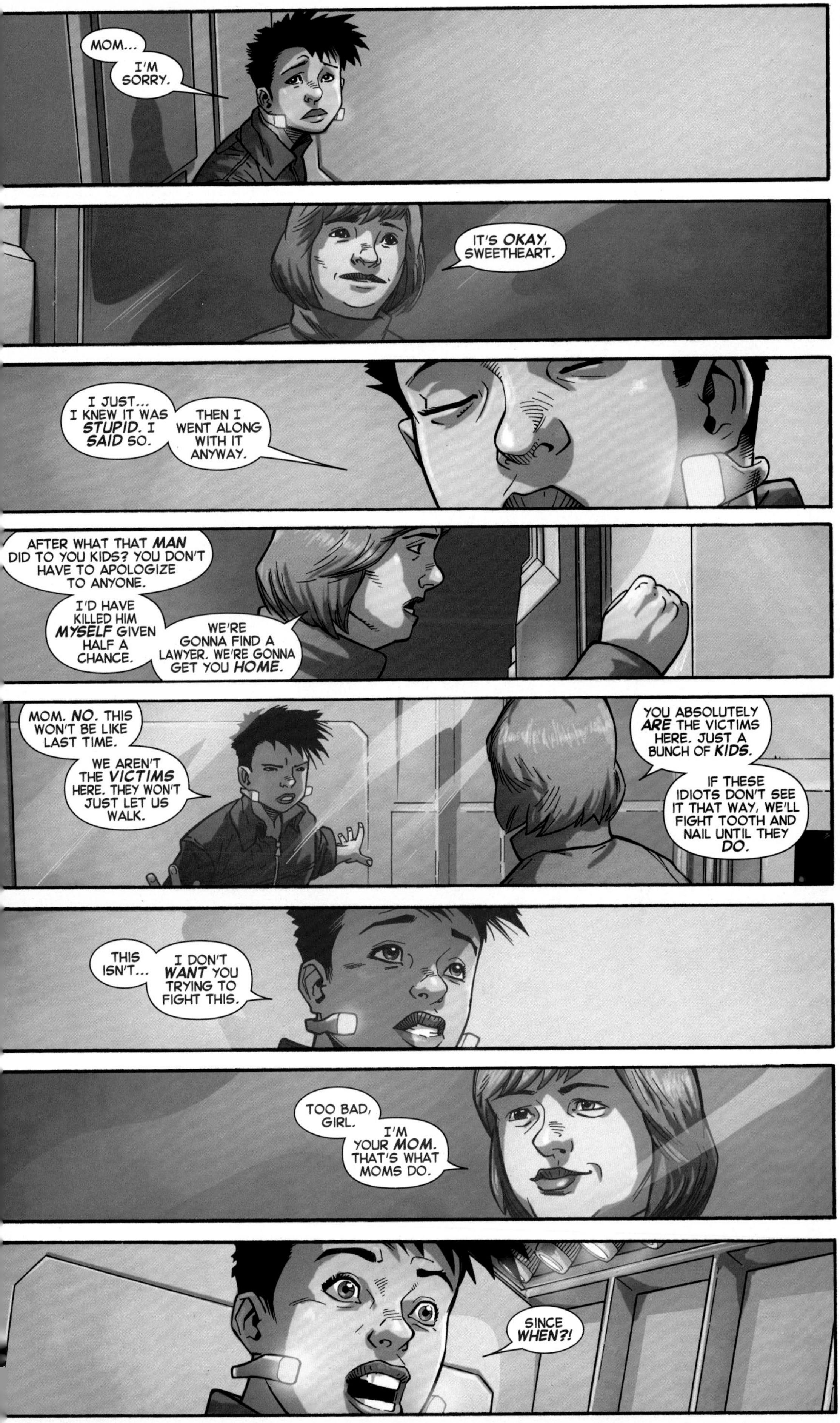

MOM...
I'M SORRY.
IT'S OKAY, SWEETHEART.
I JUST... I KNEW IT WAS STUPID. I SAID SO.
THEN I WENT ALONG WITH IT ANYWAY.
AFTER WHAT THAT MAN DID TO YOU KIDS? YOU DON'T HAVE TO APOLOGIZE TO ANYONE.
I'D HAVE KILLED HIM MYSELF GIVEN HALF A CHANCE.
WE'RE GONNA FIND A LAWYER. WE'RE GONNA GET YOU HOME.
MOM. NO. THIS WON'T BE LIKE LAST TIME.
WE AREN'T THE VICTIMS HERE. THEY WON'T JUST LET US WALK.
YOU ABSOLUTELY ARE THE VICTIMS HERE. JUST A BUNCH OF KIDS.
IF THESE IDIOTS DON'T SEE IT THAT WAY, WE'LL FIGHT TOOTH AND NAIL UNTIL THEY DO.
THIS ISN'T...
I DON'T WANT YOU TRYING TO FIGHT THIS.
TOO BAD, GIRL.
I'M YOUR MOM. THAT'S WHAT MOMS DO.
SINCE WHEN?!

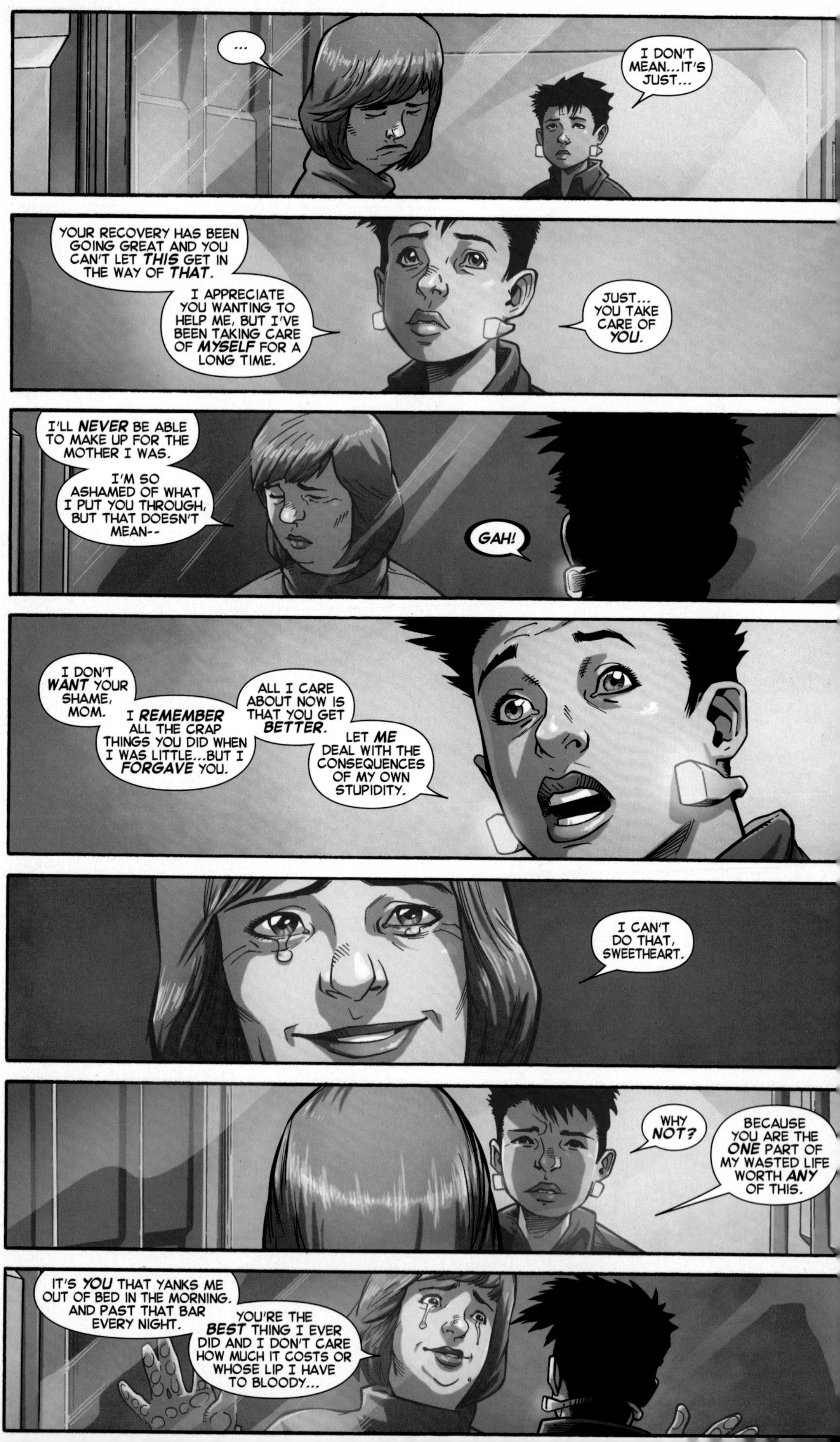
...
I DON'T MEAN...IT'S JUST...
YOUR RECOVERY HAS BEEN GOING GREAT AND YOU CAN'T LET THIS GET IN THE WAY OF THAT.
I APPRECIATE YOU WANTING TO HELP ME, BUT I'VE BEEN TAKING CARE OF MYSELF FOR A LONG TIME.
JUST... YOU TAKE CARE OF YOU.
I'LL NEVER BE ABLE TO MAKE UP FOR THE MOTHER I WAS.
I'M SO ASHAMED OF WHAT I PUT YOU THROUGH, BUT THAT DOESN'T MEAN--
GAH!
I DON'T WANT YOUR SHAME, MOM.
I REMEMBER ALL THE CRAP THINGS YOU DID WHEN I WAS LITTLE...BUT I FORGAVE YOU.
ALL I CARE ABOUT NOW IS THAT YOU GET BETTER.
LET ME DEAL WITH THE CONSEQUENCES OF MY OWN STUPIDITY.
I CAN'T DO THAT, SWEETHEART.
WHY NOT?
BECAUSE YOU ARE THE ONE PART OF MY WASTED LIFE WORTH ANY OF THIS.
IT'S YOU THAT YANKS ME OUT OF BED IN THE MORNING. AND PAST THAT BAR EVERY NIGHT.
YOU'RE THE BEST THING I EVER DID AND I DON'T CARE HOW MUCH IT COSTS OR WHOSE LIP I HAVE TO BLOODY...

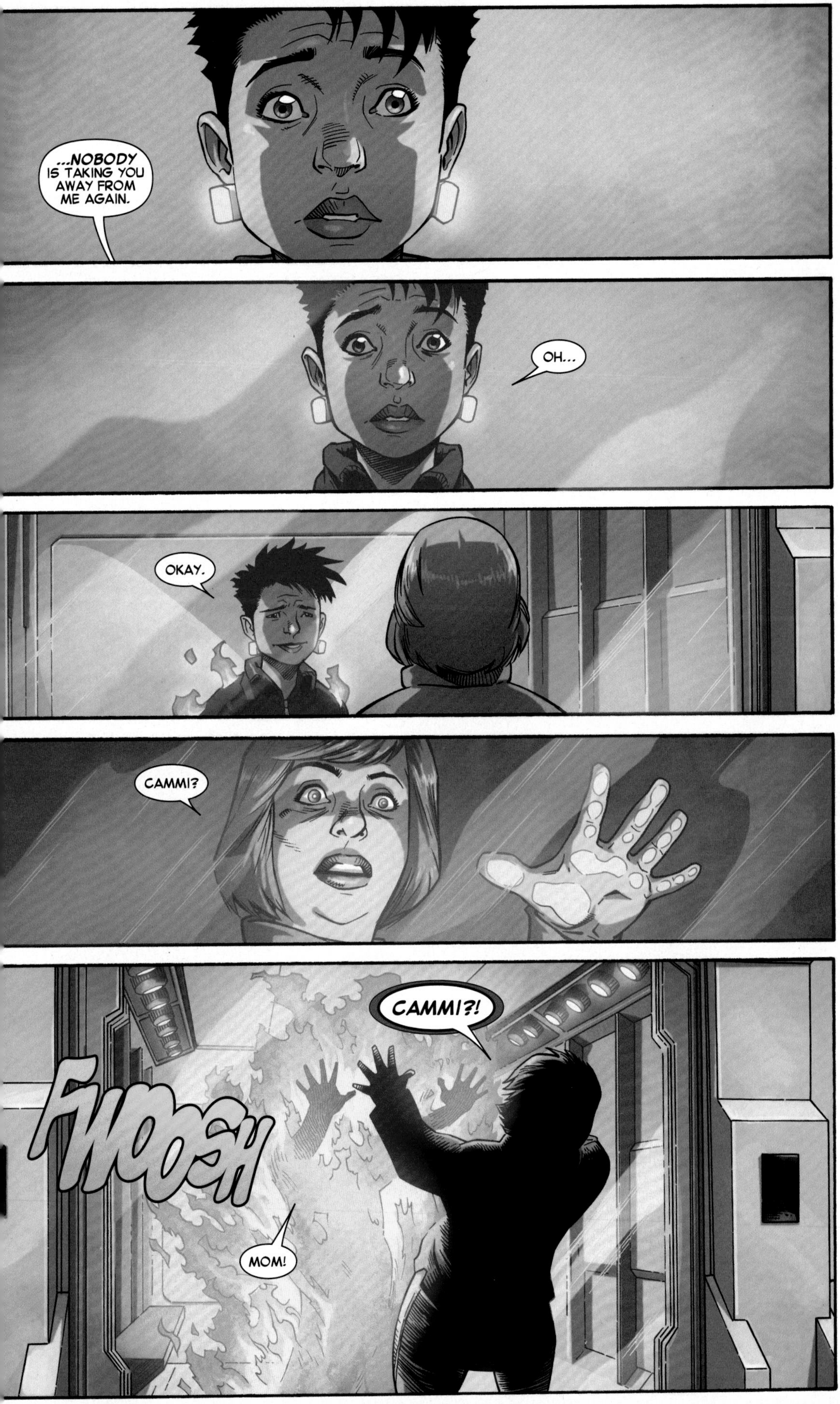
...NOBODY IS TAKING YOU AWAY FROM ME AGAIN.
OH...
OKAY.
CAMMI?
CAMMI?!
FWOOSH
MOM!

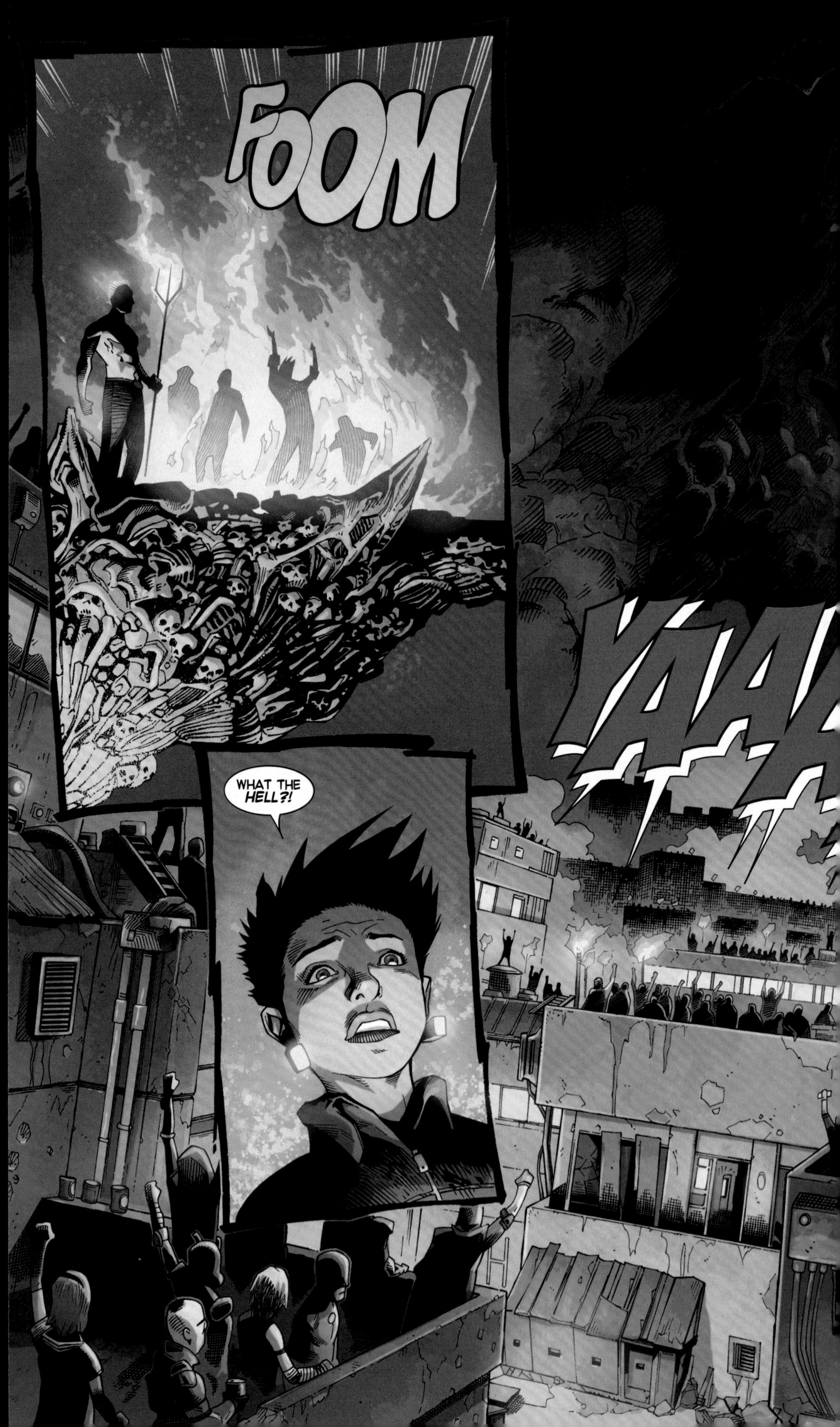
FOOM
WHAT THE HELL?!

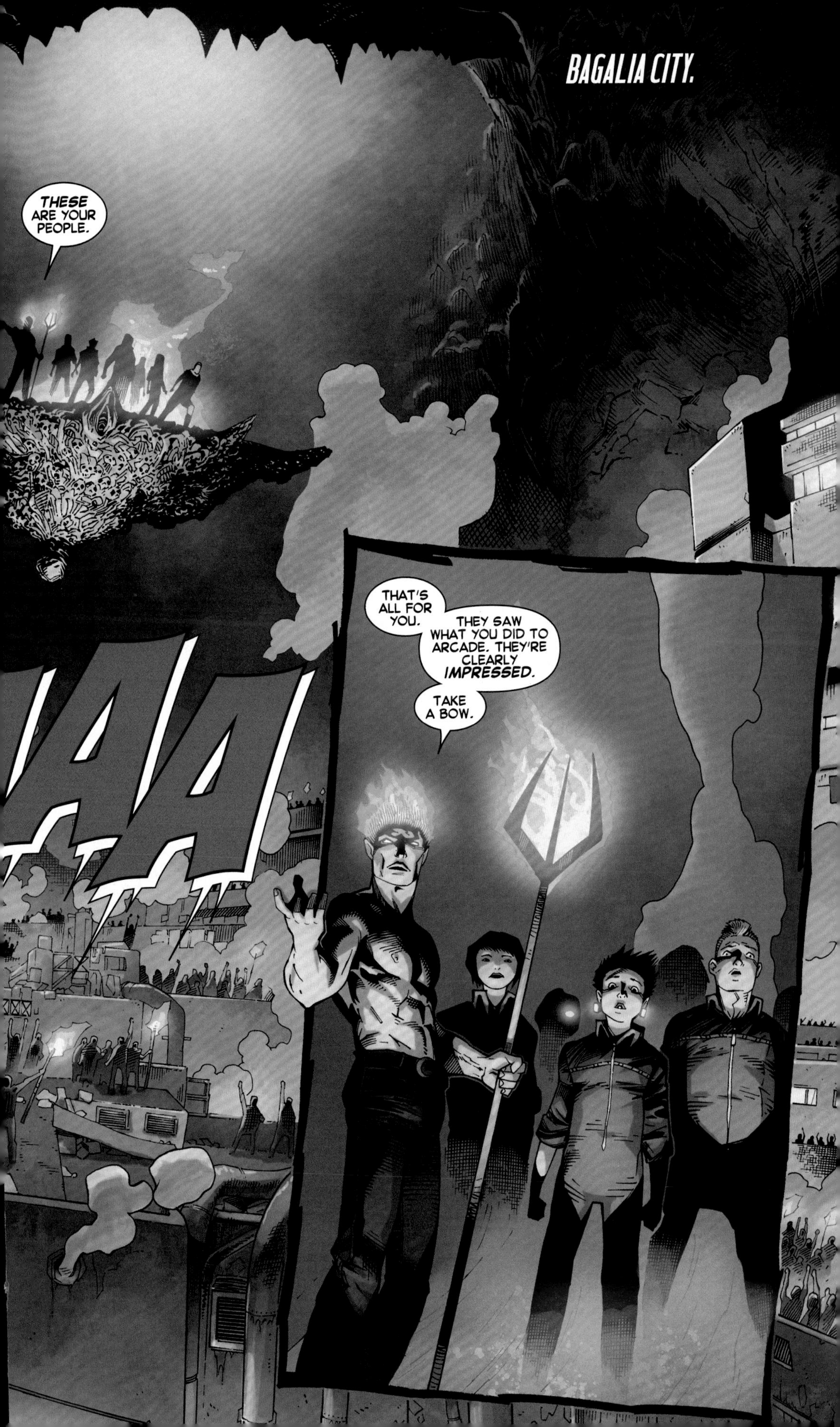
BAGALIA CITY.
THESE ARE YOUR PEOPLE.
THAT'S ALL FOR YOU.
THEY SAW WHAT YOU DID TO ARCADE. THEY'RE CLEARLY IMPRESSED.
TAKE A BOW.

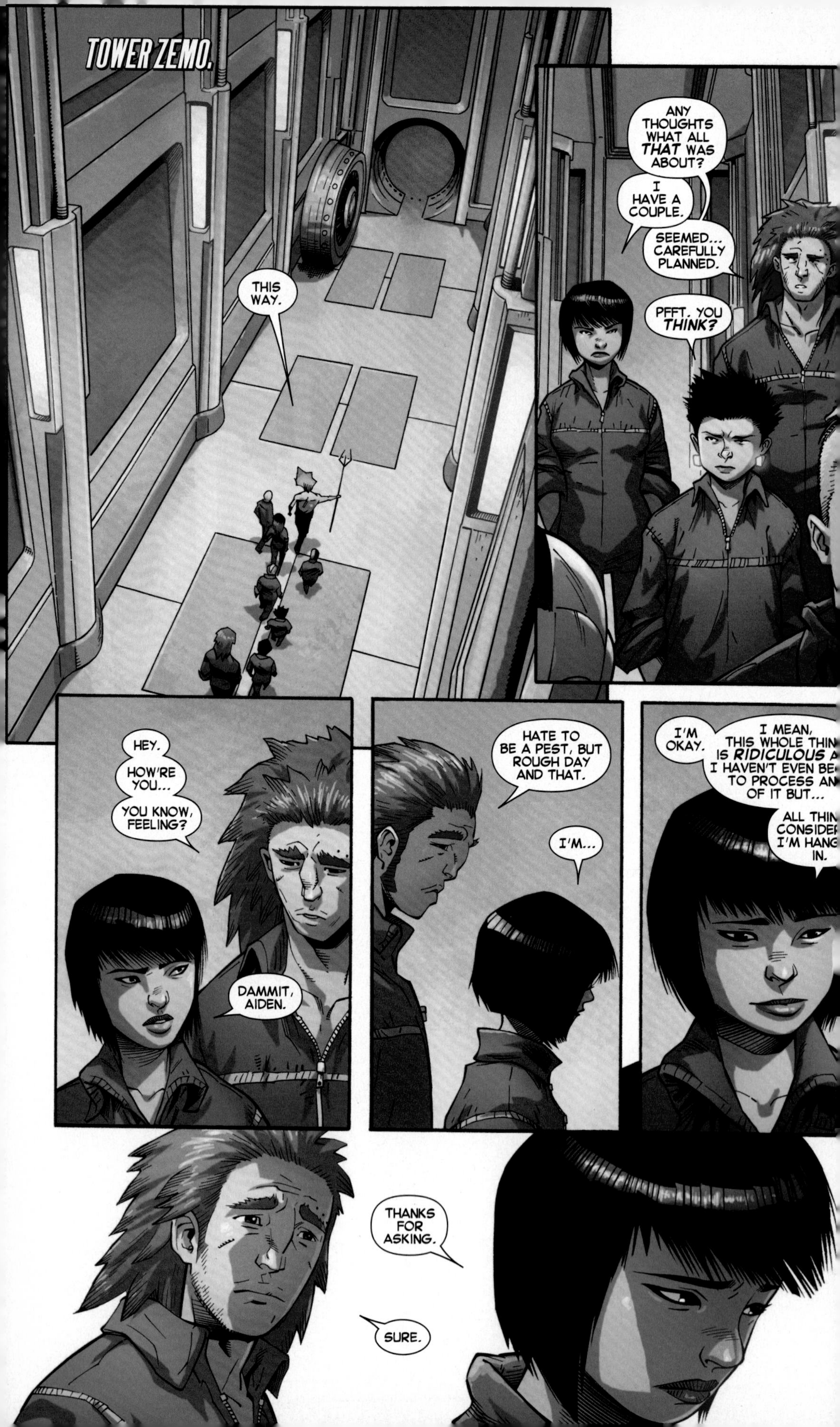
TOWER ZEMO.
THIS WAY.
ANY THOUGHTS WHAT ALL THAT WAS ABOUT?
I HAVE A COUPLE.
SEEMED... CAREFULLY PLANNED.
PFFT. YOU THINK?
HEY.
HOW'RE YOU...
YOU KNOW, FEELING?
DAMMIT, AIDEN.
HATE TO BE A PEST, BUT ROUGH DAY AND THAT.
I'M...
I'M OKAY.
I MEAN, THIS WHOLE THIN IS RIDICULOUS A I HAVEN'T EVEN BE TO PROCESS AN OF IT BUT...
ALL THIN CONSIDER I'M HANG IN.
THANKS FOR ASKING.
SURE.

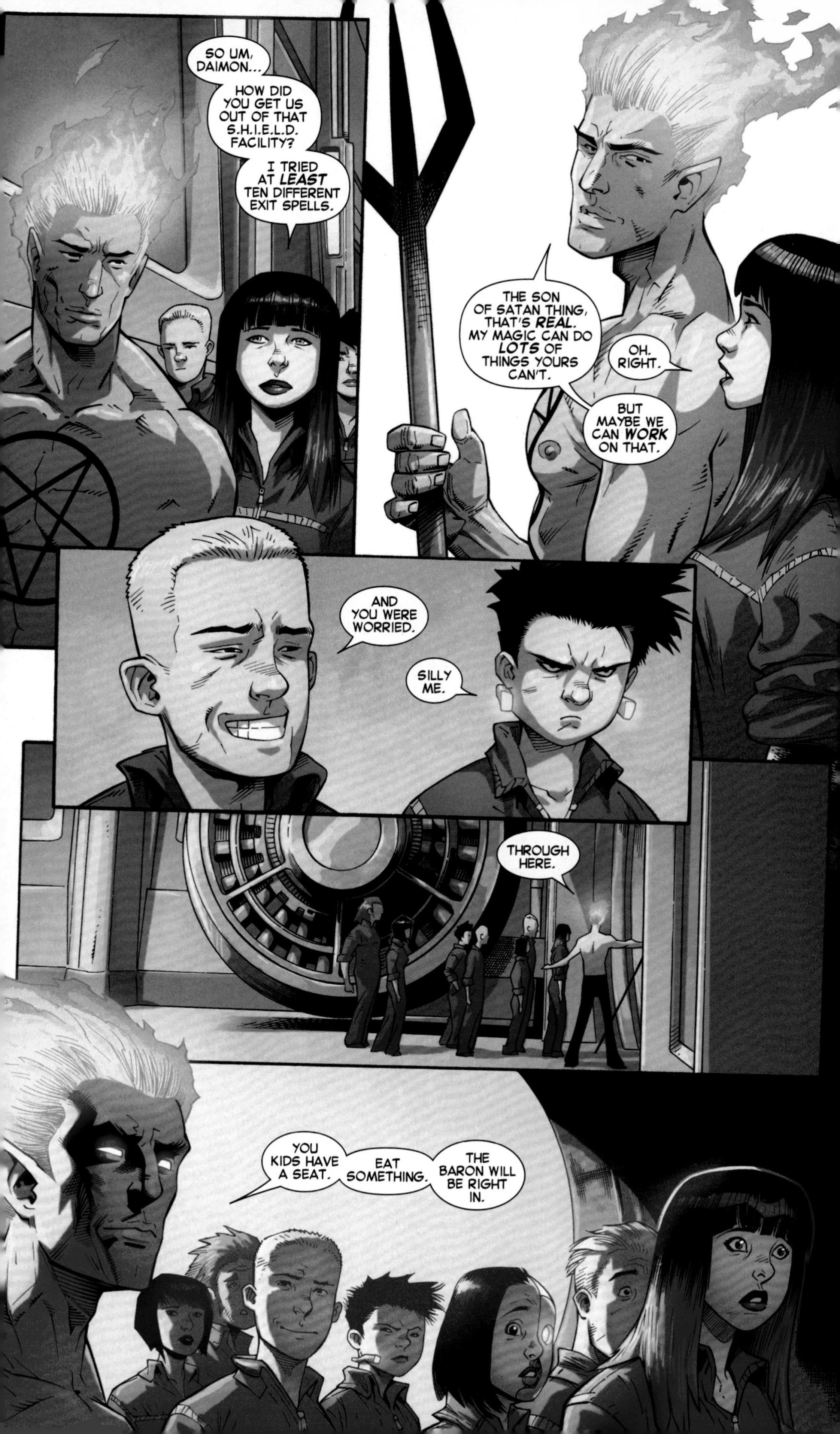
SO UM, DAIMON...
HOW DID YOU GET US OUT OF THAT S.H.I.E.L.D. FACILITY?
I TRIED AT LEAST TEN DIFFERENT EXIT SPELLS.
THE SON OF SATAN THING, THAT'S REAL. MY MAGIC CAN DO LOTS OF THINGS YOURS CAN'T.
OH. RIGHT.
BUT MAYBE WE CAN WORK ON THAT.
AND YOU WERE WORRIED.
SILLY ME.
THROUGH HERE.
YOU KIDS HAVE A SEAT.
EAT SOMETHING.
THE BARON WILL BE RIGHT IN.

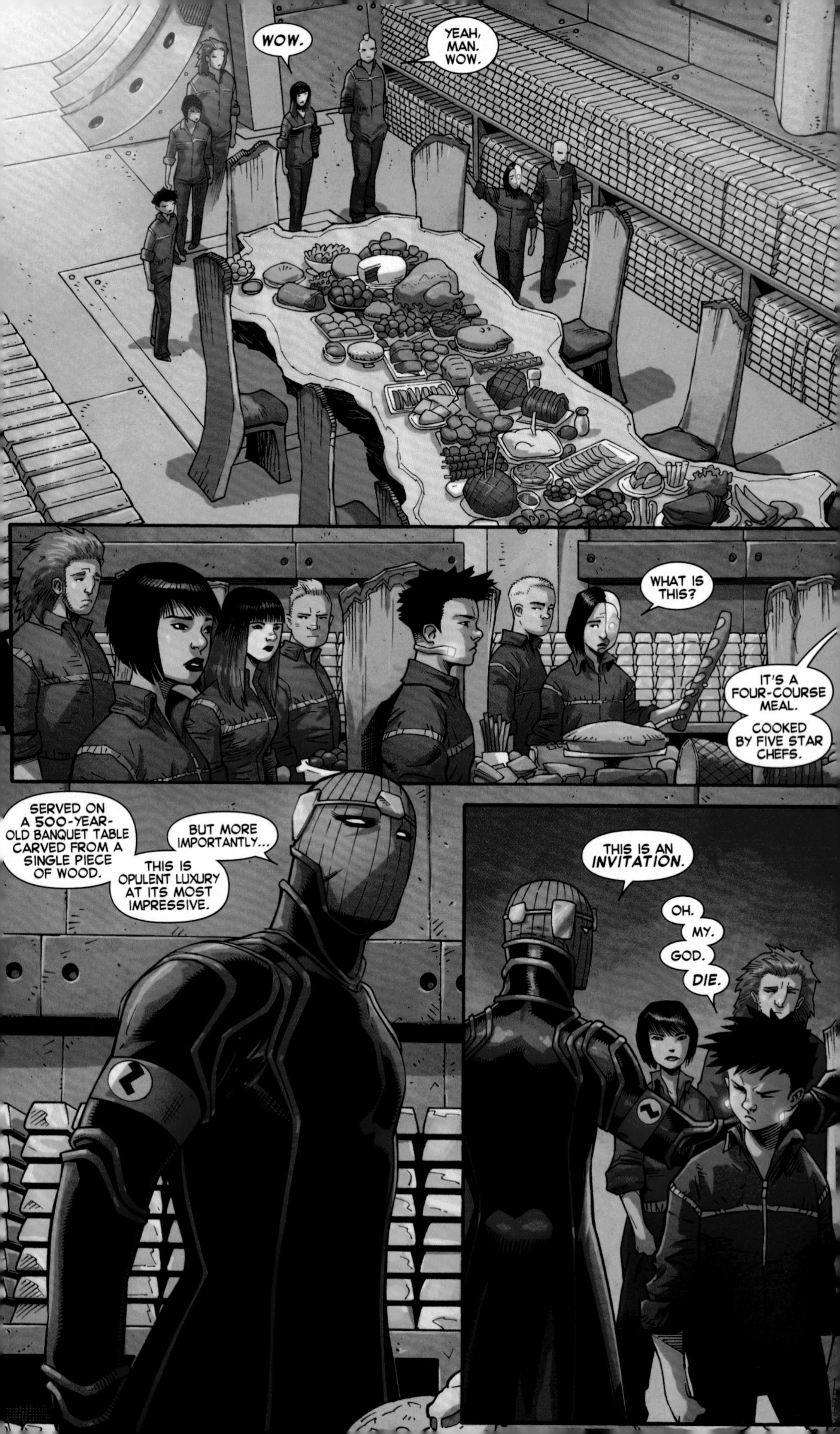
WOW.
YEAH, MAN. WOW.
WHAT IS THIS?
IT'S A FOUR-COURSE MEAL.
COOKED BY FIVE STAR CHEFS.
SERVED ON A 500-YEAR-OLD BANQUET TABLE CARVED FROM A SINGLE PIECE OF WOOD.
THIS IS OPULENT LUXURY AT ITS MOST IMPRESSIVE.
BUT MORE IMPORTANTLY...
THIS IS AN INVITATION.
OH.
MY.
GOD.
DIE.

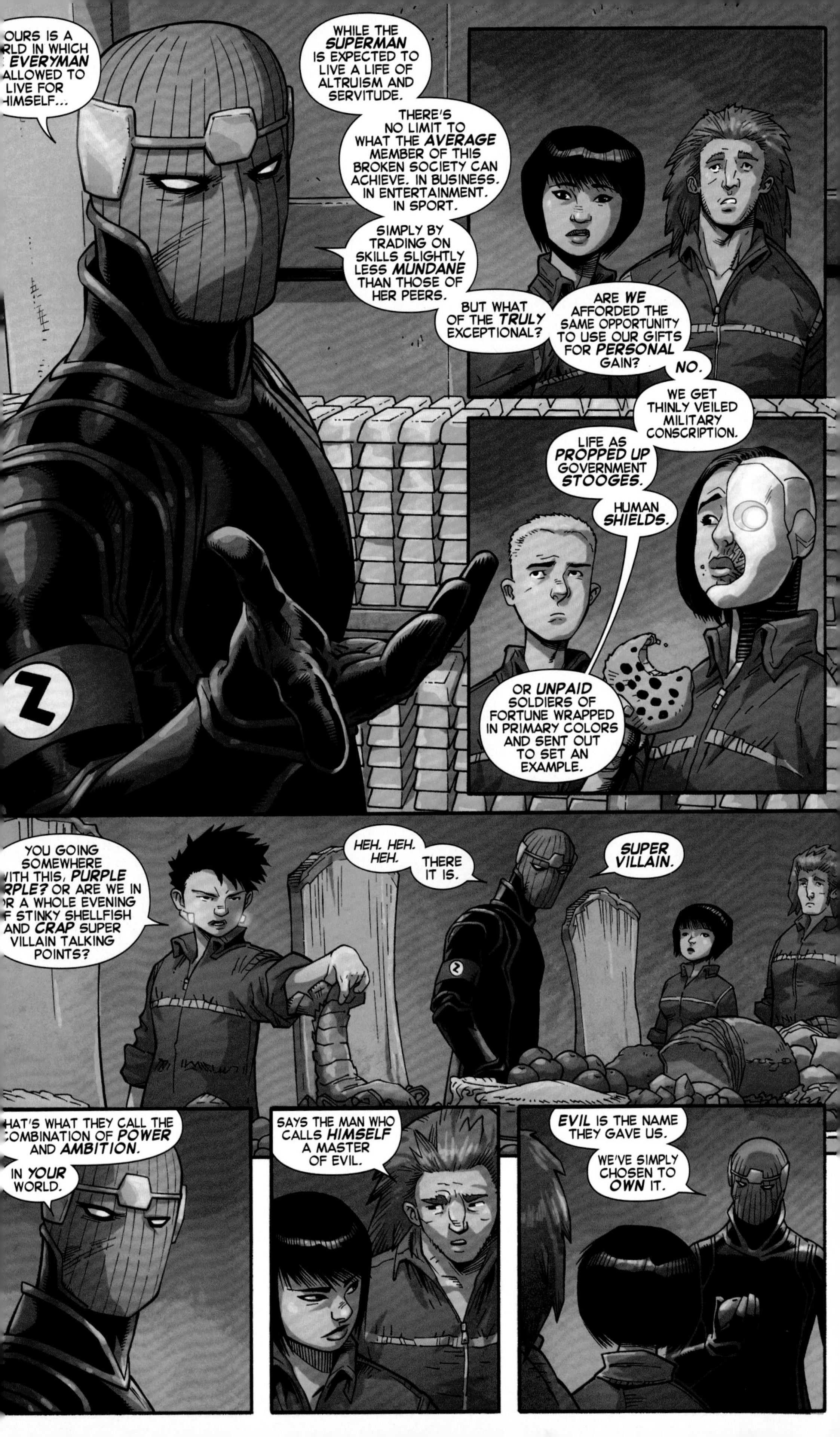
OURS IS A
RLD IN WHICH
EVERYMAN
ALLOWED TO
LIVE FOR
HIMSELF...
WHILE THE SUPERMAN IS EXPECTED TO LIVE A LIFE OF ALTRUISM AND SERVITUDE.
THERE'S NO LIMIT TO WHAT THE AVERAGE MEMBER OF THIS BROKEN SOCIETY CAN ACHIEVE. IN BUSINESS. IN ENTERTAINMENT. IN SPORT.
SIMPLY BY TRADING ON SKILLS SLIGHTLY LESS MUNDANE THAN THOSE OF HER PEERS.
BUT WHAT OF THE TRULY EXCEPTIONAL?
ARE WE AFFORDED THE SAME OPPORTUNITY TO USE OUR GIFTS FOR PERSONAL GAIN?
NO.
WE GET THINLY VEILED MILITARY CONSCRIPTION.
LIFE AS PROPPED UP GOVERNMENT STOOGES.
HUMAN SHIELDS.
OR UNPAID SOLDIERS OF FORTUNE WRAPPED IN PRIMARY COLORS AND SENT OUT TO SET AN EXAMPLE.
YOU GOING SOMEWHERE
VITH THIS, PURPLE
RPLE? OR ARE WE IN
R A WHOLE EVENING
F STINKY SHELLFISH
AND CRAP SUPER
VILLAIN TALKING
POINTS?
HEH. HEH. HEH.
THERE IT IS.
SUPER VILLAIN.
HAT'S WHAT THEY CALL THE
OMBINATION OF POWER
AND AMBITION.
IN YOUR WORLD.
SAYS THE MAN WHO CALLS HIMSELF A MASTER OF EVIL.
EVIL IS THE NAME THEY GAVE US.
WE'VE SIMPLY CHOSEN TO OWN IT.

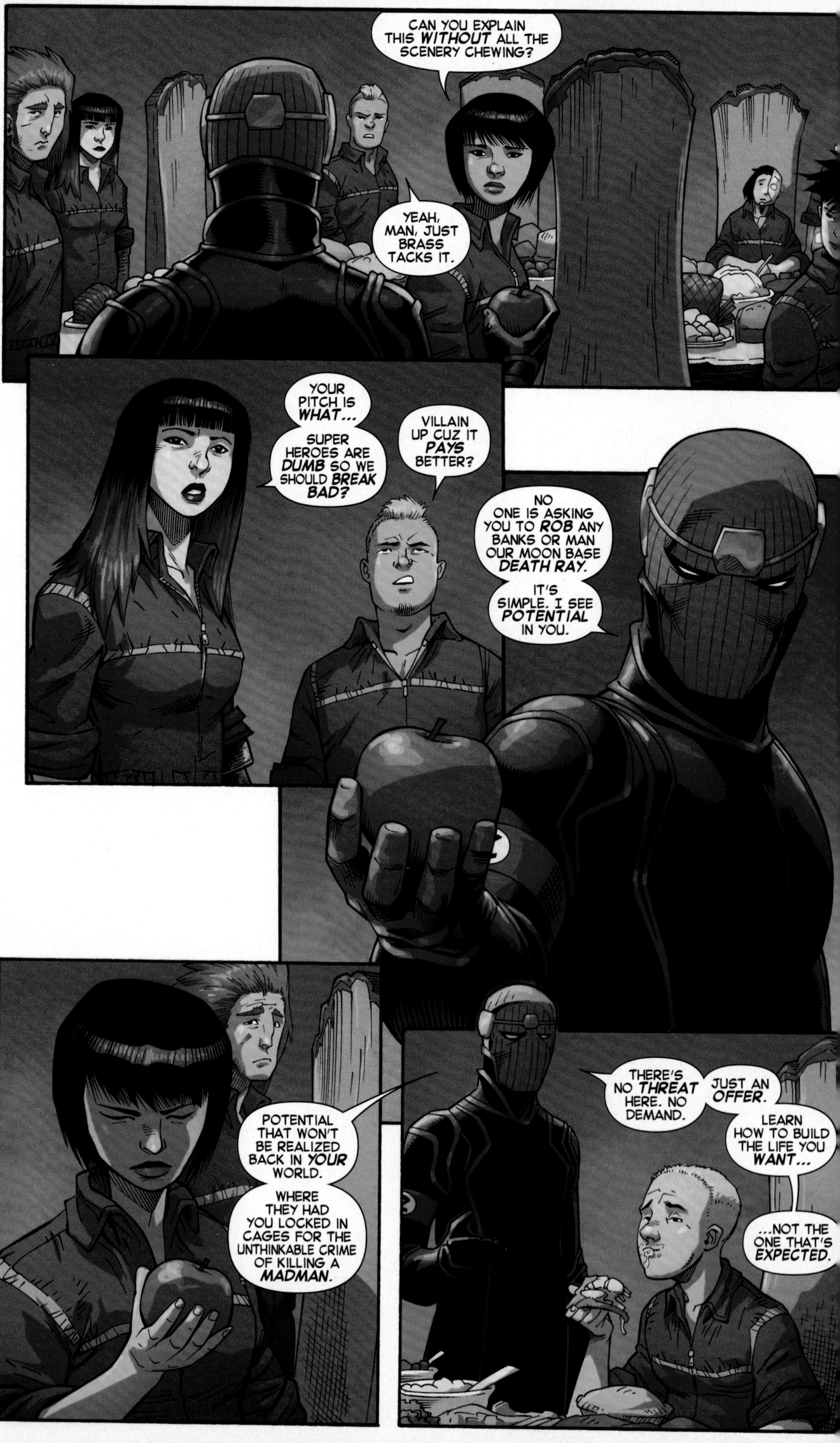
CAN YOU EXPLAIN THIS WITHOUT ALL THE SCENERY CHEWING?
YEAH, MAN, JUST BRASS TACKS IT.
YOUR PITCH IS WHAT...
SUPER HEROES ARE DUMB SO WE SHOULD BREAK BAD?
VILLAIN UP CUZ IT PAYS BETTER?
NO ONE IS ASKING YOU TO ROB ANY BANKS OR MAN OUR MOON BASE DEATH RAY.
IT'S SIMPLE. I SEE POTENTIAL IN YOU.
POTENTIAL THAT WON'T BE REALIZED BACK IN YOUR WORLD.
WHERE THEY HAD YOU LOCKED IN CAGES FOR THE UNTHINKABLE CRIME OF KILLING A MADMAN.
THERE'S NO THREAT HERE. NO DEMAND.
JUST AN OFFER.
LEARN HOW TO BUILD THE LIFE YOU WANT...
...NOT THE ONE THAT'S EXPECTED.

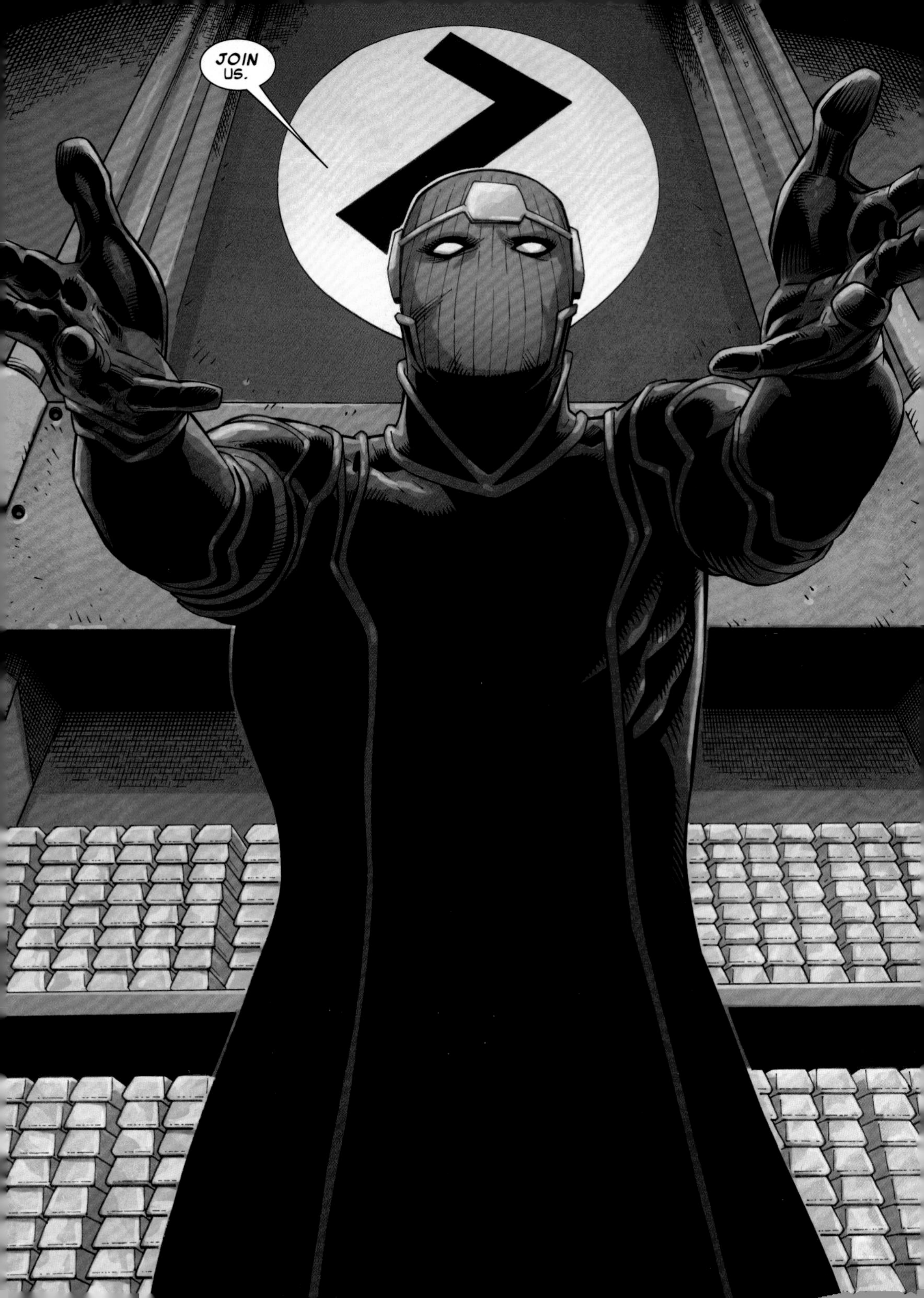
JOIN US.

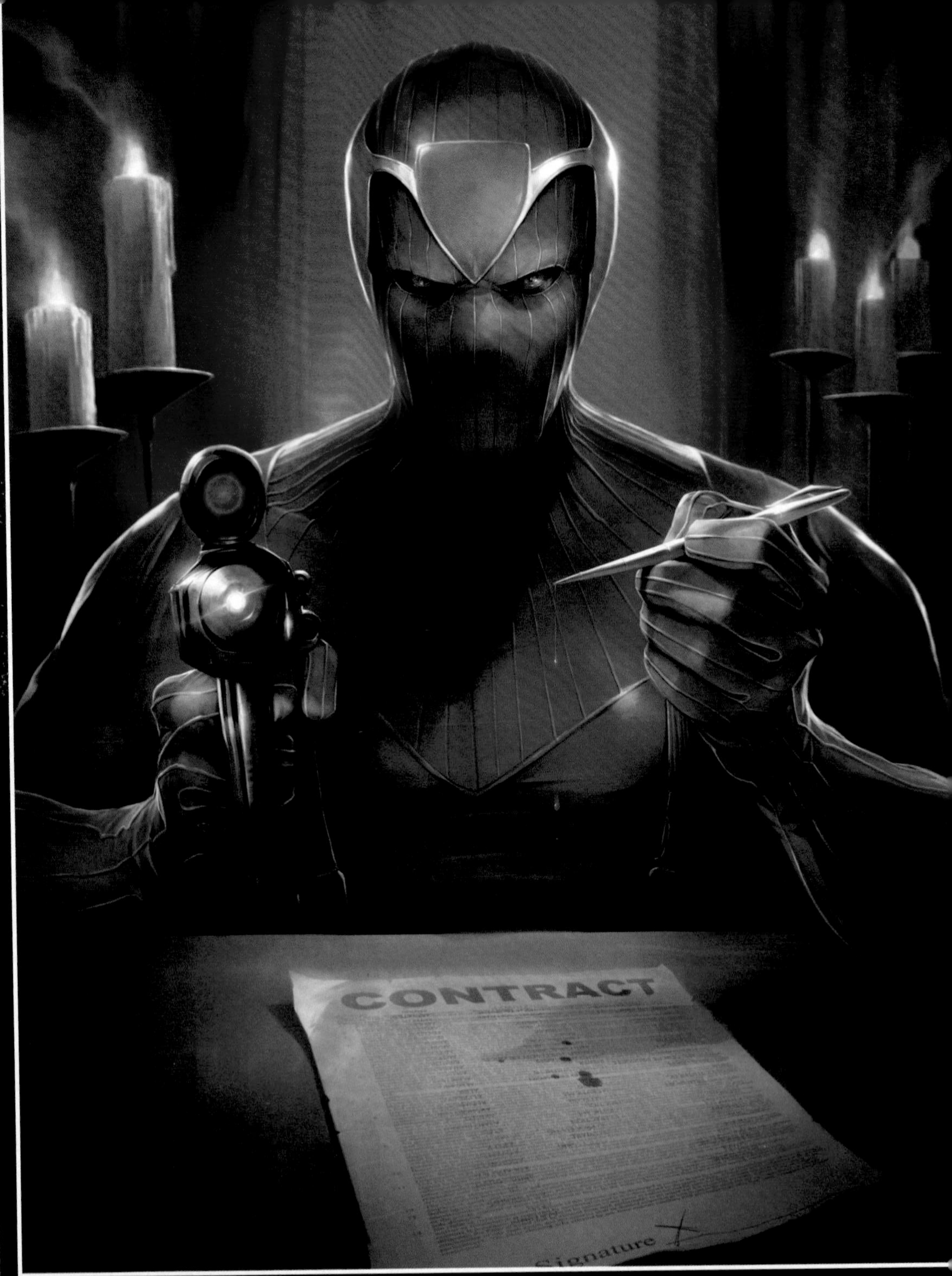
CONTRACT
Signature

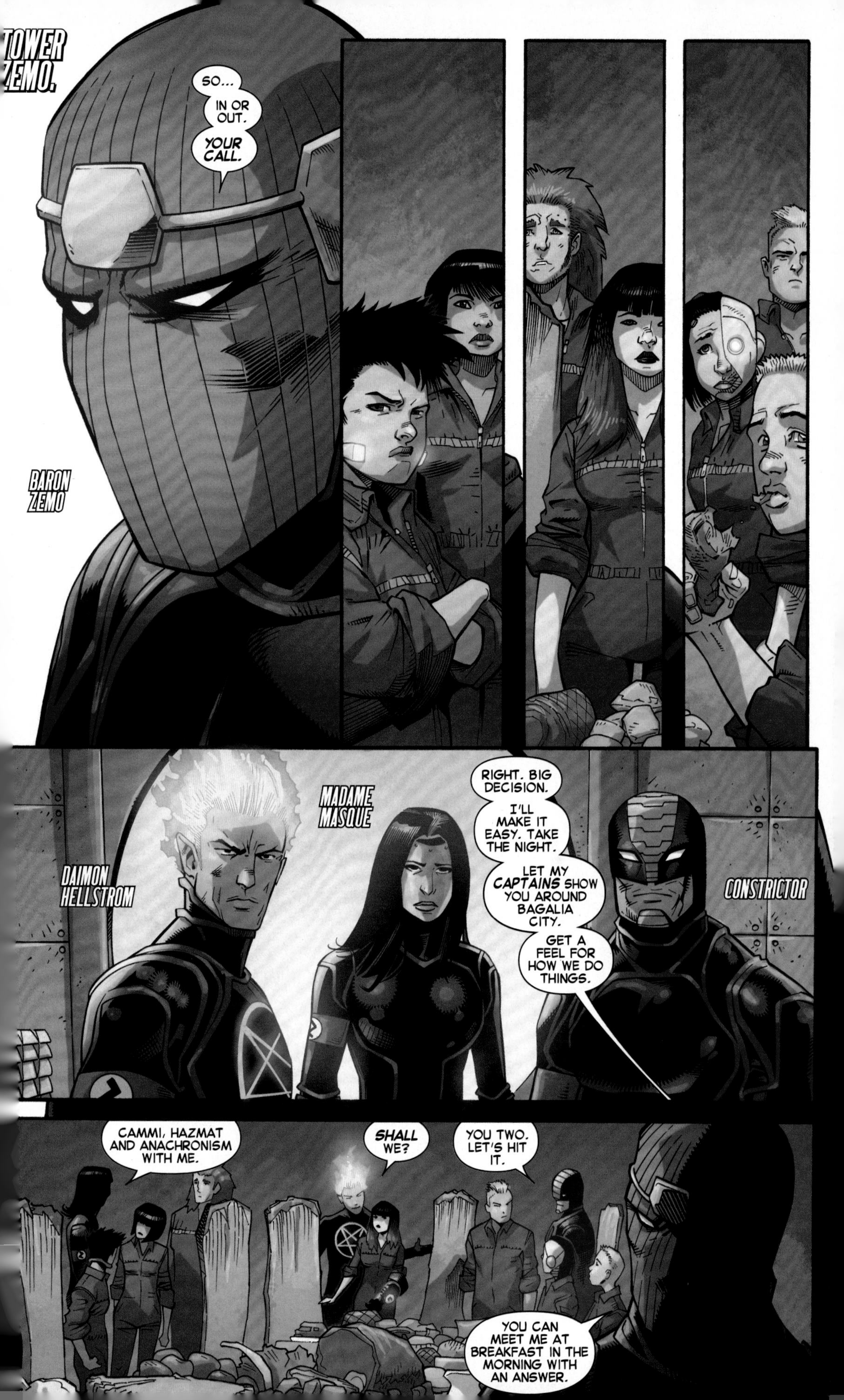
TOWER
ZEMO.
SO...
IN OR OUT.
YOUR CALL.
BARON ZEMO
MADAME MASQUE
RIGHT. BIG DECISION.
I'LL MAKE IT EASY. TAKE THE NIGHT.
LET MY CAPTAINS SHOW YOU AROUND BAGALIA CITY.
GET A FEEL FOR HOW WE DO THINGS.
DAIMON HELLSTROM
CONSTRICTOR
CAMMI, HAZMAT AND ANACHRONISM WITH ME.
SHALL WE?
YOU TWO. LET'S HIT IT.
YOU CAN MEET ME AT BREAKFAST IN THE MORNING WITH AN ANSWER.

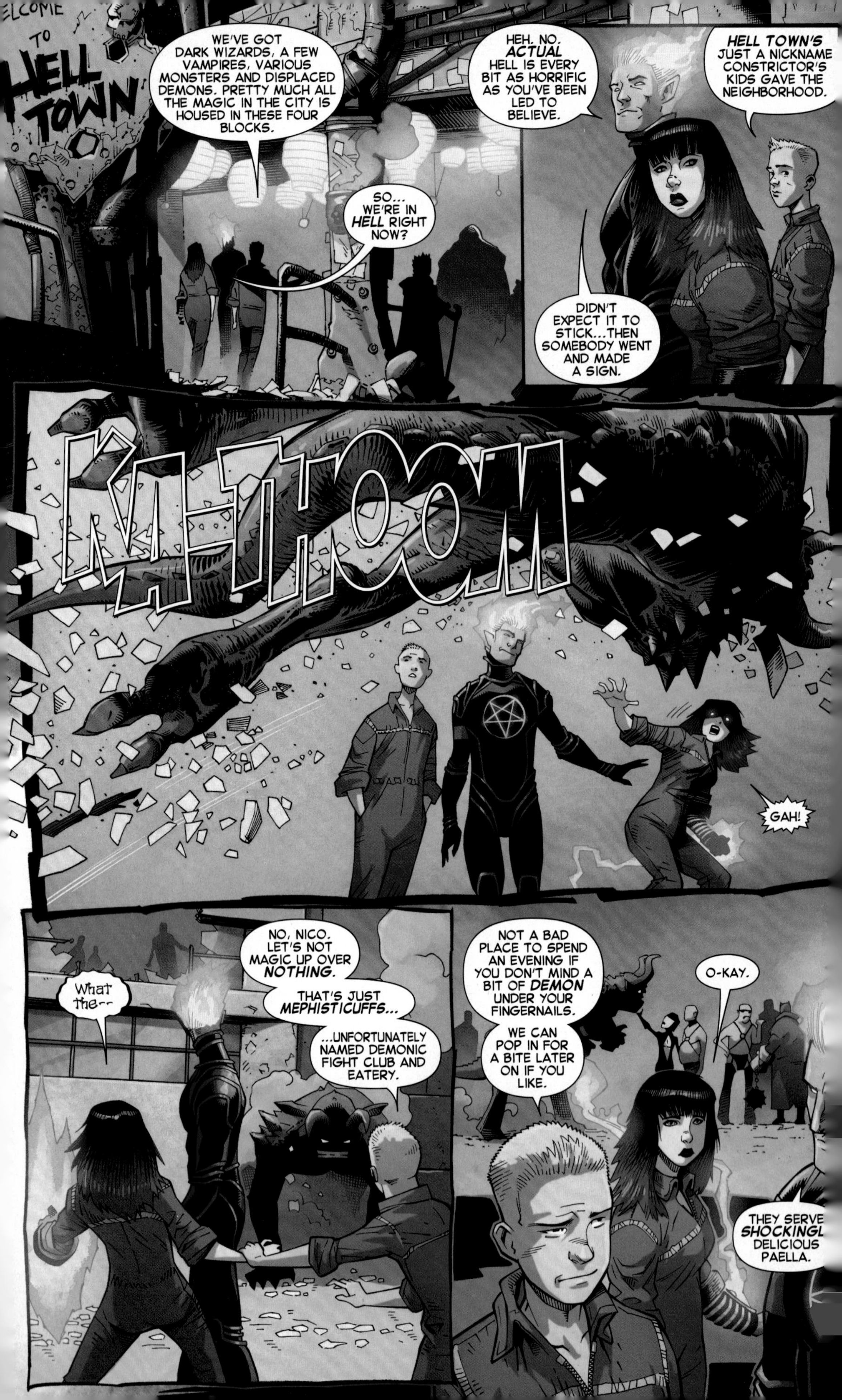

WELCOME TO HELL TOWN
WE'VE GOT DARK WIZARDS, A FEW VAMPIRES, VARIOUS MONSTERS AND DISPLACED DEMONS. PRETTY MUCH ALL THE MAGIC IN THE CITY IS HOUSED IN THESE FOUR BLOCKS.
SO... WE'RE IN HELL RIGHT NOW?
HEH. NO. ACTUAL HELL IS EVERY BIT AS HORRIFIC AS YOU'VE BEEN LED TO BELIEVE.
HELL TOWN'S JUST A NICKNAME CONSTRICTOR'S KIDS GAVE THE NEIGHBORHOOD.
DIDN'T EXPECT IT TO STICK...THEN SOMEBODY WENT AND MADE A SIGN.
KA-THOOM
GAH!
What the--
NO, NICO. LET'S NOT MAGIC UP OVER NOTHING.
THAT'S JUST MEPHISTICUFFS...
...UNFORTUNATELY NAMED DEMONIC FIGHT CLUB AND EATERY.
NOT A BAD PLACE TO SPEND AN EVENING IF YOU DON'T MIND A BIT OF DEMON UNDER YOUR FINGERNAILS.
WE CAN POP IN FOR A BITE LATER ON IF YOU LIKE.
O-KAY.
THEY SERVE SHOCKINGL DELICIOUS PAELLA.

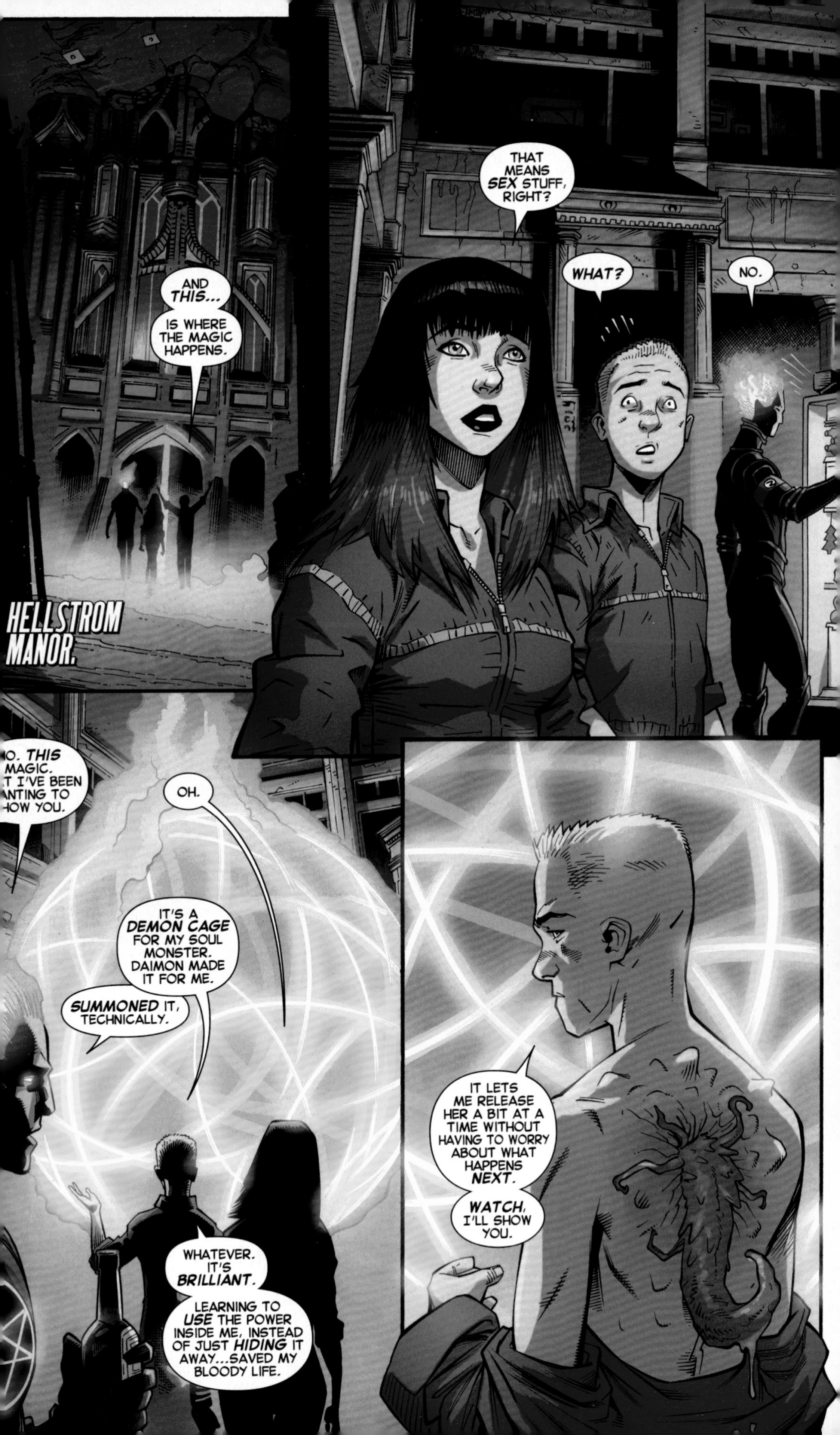

HELLSTROM MANOR.
AND THIS...
IS WHERE THE MAGIC HAPPENS.
THAT MEANS SEX STUFF, RIGHT?
WHAT?
NO.
O. THIS MAGIC. T I'VE BEEN ANTING TO HOW YOU.
OH.
IT'S A DEMON CAGE FOR MY SOUL MONSTER. DAIMON MADE IT FOR ME.
SUMMONED IT, TECHNICALLY.
WHATEVER. IT'S BRILLIANT.
LEARNING TO USE THE POWER INSIDE ME, INSTEAD OF JUST HIDING IT AWAY...SAVED MY BLOODY LIFE.
IT LETS ME RELEASE HER A BIT AT A TIME WITHOUT HAVING TO WORRY ABOUT WHAT HAPPENS NEXT.
WATCH, I'LL SHOW YOU.

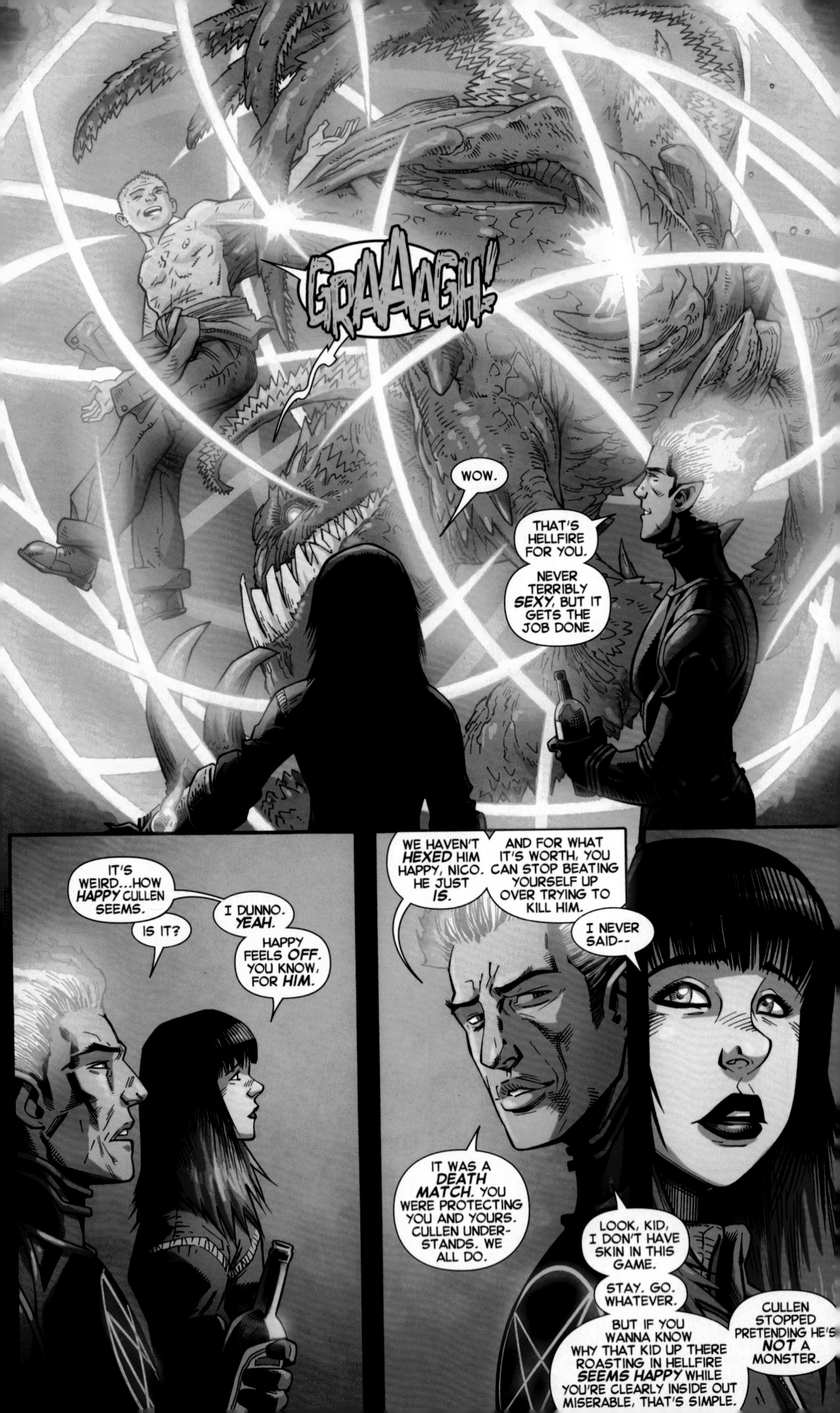
GRAAAGH!
WOW.
THAT'S HELLFIRE FOR YOU.
NEVER TERRIBLY SEXY, BUT IT GETS THE JOB DONE.
IT'S WEIRD...HOW HAPPY CULLEN SEEMS.
I DUNNO. YEAH.
IS IT?
HAPPY FEELS OFF. YOU KNOW, FOR HIM.
WE HAVEN'T HEXED HIM HAPPY, NICO. HE JUST IS.
AND FOR WHAT IT'S WORTH, YOU CAN STOP BEATING YOURSELF UP OVER TRYING TO KILL HIM.
I NEVER SAID--
IT WAS A DEATH MATCH. YOU WERE PROTECTING YOU AND YOURS. CULLEN UNDER-STANDS. WE ALL DO.
LOOK, KID, I DON'T HAVE SKIN IN THIS GAME.
STAY. GO. WHATEVER.
BUT IF YOU WANNA KNOW WHY THAT KID UP THERE ROASTING IN HELLFIRE SEEMS HAPPY WHILE YOU'RE CLEARLY INSIDE OUT MISERABLE, THAT'S SIMPLE.
CULLEN STOPPED PRETENDING HE'S NOT A MONSTER.

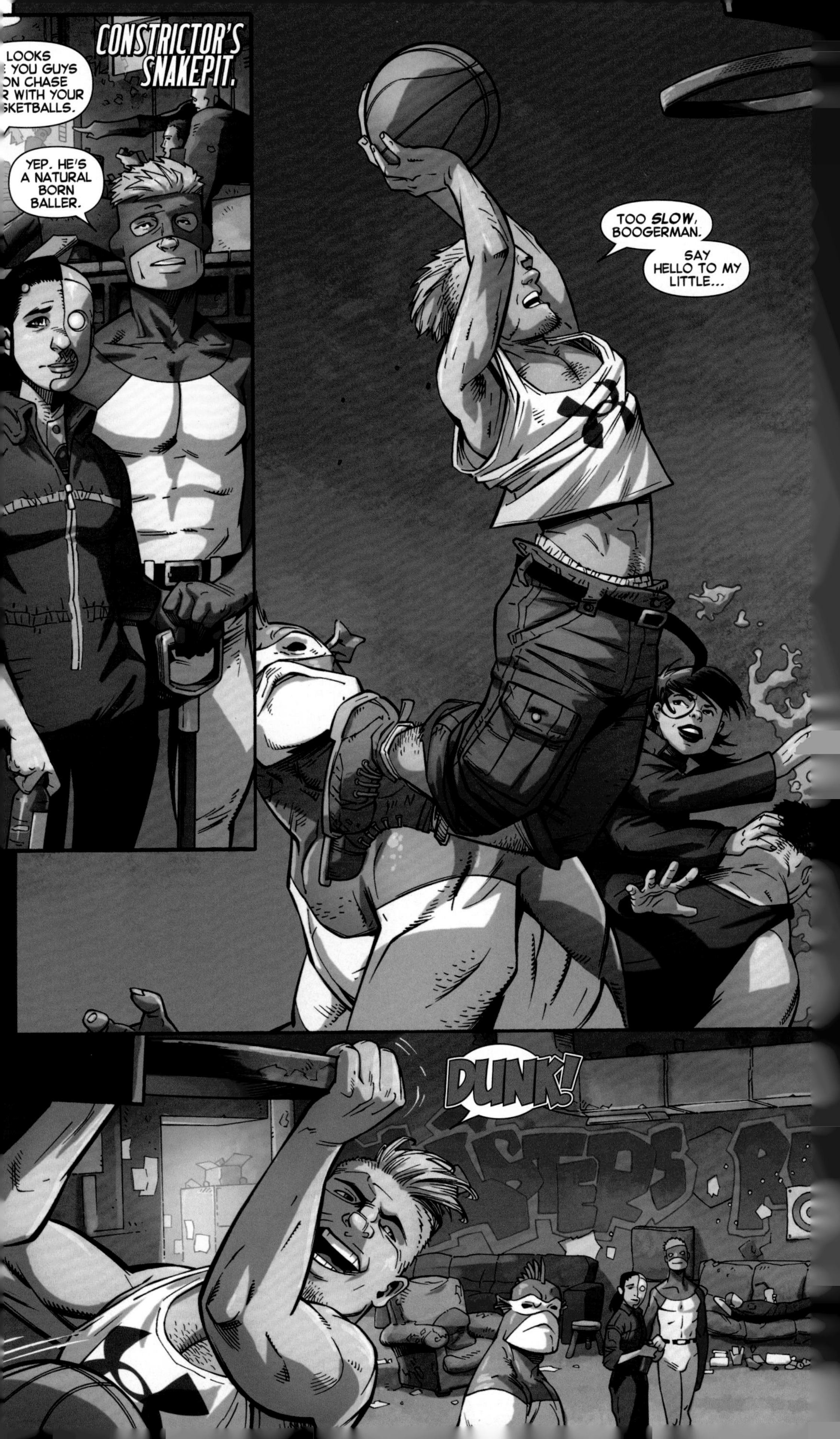
CONSTRICTOR'S SNAKEPIT.
LOOKS
E YOU GUYS
ON CHASE
R WITH YOUR
SKETBALLS.
YEP. HE'S A NATURAL BORN BALLER.
TOO SLOW, BOOGERMAN.
SAY HELLO TO MY LITTLE...
DUNK!

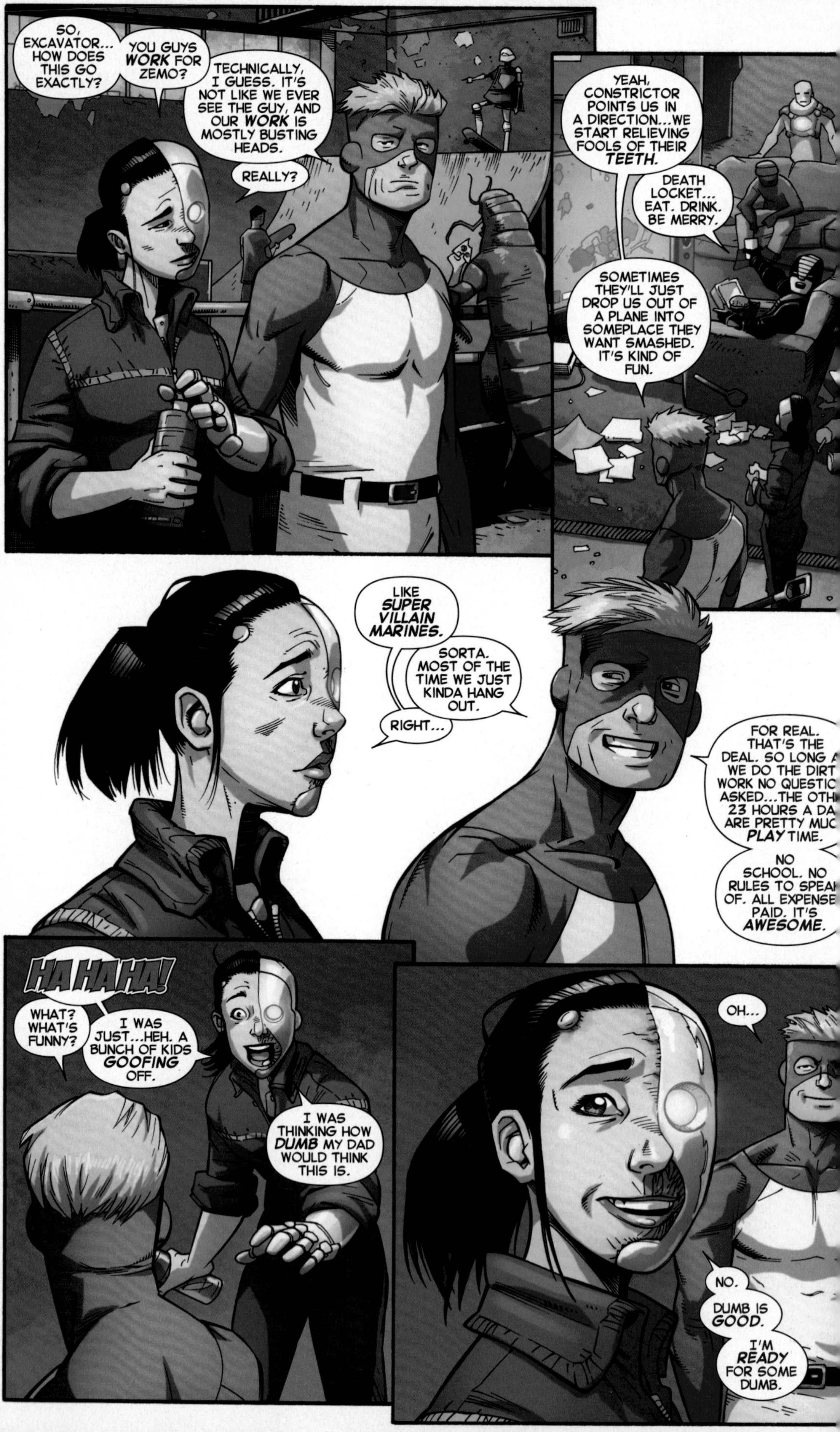
SO, EXCAVATOR... HOW DOES THIS GO EXACTLY?
YOU GUYS WORK FOR ZEMO?
TECHNICALLY, I GUESS. IT'S NOT LIKE WE EVER SEE THE GUY, AND OUR WORK IS MOSTLY BUSTING HEADS.
REALLY?
YEAH, CONSTRICTOR POINTS US IN A DIRECTION...WE START RELIEVING FOOLS OF THEIR TEETH.
DEATH LOCKET... EAT. DRINK. BE MERRY.
SOMETIMES THEY'LL JUST DROP US OUT OF A PLANE INTO SOMEPLACE THEY WANT SMASHED. IT'S KIND OF FUN.
LIKE SUPER VILLAIN MARINES.
SORTA. MOST OF THE TIME WE JUST KINDA HANG OUT.
RIGHT...
NO SCHOOL. NO
HA HA HA!
WHAT? WHAT'S FUNNY?
I WAS JUST...HEH. A BUNCH OF KIDS GOOFING OFF.
I WAS THINKING HOW DUMB MY DAD WOULD THINK THIS IS.
OH...
NO.
DUMB IS GOOD.
I'M READY FOR SOME DUMB.

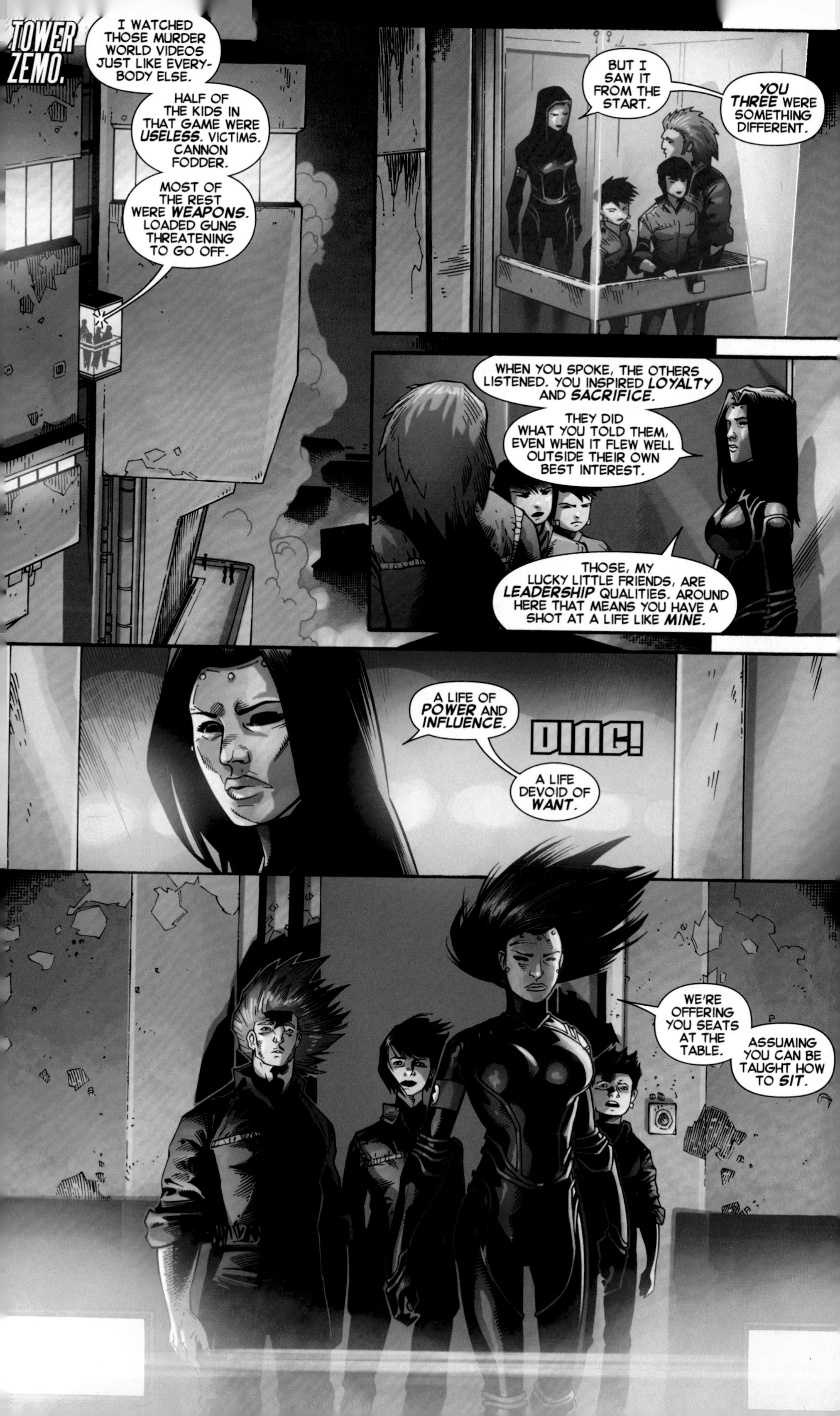
TOWER ZEMO.
I WATCHED THOSE MURDER WORLD VIDEOS JUST LIKE EVERY-BODY ELSE.
HALF OF THE KIDS IN THAT GAME WERE USELESS. VICTIMS. CANNON FODDER.
MOST OF THE REST WERE WEAPONS. LOADED GUNS THREATENING TO GO OFF.
BUT I SAW IT FROM THE START.
YOU THREE WERE SOMETHING DIFFERENT.
WHEN YOU SPOKE, THE OTHERS LISTENED. YOU INSPIRED LOYALTY AND SACRIFICE.
THEY DID WHAT YOU TOLD THEM, EVEN WHEN IT FLEW WELL OUTSIDE THEIR OWN BEST INTEREST.
THOSE, MY LUCKY LITTLE FRIENDS, ARE LEADERSHIP QUALITIES. AROUND HERE THAT MEANS YOU HAVE A SHOT AT A LIFE LIKE MINE.
A LIFE OF POWER AND INFLUENCE.
DING!
A LIFE DEVOID OF WANT.
WE'RE OFFERING YOU SEATS AT THE TABLE.
ASSUMING YOU CAN BE TAUGHT HOW TO SIT.

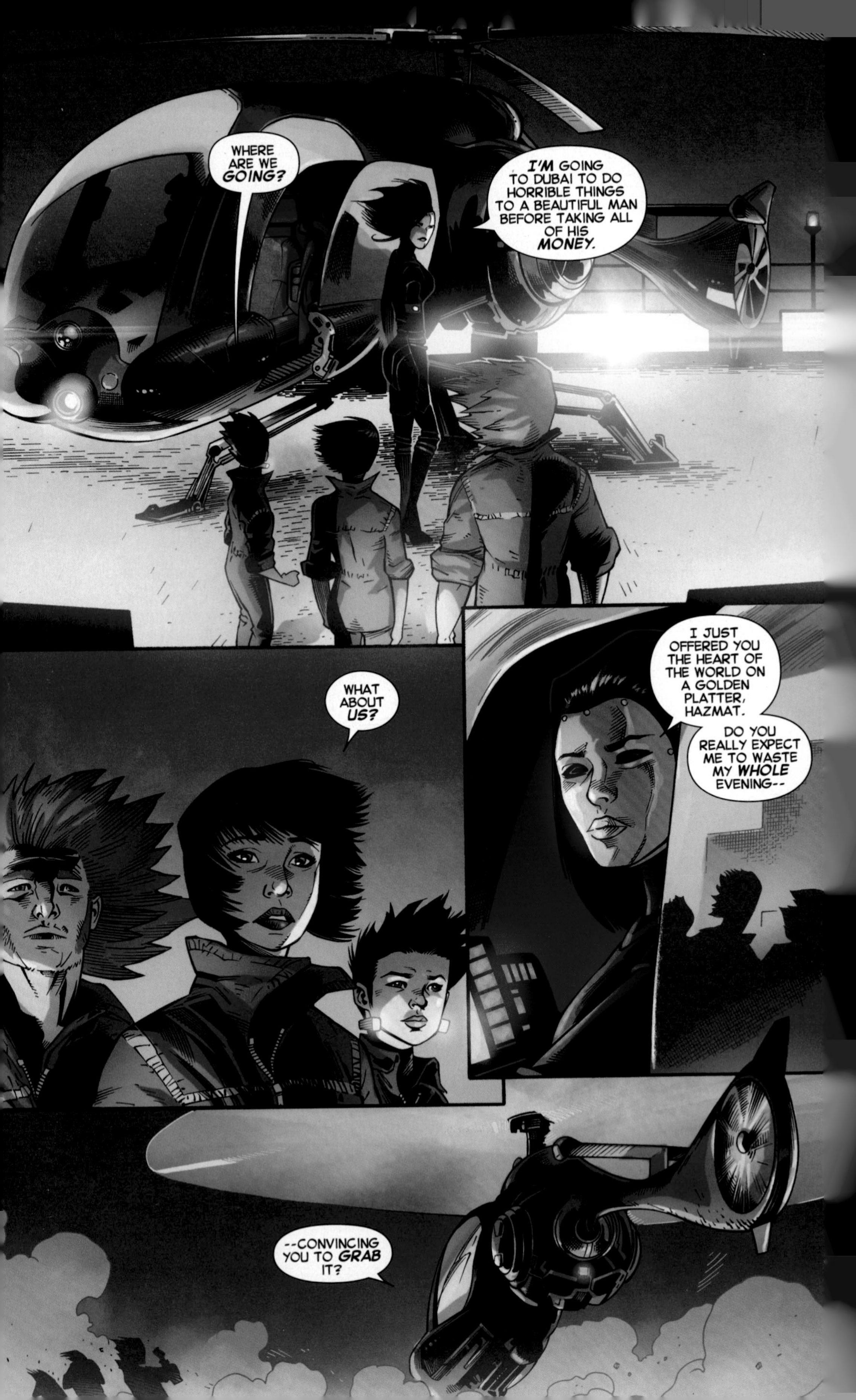
WHERE ARE WE GOING?
I'M GOING TO DUBAI TO DO HORRIBLE THINGS TO A BEAUTIFUL MAN BEFORE TAKING ALL OF HIS MONEY.
WHAT ABOUT US?
I JUST OFFERED YOU THE HEART OF THE WORLD ON A GOLDEN PLATTER, HAZMAT.
DO YOU REALLY EXPECT ME TO WASTE MY WHOLE EVENING--
--CONVINCING YOU TO GRAB IT?

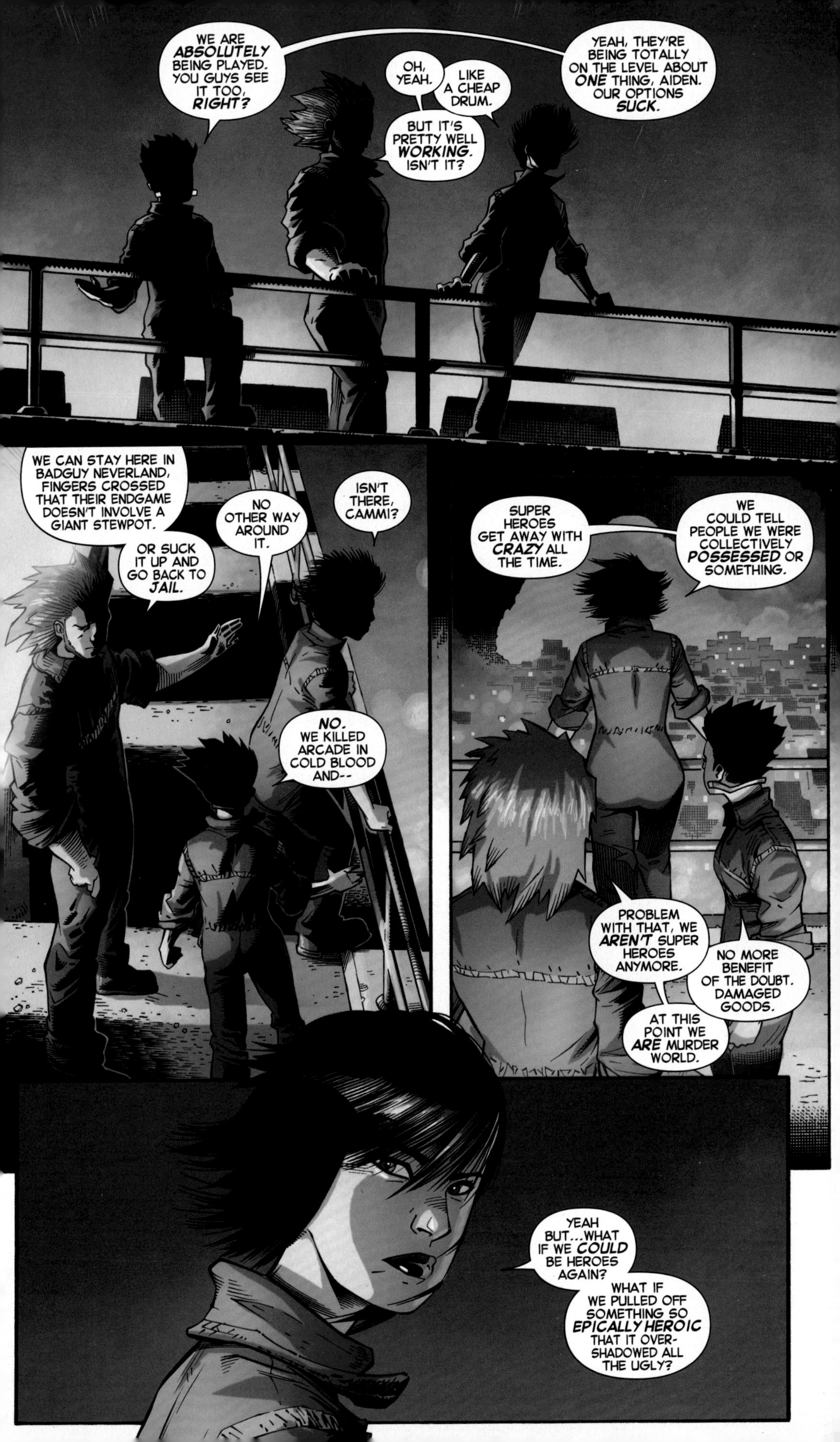
WE ARE ABSOLUTELY BEING PLAYED. YOU GUYS SEE IT TOO, RIGHT?
OH, YEAH.
LIKE A CHEAP DRUM.
BUT IT'S PRETTY WELL WORKING. ISN'T IT?
YEAH, THEY'RE BEING TOTALLY ON THE LEVEL ABOUT ONE THING, AIDEN. OUR OPTIONS SUCK.
WE CAN STAY HERE IN BADGUY NEVERLAND, FINGERS CROSSED THAT THEIR ENDGAME DOESN'T INVOLVE A GIANT STEWPOT.
OR SUCK IT UP AND GO BACK TO JAIL.
NO OTHER WAY AROUND IT.
ISN'T THERE, CAMMI?
NO. WE KILLED ARCADE IN COLD BLOOD AND--
SUPER HEROES GET AWAY WITH CRAZY ALL THE TIME.
WE COULD TELL PEOPLE WE WERE COLLECTIVELY POSSESSED OR SOMETHING.
PROBLEM WITH THAT, WE AREN'T SUPER HEROES ANYMORE.
NO MORE BENEFIT OF THE DOUBT. DAMAGED GOODS.
AT THIS POINT WE ARE MURDER WORLD.
YEAH BUT...WHAT IF WE COULD BE HEROES AGAIN?
WHAT IF WE PULLED OFF SOMETHING SO EPICALLY HEROIC THAT IT OVER-SHADOWED ALL THE UGLY?

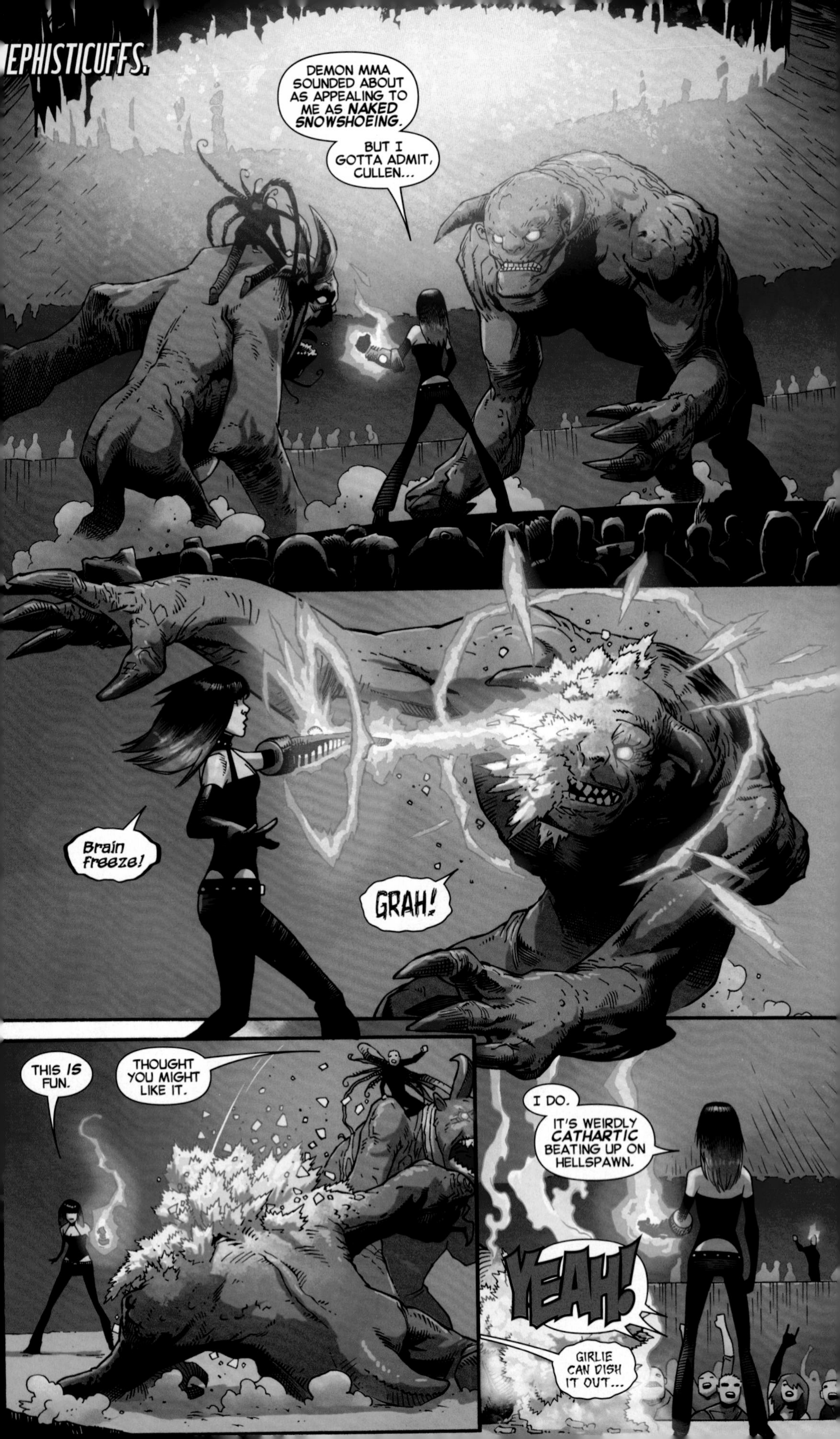
EPHISTICUFFS.
DEMON MMA SOUNDED ABOUT AS APPEALING TO ME AS NAKED SNOWSHOEING.
BUT I GOTTA ADMIT, CULLEN...
Brain freeze!
GRAH!
THIS IS FUN.
THOUGHT YOU MIGHT LIKE IT.
I DO.
IT'S WEIRDLY CATHARTIC BEATING UP ON HELLSPAWN.
YEAH!
GIRLIE CAN DISH IT OUT...

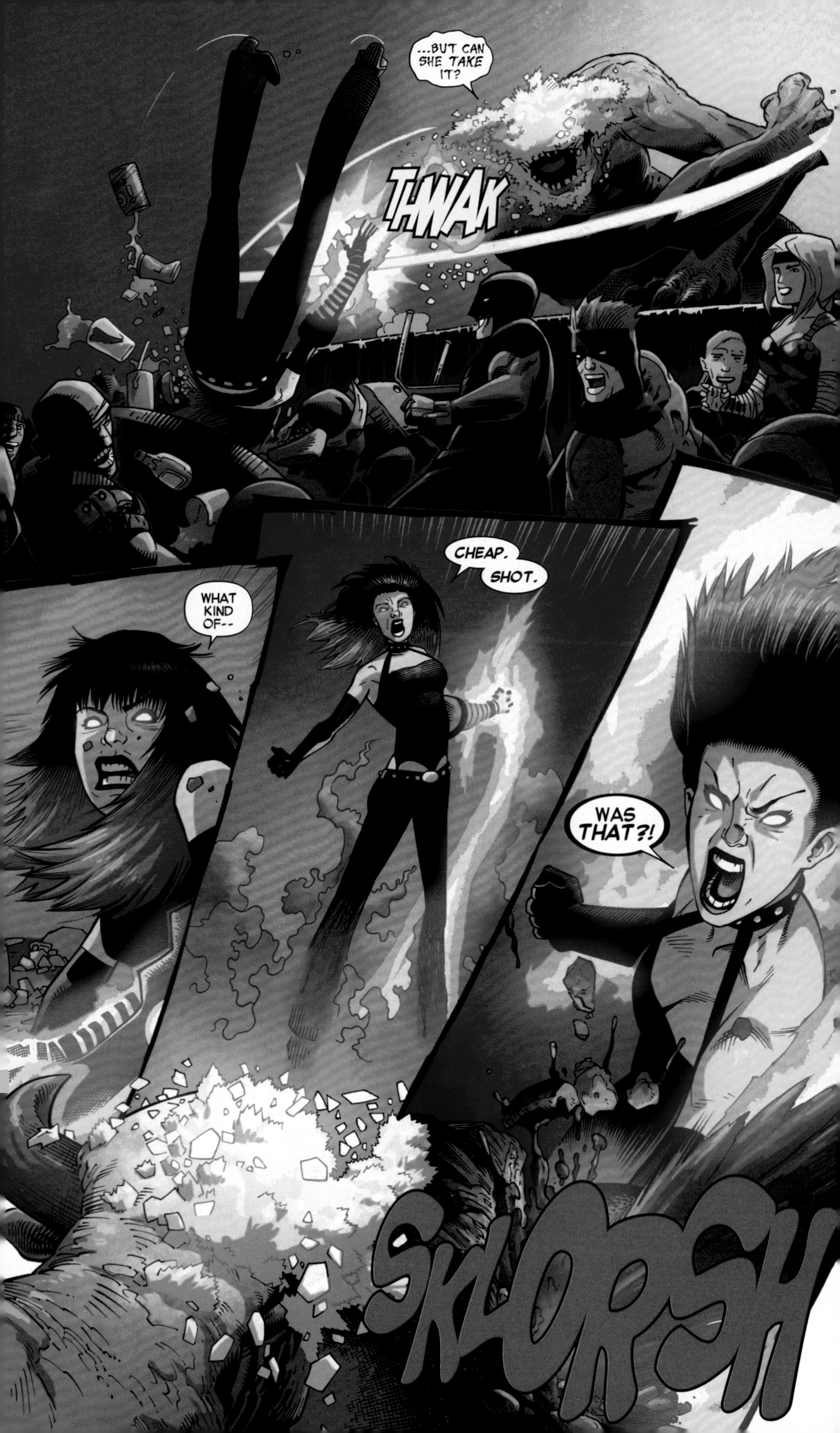
...BUT CAN SHE TAKE IT?
THWAK
WHAT KIND OF--
CHEAP.
SHOT.
WAS THAT?!
SKLORSH

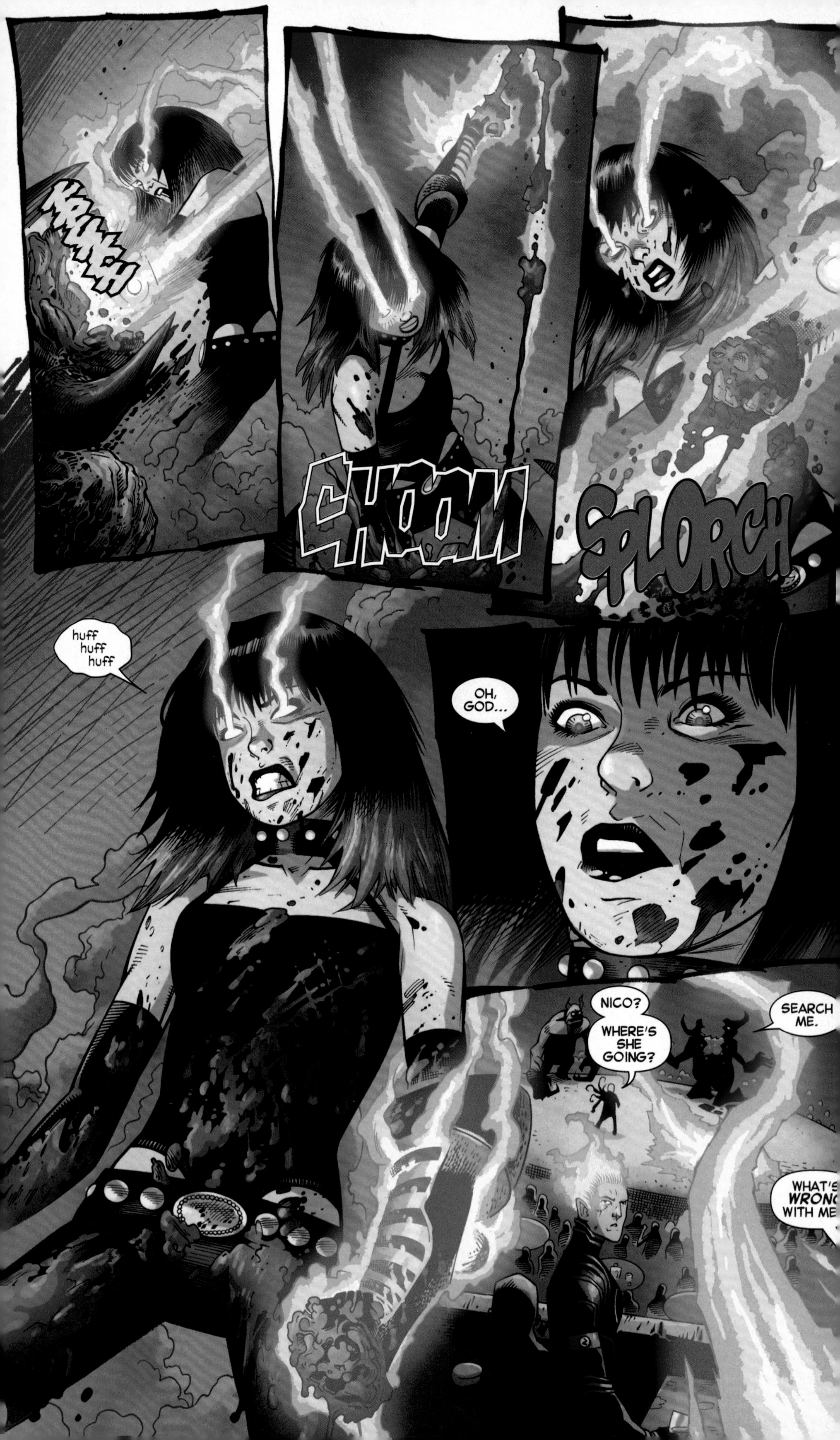
KRUNCH
CHOOM
SPLORCH
huff huff huff
OH, GOD...
NICO? WHERE'S SHE GOING?
SEARCH ME.

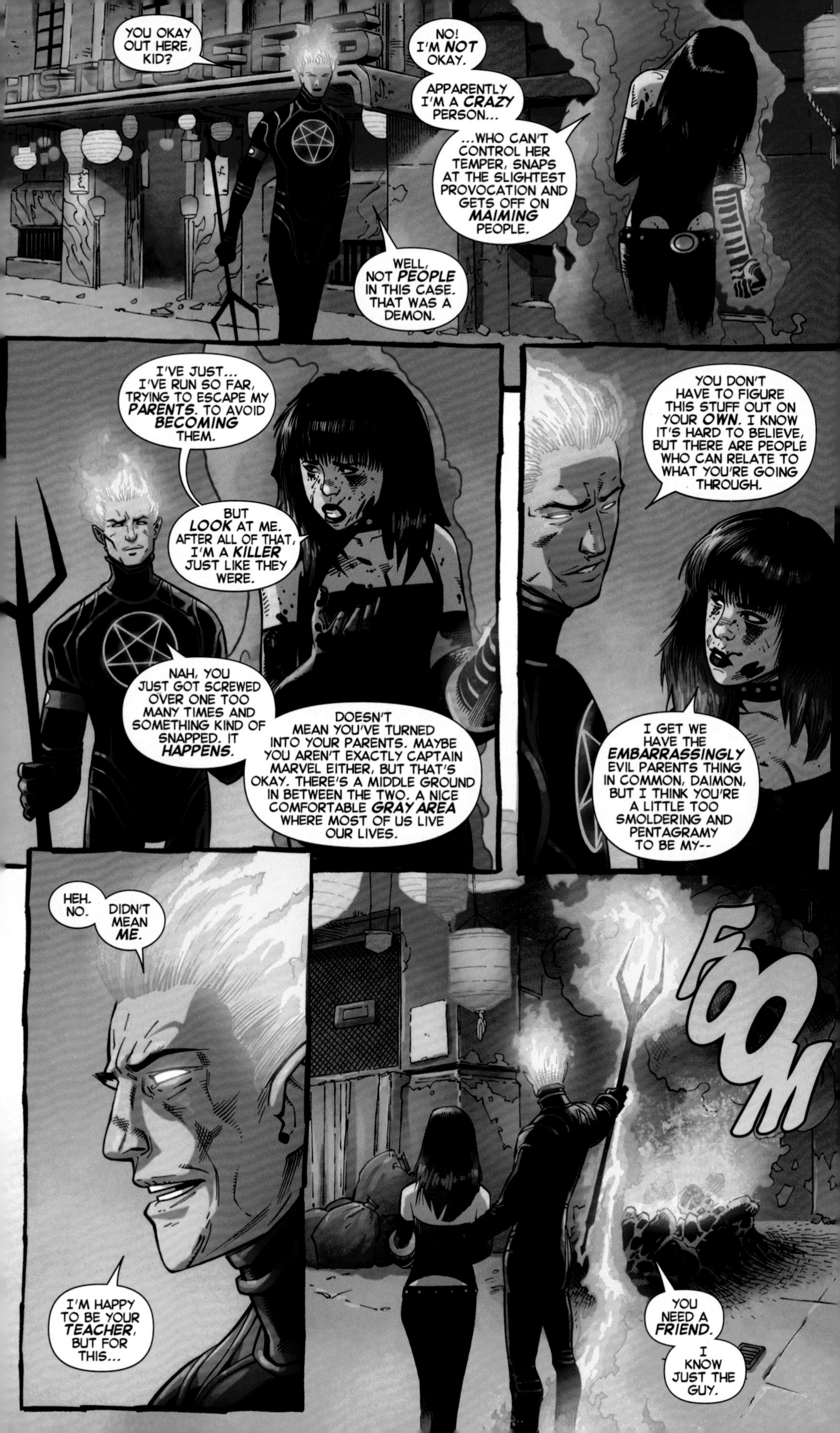
YOU OKAY OUT HERE, KID?
NO! I'M NOT OKAY.
APPARENTLY I'M A CRAZY PERSON...
...WHO CAN'T CONTROL HER TEMPER, SNAPS AT THE SLIGHTEST PROVOCATION AND GETS OFF ON MAIMING PEOPLE.
WELL, NOT PEOPLE IN THIS CASE. THAT WAS A DEMON.
I'VE JUST... I'VE RUN SO FAR, TRYING TO ESCAPE MY PARENTS. TO AVOID BECOMING THEM.
BUT LOOK AT ME. AFTER ALL OF THAT, I'M A KILLER JUST LIKE THEY WERE.
NAH, YOU JUST GOT SCREWED OVER ONE TOO MANY TIMES AND SOMETHING KIND OF SNAPPED. IT HAPPENS.
DOESN'T MEAN YOU'VE TURNED INTO YOUR PARENTS. MAYBE YOU AREN'T EXACTLY CAPTAIN MARVEL EITHER, BUT THAT'S OKAY. THERE'S A MIDDLE GROUND IN BETWEEN THE TWO. A NICE COMFORTABLE GRAY AREA WHERE MOST OF US LIVE OUR LIVES.
YOU DON'T HAVE TO FIGURE THIS STUFF OUT ON YOUR OWN. I KNOW IT'S HARD TO BELIEVE, BUT THERE ARE PEOPLE WHO CAN RELATE TO WHAT YOU'RE GOING THROUGH.
I GET WE HAVE THE EMBARRASSINGLY EVIL PARENTS THING IN COMMON, DAIMON, BUT I THINK YOU'RE A LITTLE TOO SMOLDERING AND PENTAGRAMY TO BE MY--
HEH. NO.
DIDN'T MEAN ME.
I'M HAPPY TO BE YOUR TEACHER, BUT FOR THIS...
FOOM
YOU NEED A FRIEND.
I KNOW JUST THE GUY.

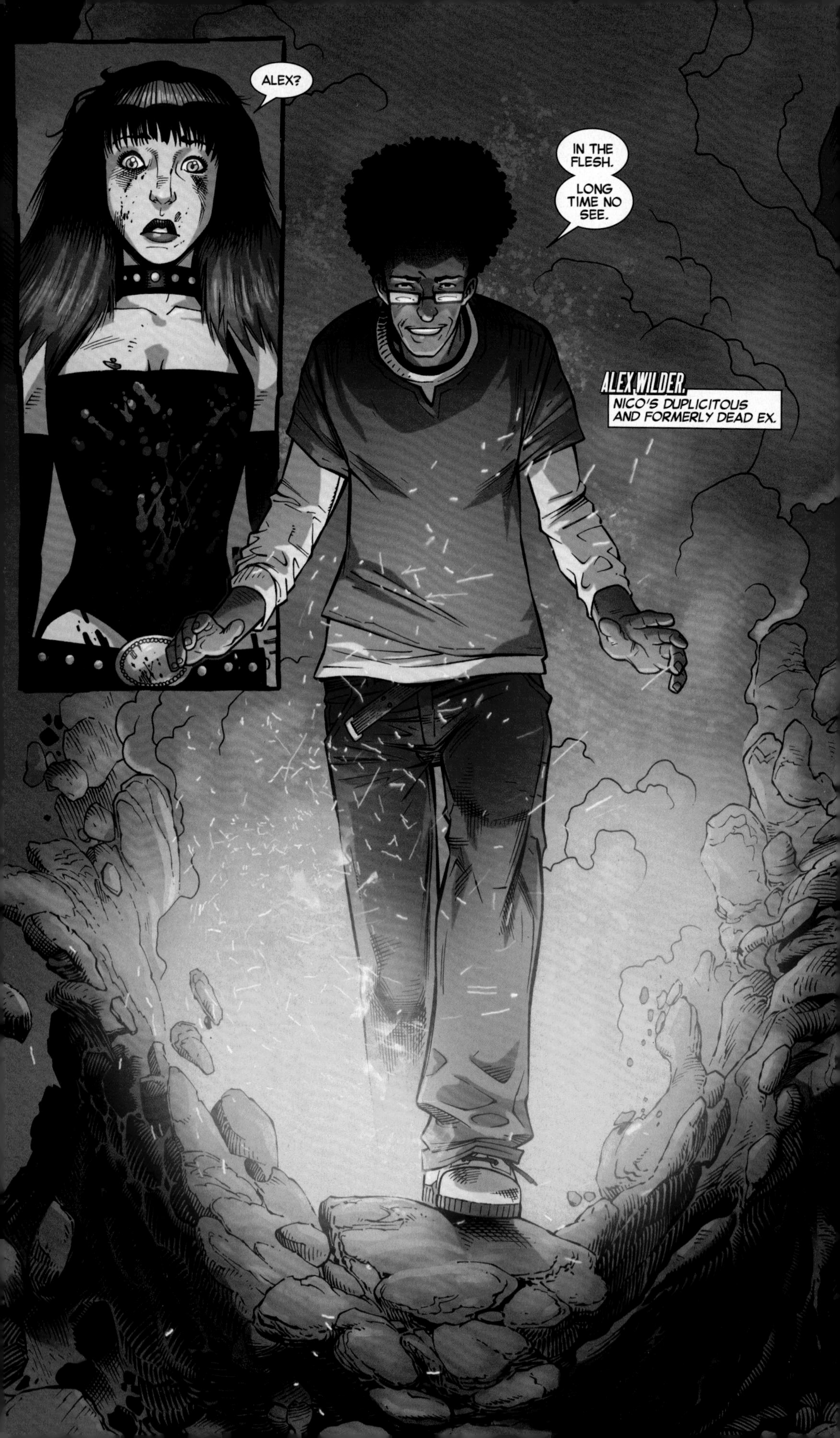
ALEX?
IN THE FLESH.
LONG TIME NO SEE.
ALEX WILDER.
NICO'S DUPLICITOUS AND FORMERLY DEAD EX.

THE HOLE.

I'M SAYING THIS IS GONNA LOOK UGLY FROM THE OUTSIDE. REAL UGLY.

I DON'T DISAGREE, CAMMI. BUT SERIOUSLY, WHAT *ELSE'S* NEW? PEOPLE HAVE BEEN HATING OUT LOUD FOR SIX MONTHS. *LET* 'EM HATE.

YOU THINK THEY HATE US *NOW*...

THERE'S NICO AND CHASE.

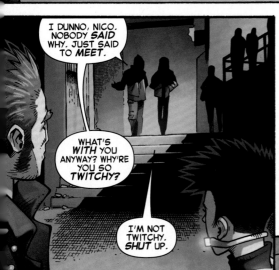

I DUNNO, NICO. NOBODY *SAID* WHY. JUST SAID TO *MEET*.

WHAT'S *WITH* YOU ANYWAY? WHY'RE YOU SO *TWITCHY?*

I'M NOT TWITCHY. *SHUT* UP.

WE'RE HERE, YO, BUT FAIR WARNING... NICO'S ALL TWITCHY AND WON'T SAY WHY.

I *AM* NOT.

CHASE, WHERE'S DEATH LOCKET?

OVER THERE, HUGGED UP WITH *CAPTAIN SHOVEL* LIKE SHE HAS BEEN ALL DAY.

WOULD'VE GRABBED HER BUT I DIDN'T FIGURE YOU WANTED HALF THE YOUNG MASTERS COMING WITH.

IT'S ALL RIGHT. WE CAN TALK TO HER *LATER.*

OKAY, HERE'S THE DEAL. ZEMO SAYS WE HAVE TWO OPTIONS. JAIL OR JOIN.

BUT WE'VE BEEN TALKING, AND WE THINK THERE MIGHT BE A *THIRD.*

JAIL, JOIN OR...

INFILTRATE THE MASTERS OF EVIL AND BRING ZEMO'S EMPIRE DOWN *FROM THE INSIDE.*

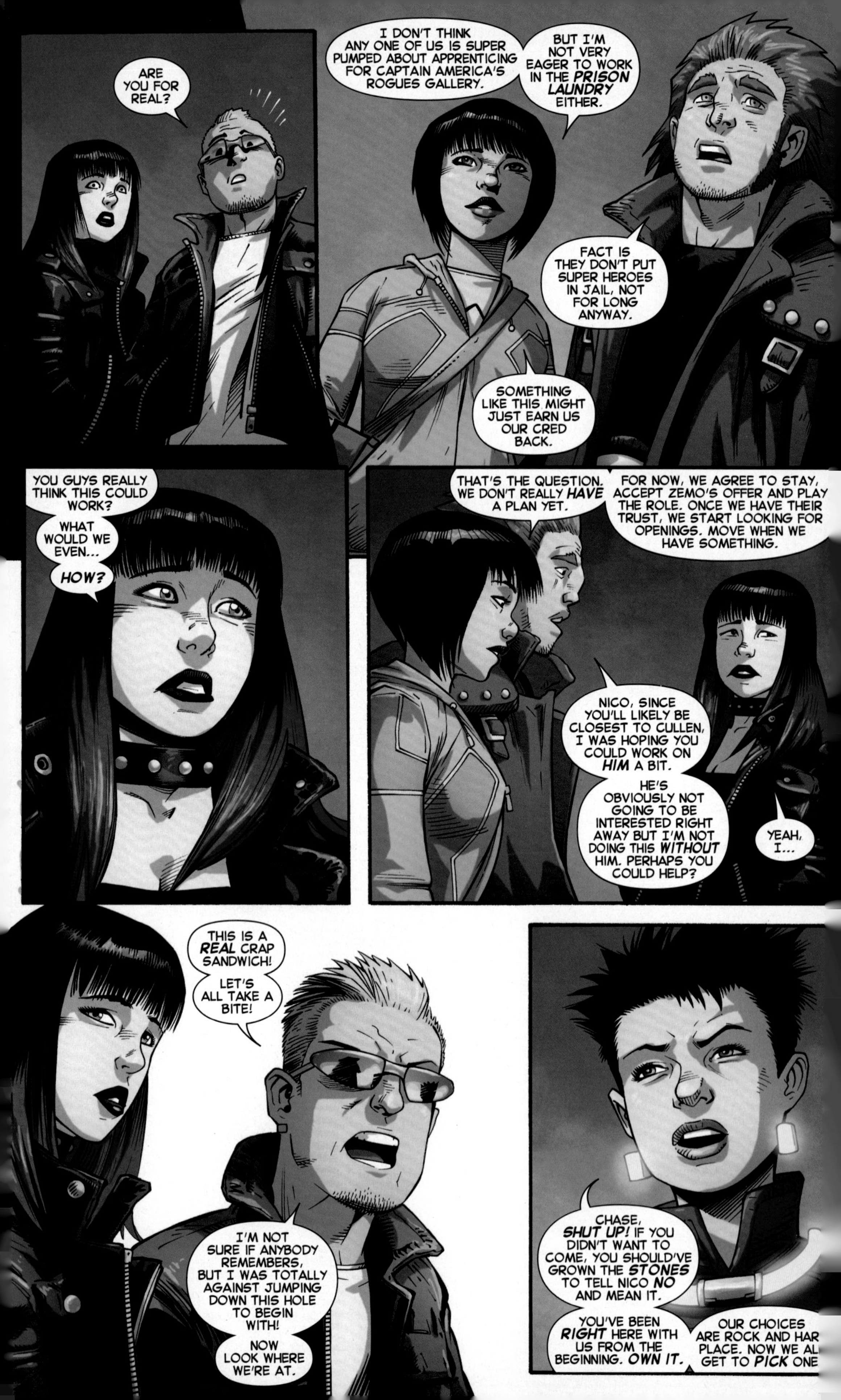
ARE YOU FOR REAL?
I DON'T THINK ANY ONE OF US IS SUPER PUMPED ABOUT APPRENTICING FOR CAPTAIN AMERICA'S ROGUES GALLERY.
BUT I'M NOT VERY EAGER TO WORK IN THE PRISON LAUNDRY EITHER.
FACT IS THEY DON'T PUT SUPER HEROES IN JAIL, NOT FOR LONG ANYWAY.
SOMETHING LIKE THIS MIGHT JUST EARN US OUR CRED BACK.
YOU GUYS REALLY THINK THIS COULD WORK?
WHAT WOULD WE EVEN...
HOW?
THAT'S THE QUESTION. WE DON'T REALLY HAVE A PLAN YET.
FOR NOW, WE AGREE TO STAY, ACCEPT ZEMO'S OFFER AND PLAY THE ROLE. ONCE WE HAVE THEIR TRUST, WE START LOOKING FOR OPENINGS. MOVE WHEN WE HAVE SOMETHING.
NICO, SINCE YOU'LL LIKELY BE CLOSEST TO CULLEN, I WAS HOPING YOU COULD WORK ON HIM A BIT.
HE'S OBVIOUSLY NOT GOING TO BE INTERESTED RIGHT AWAY BUT I'M NOT DOING THIS WITHOUT HIM. PERHAPS YOU COULD HELP?
YEAH, I...
THIS IS A REAL CRAP SANDWICH!
LET'S ALL TAKE A BITE!
I'M NOT SURE IF ANYBODY REMEMBERS, BUT I WAS TOTALLY AGAINST JUMPING DOWN THIS HOLE TO BEGIN WITH!
NOW LOOK WHERE WE'RE AT.
CHASE, SHUT UP! IF YOU DIDN'T WANT TO COME, YOU SHOULD'VE GROWN THE STONES TO TELL NICO NO AND MEAN IT.
YOU'VE BEEN RIGHT HERE WITH US FROM THE BEGINNING. OWN IT.
OUR CHOICES ARE ROCK AND HAR PLACE. NOW WE AL GET TO PICK ONE

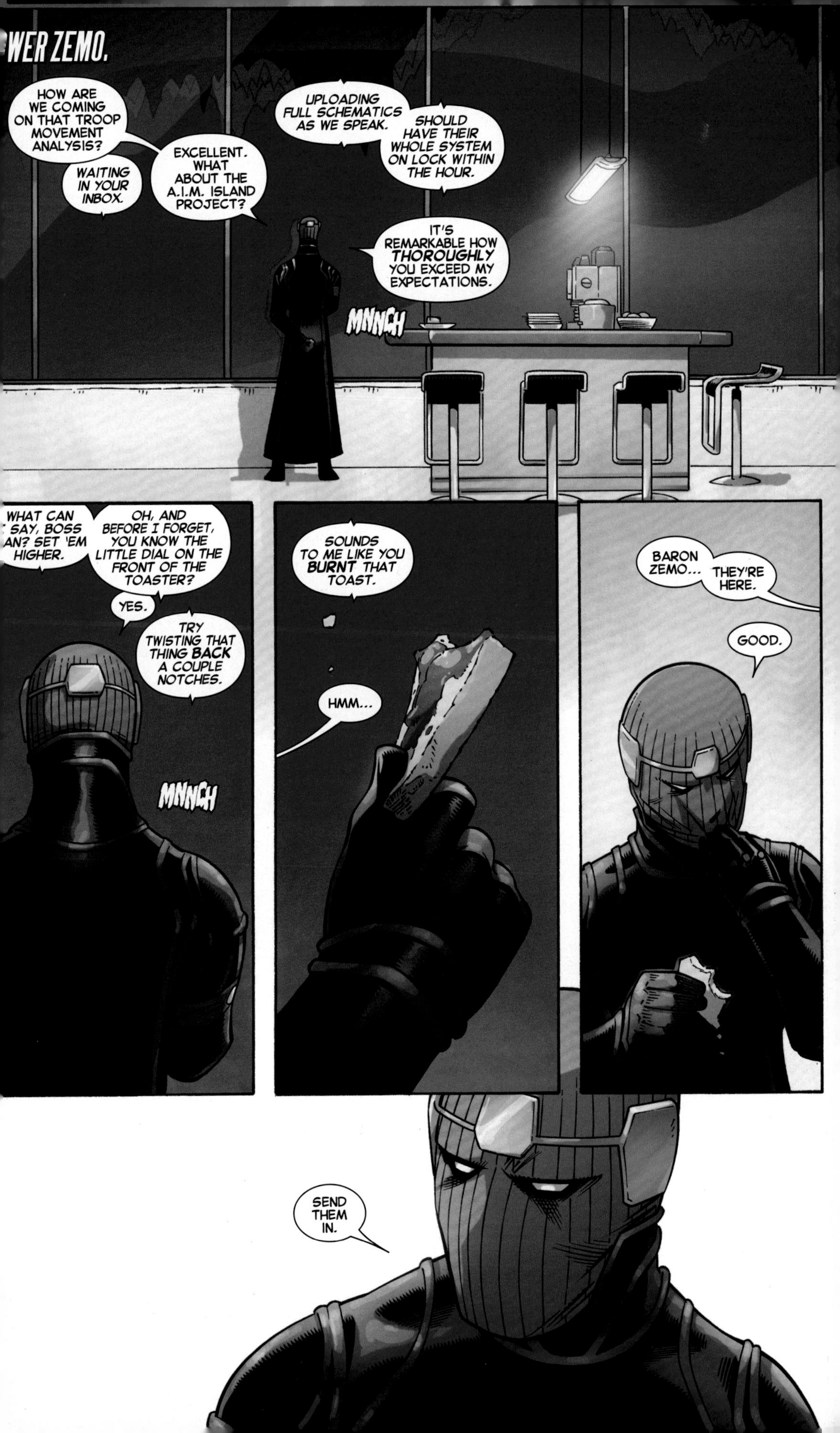
WER ZEMO.
HOW ARE WE COMING ON THAT TROOP MOVEMENT ANALYSIS?
WAITING IN YOUR INBOX.
EXCELLENT. WHAT ABOUT THE A.I.M. ISLAND PROJECT?
UPLOADING FULL SCHEMATICS AS WE SPEAK.
SHOULD HAVE THEIR WHOLE SYSTEM ON LOCK WITHIN THE HOUR.
IT'S REMARKABLE HOW THOROUGHLY YOU EXCEED MY EXPECTATIONS.
MNNCH
WHAT CAN SAY, BOSS AN? SET 'EM HIGHER.
OH, AND BEFORE I FORGET, YOU KNOW THE LITTLE DIAL ON THE FRONT OF THE TOASTER?
YES.
TRY TWISTING THAT THING BACK A COUPLE NOTCHES.
MNNCH
SOUNDS TO ME LIKE YOU BURNT THAT TOAST.
HMM...
BARON ZEMO...
THEY'RE HERE.
GOOD.
SEND THEM IN.

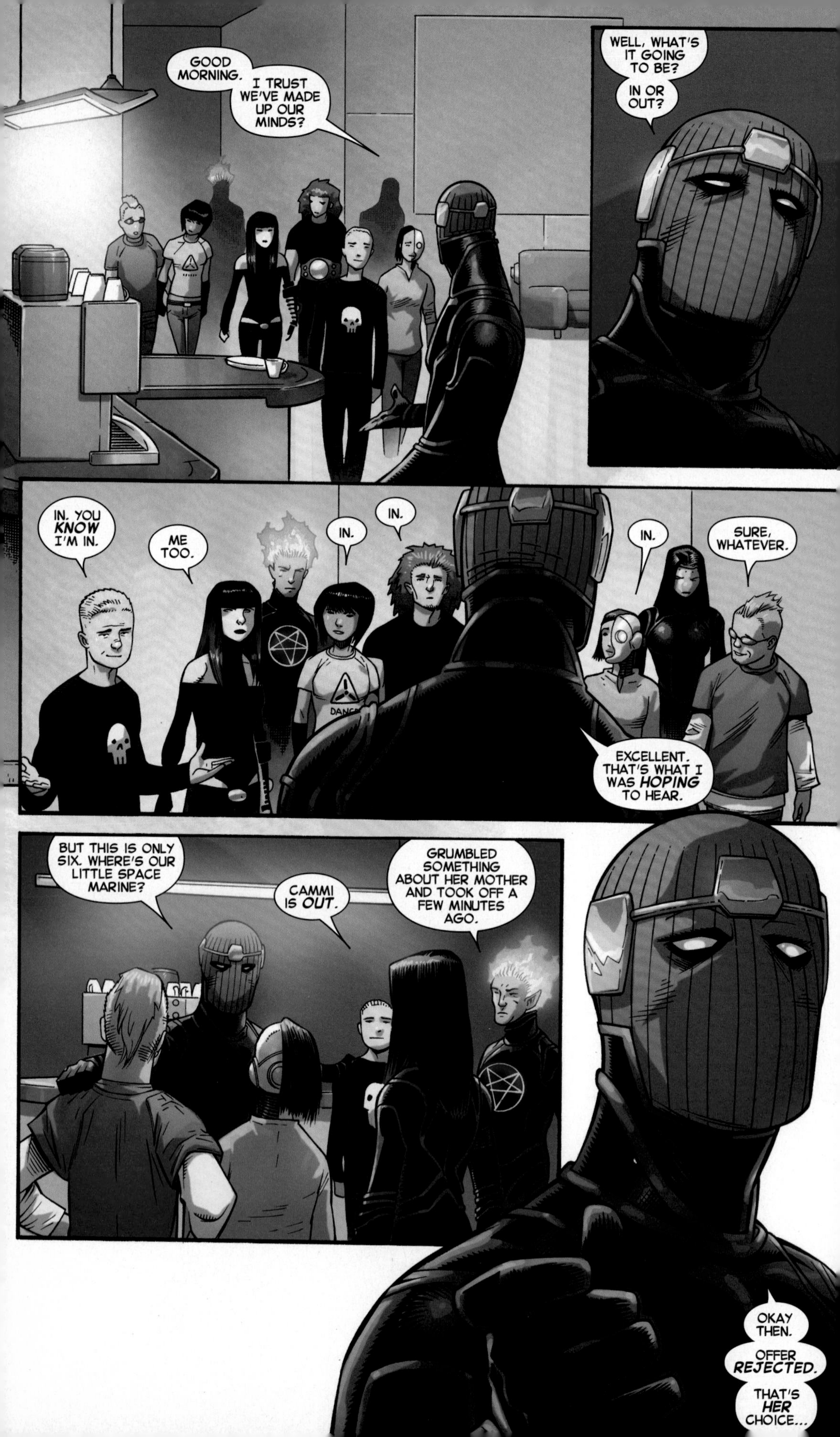
GOOD MORNING.
I TRUST WE'VE MADE UP OUR MINDS?
WELL, WHAT'S IT GOING TO BE?
IN OR OUT?
IN. YOU KNOW I'M IN.
ME TOO.
IN.
IN.
IN.
SURE, WHATEVER.
EXCELLENT. THAT'S WHAT I WAS HOPING TO HEAR.
BUT THIS IS ONLY SIX. WHERE'S OUR LITTLE SPACE MARINE?
CAMMI IS OUT.
GRUMBLED SOMETHING ABOUT HER MOTHER AND TOOK OFF A FEW MINUTES AGO.
OKAY THEN.
OFFER REJECTED.
THAT'S HER CHOICE...

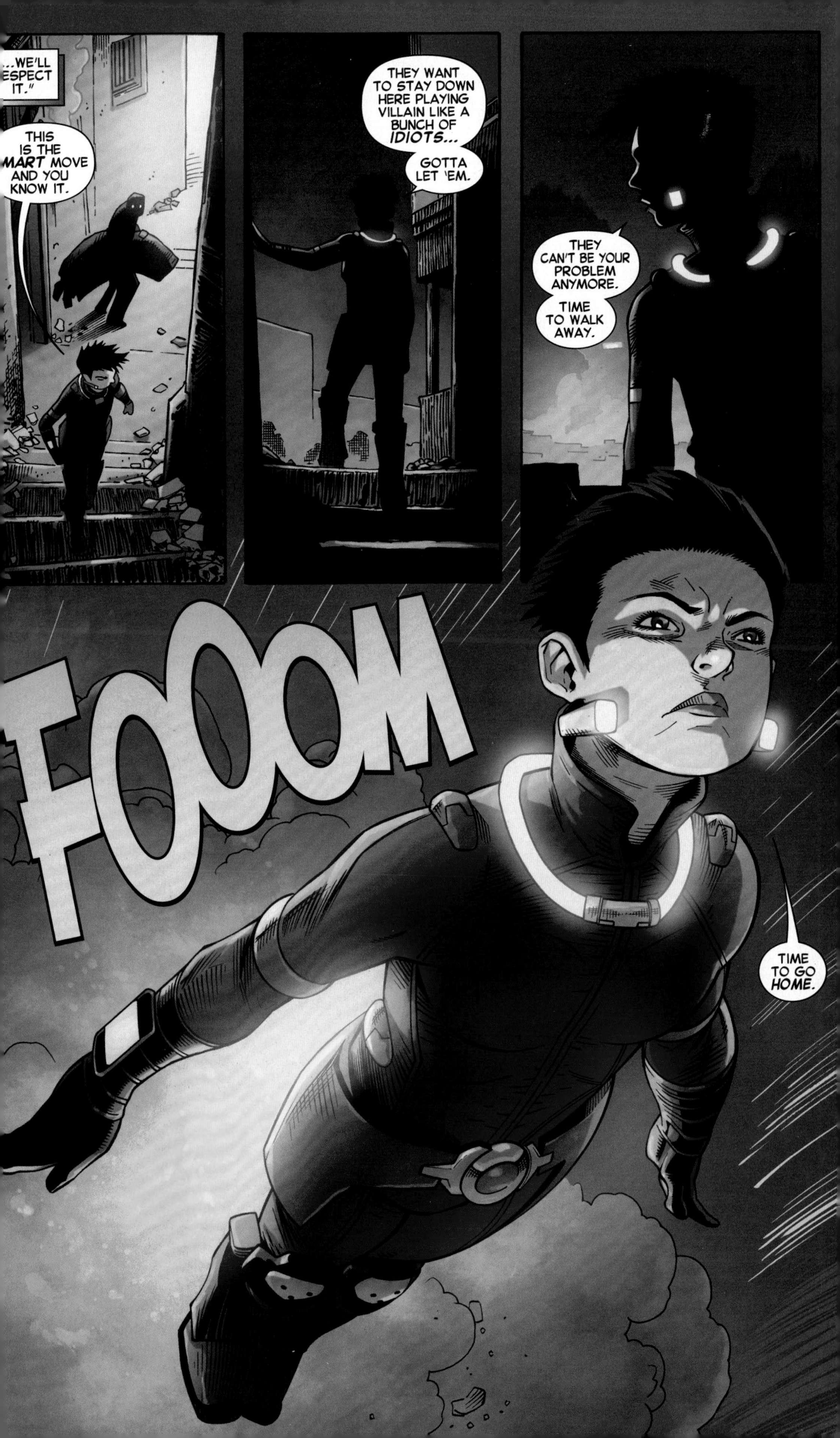

...WE'LL
ESPECT
IT."
THIS IS THE MART MOVE AND YOU KNOW IT.
THEY WANT TO STAY DOWN HERE PLAYING VILLAIN LIKE A BUNCH OF *IDIOTS...*
GOTTA LET 'EM.
THEY CAN'T BE YOUR PROBLEM ANYMORE.
TIME TO WALK AWAY.
FOOOM
TIME TO GO *HOME.*

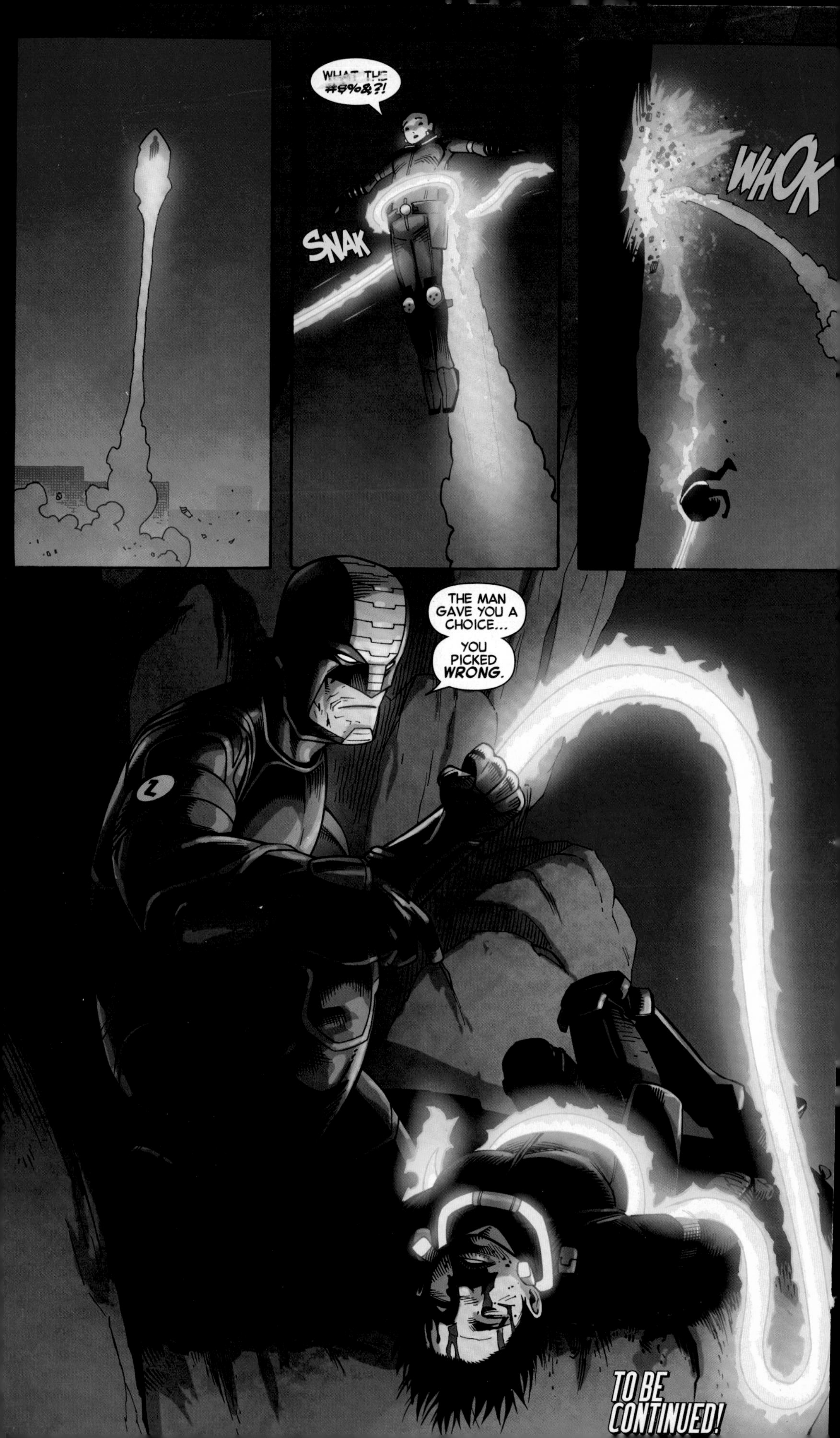
WHAT THE #$%&?!
SNAK
WHOK
THE MAN GAVE YOU A CHOICE...
YOU PICKED WRONG.
TO BE CONTINUED!

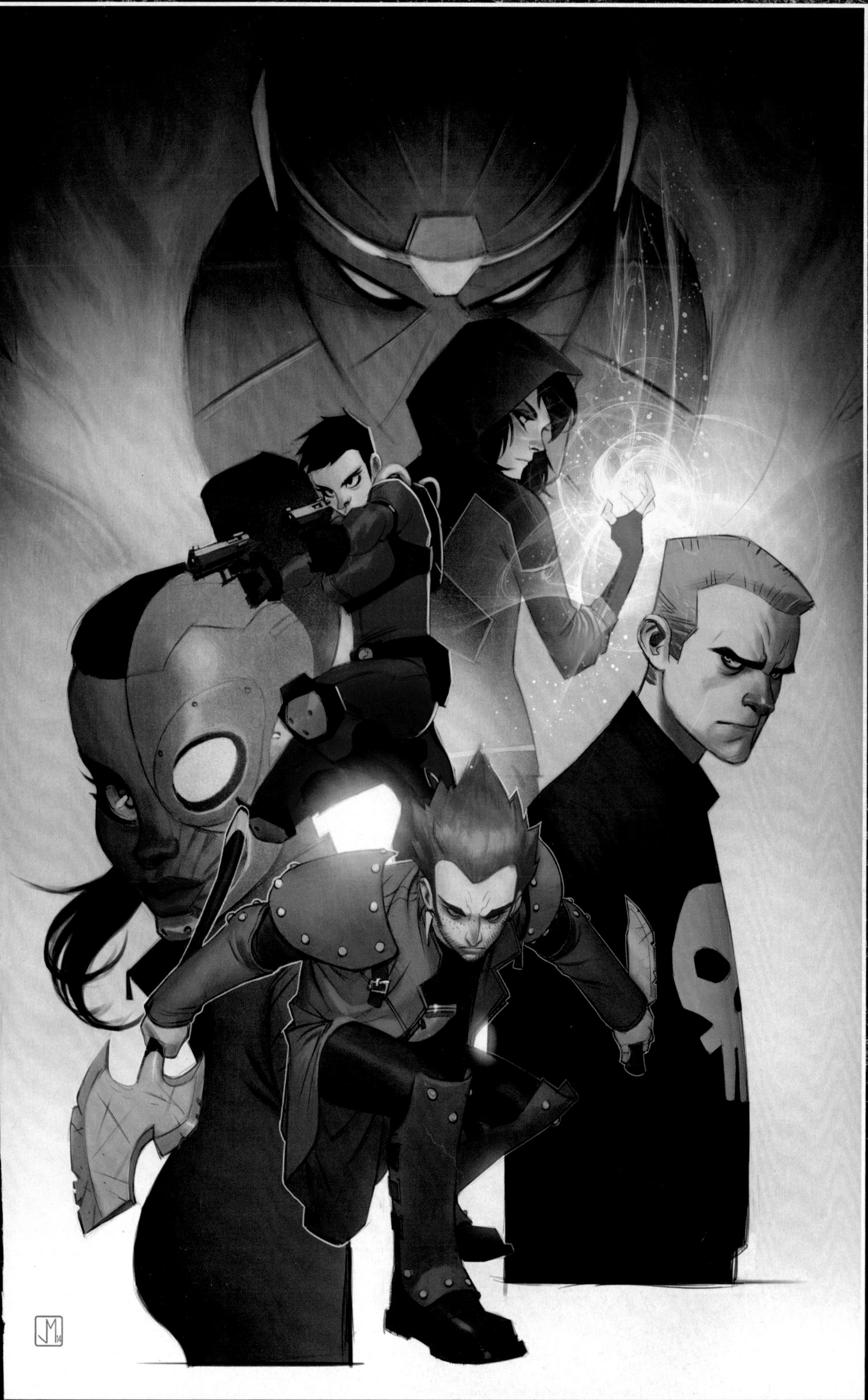

#3 VARIANT BY JORGE MOLINA

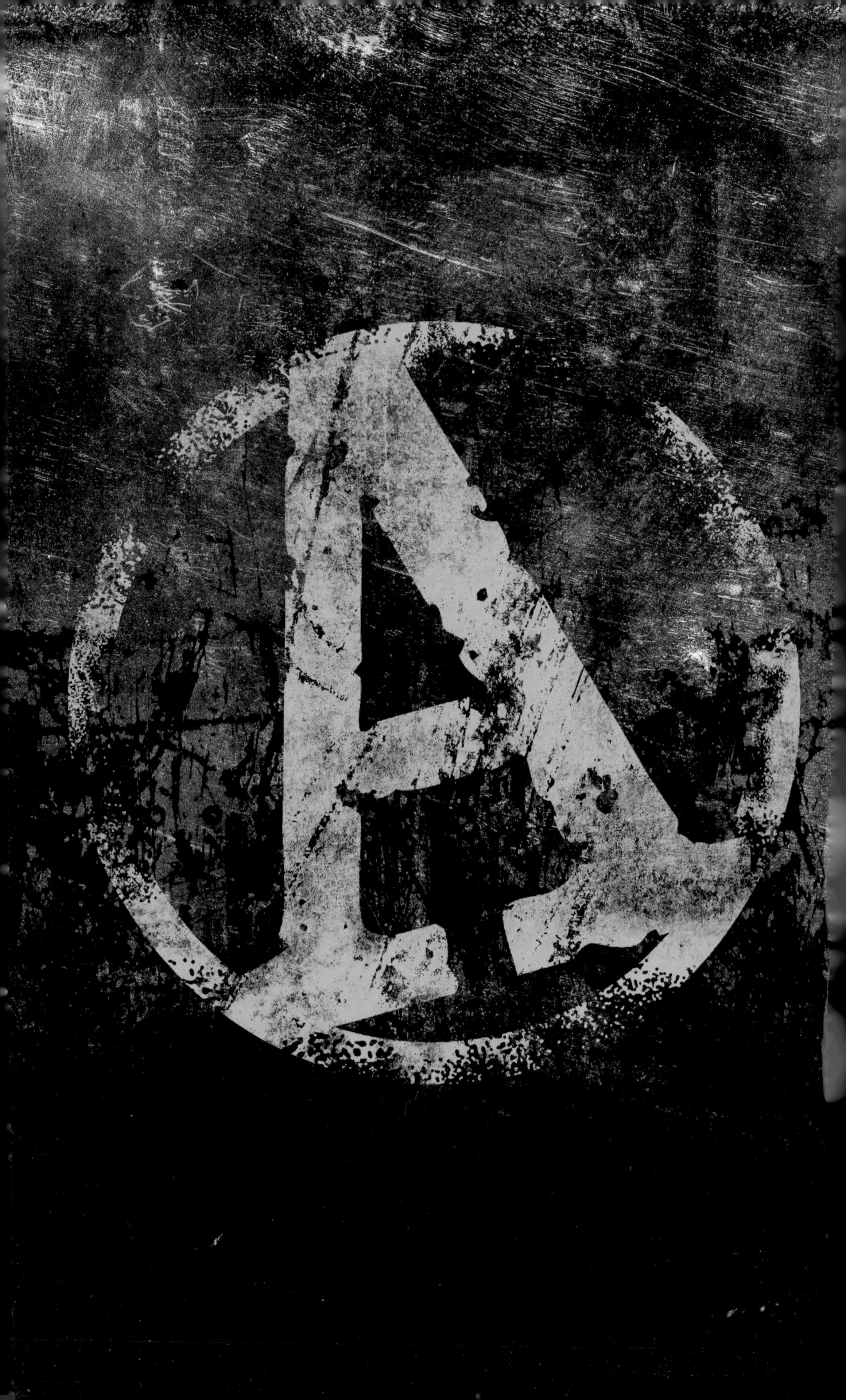